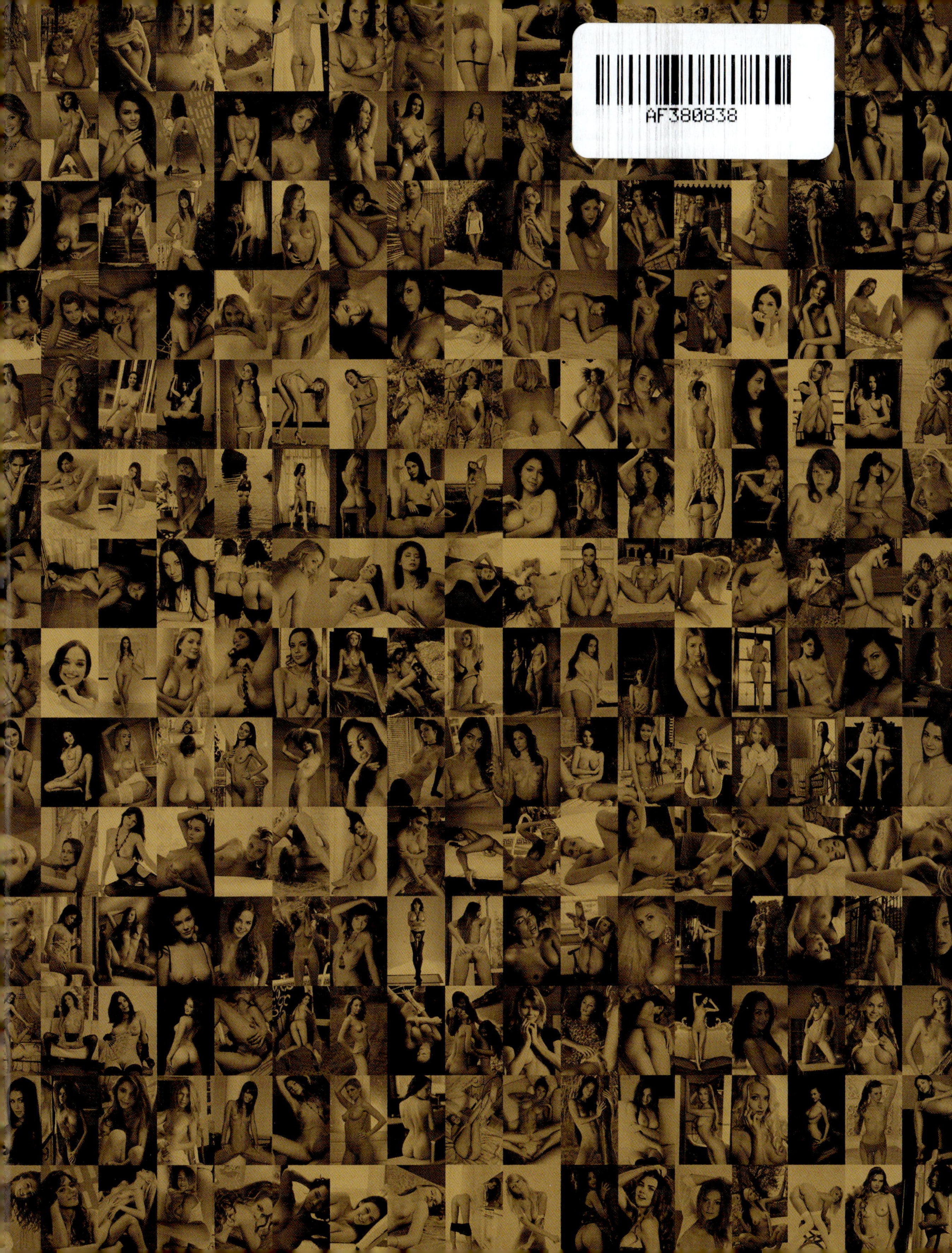
AF380838

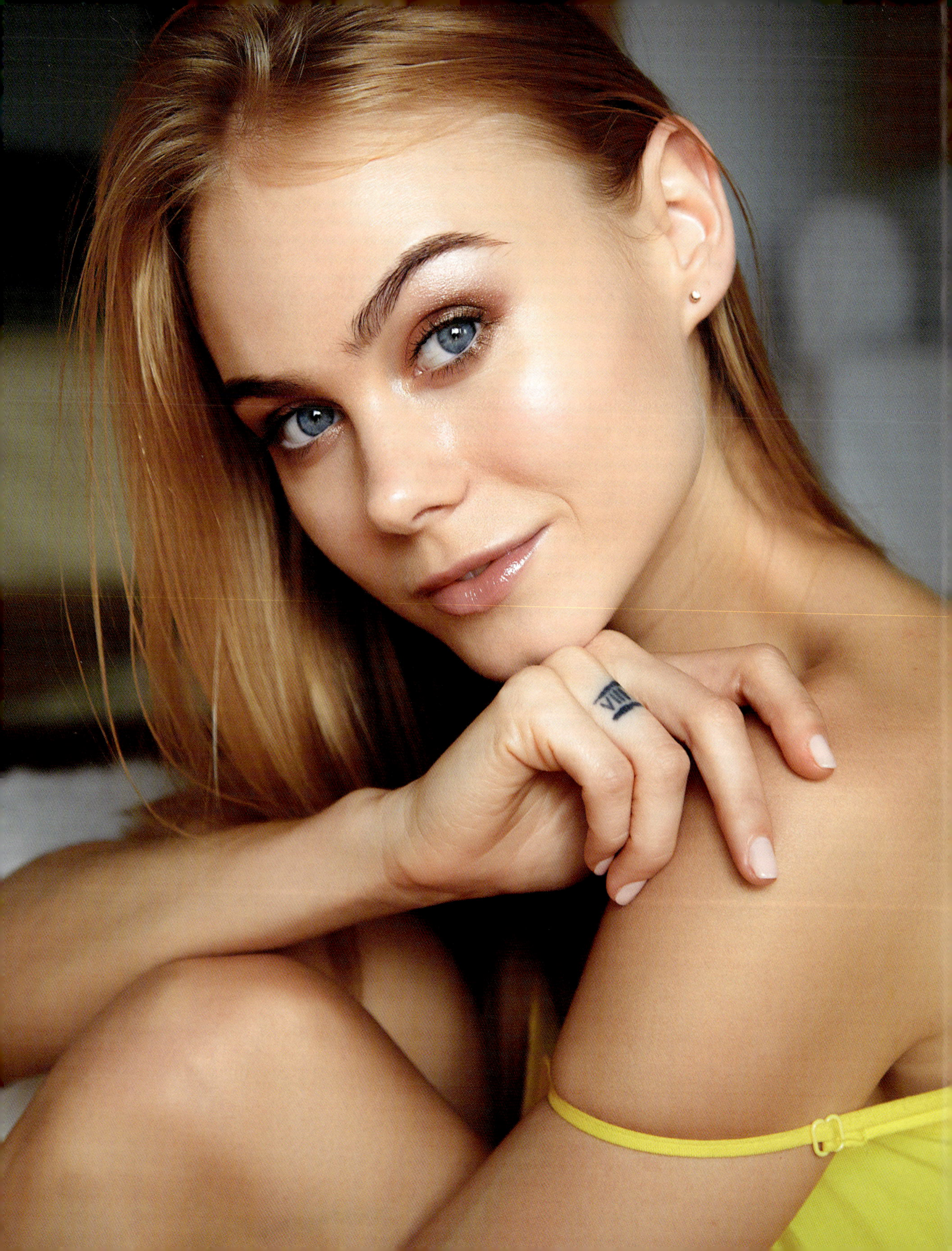

TOP MODELS OF
MetArt.com
WHERE FLAWLESS BEAUTY MEETS ART

NANCY A

COLLECTED AND EDITED BY ISABELLA CATALINA

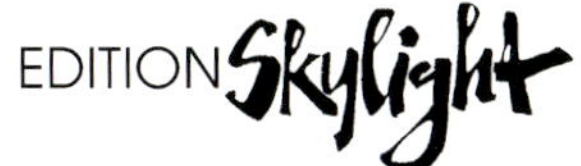

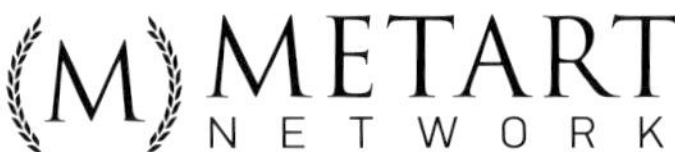

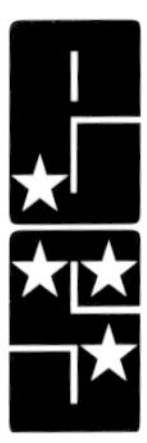

2nd Edition 2024
1st Edition 2023
Copyright © 2023 by Edition Skylight

EDITION SKYLIGHT
Rosengartenstrasse 13B
CH-8608 Bubikon / Zürich
Switzerland
info@edition-skylight.com
www.edition-skylight.com

ISBN 978-3-03766-687-6

Bibliographic information published by Die Deutsche Bibliothek
Die Deutsche Bibliothek lists this publication in the
Deutsche Nationalbibliografie; detailed bibliographic data
are available in the Internet at http://dnb.ddb.de.

Printed in Bosnia and Herzogovina

SEXY AND ALL JUST PURE NATURAL CURVES

Everything about **Nancy A** is perfect. She's got perfect tits, long legs, a slammin' body and she is sexy as hell. Nancy is also a budding entrepreneur, having launched her own lingerie line for women that want to feel sexy and classy at the same time. Nancy is a lingerie connoisseur and she has worked at many high end lingerie shops over the years. As a matter of fact, that is what lead her to become a Diva. Men would ask her to model sexy intimates for their wives as they were shopping and Nancy got a huge charge out of parading around half naked in front of strangers. Now she is at the top of her game with fans around the world and we are proud to have her as one of our featured divas.

Alles an **Nancy A** ist einfach perfekt. Sie hat perfekte Brüste, lange Beine, einen knallharten, durchtrainierten Körper und besitzt diese gewisse sexy Ausstrahlung. Nancy kann sehr unterhaltsam sein, sie hat ihre eigene Lingerie-Modelinie entworfen und bietet ihre zarte Wäsche Frauen an, die sich ebenso sexy fühlen wollen wie sie. Nancy hat in diversen teuren Lingerie-Geschäften gearbeitet und ist eine verrückte Lingerie-Liebhaberin. Dabei wandelte sie sich wohl zu einer richtigen kleinen Diva. Männer wollten, dass sie die Wäsche den Ehefrauen vorführt, und plötzlich war die Aufmerksamkeit ganz bei ihr und sie hatte noch Spass dazu, sich vor fremden Paaren auszuziehen. Jetzt ist sie unsere Diva und wir sind stolz auf diese extravagante Verführerin.

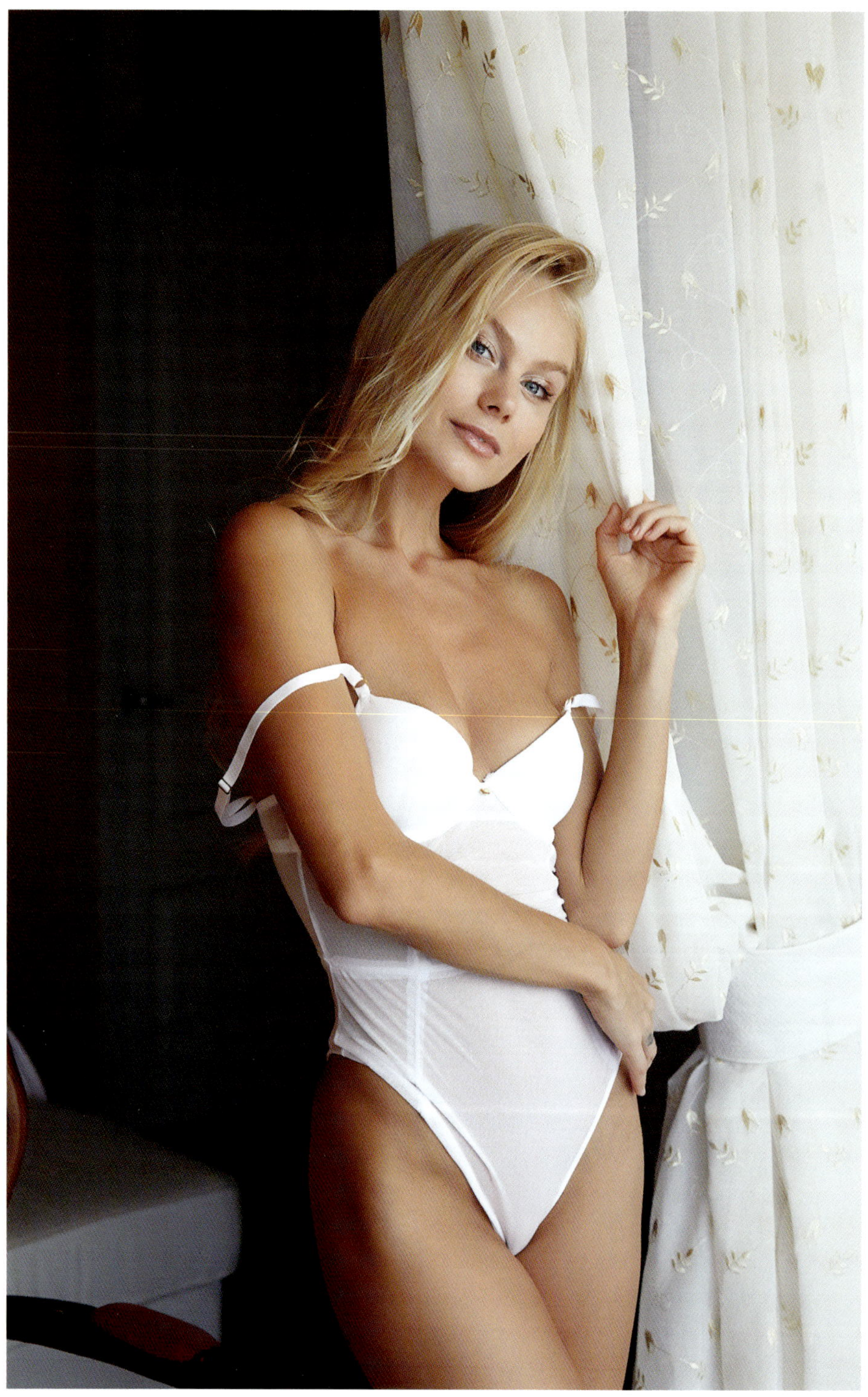

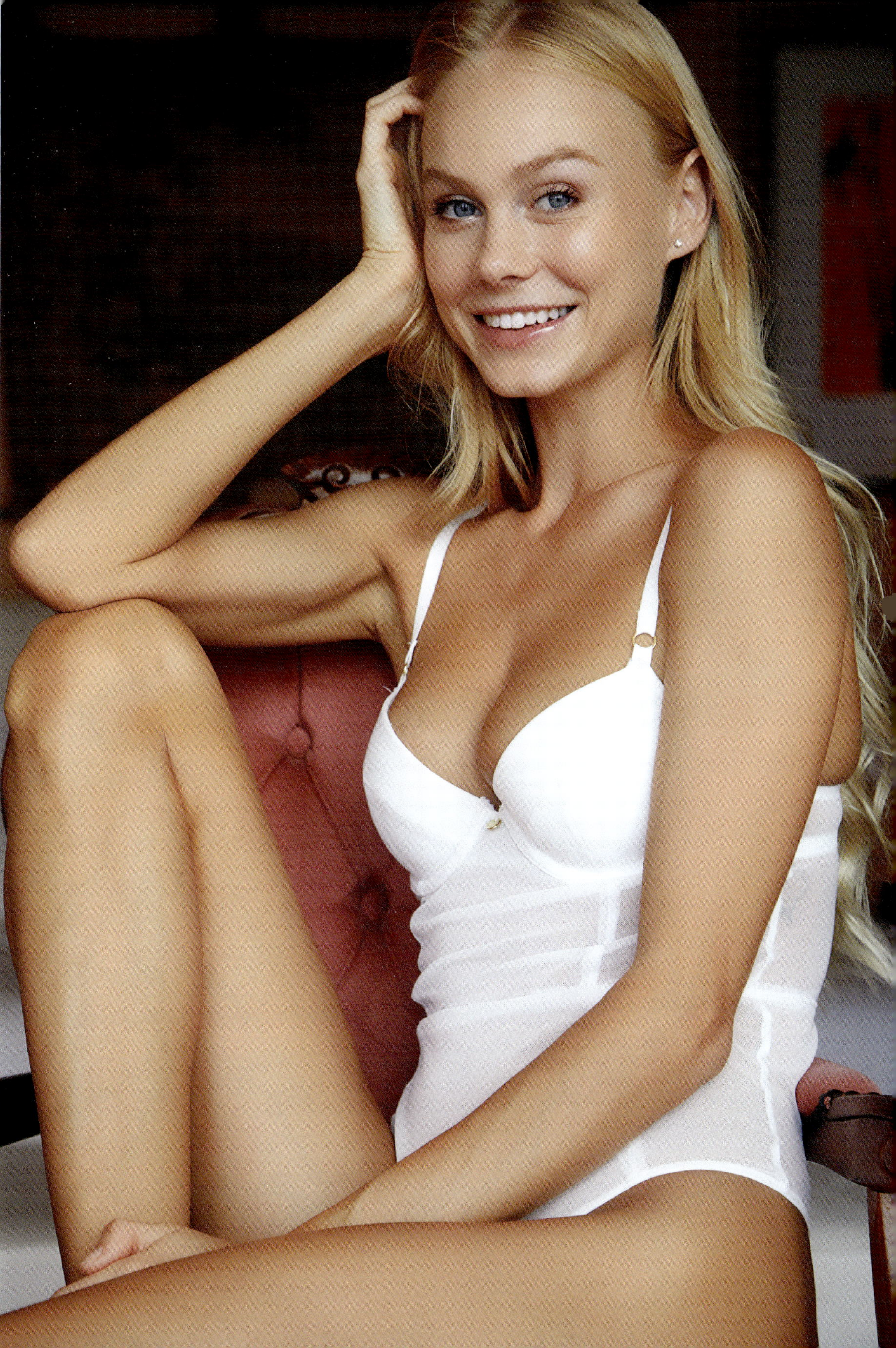

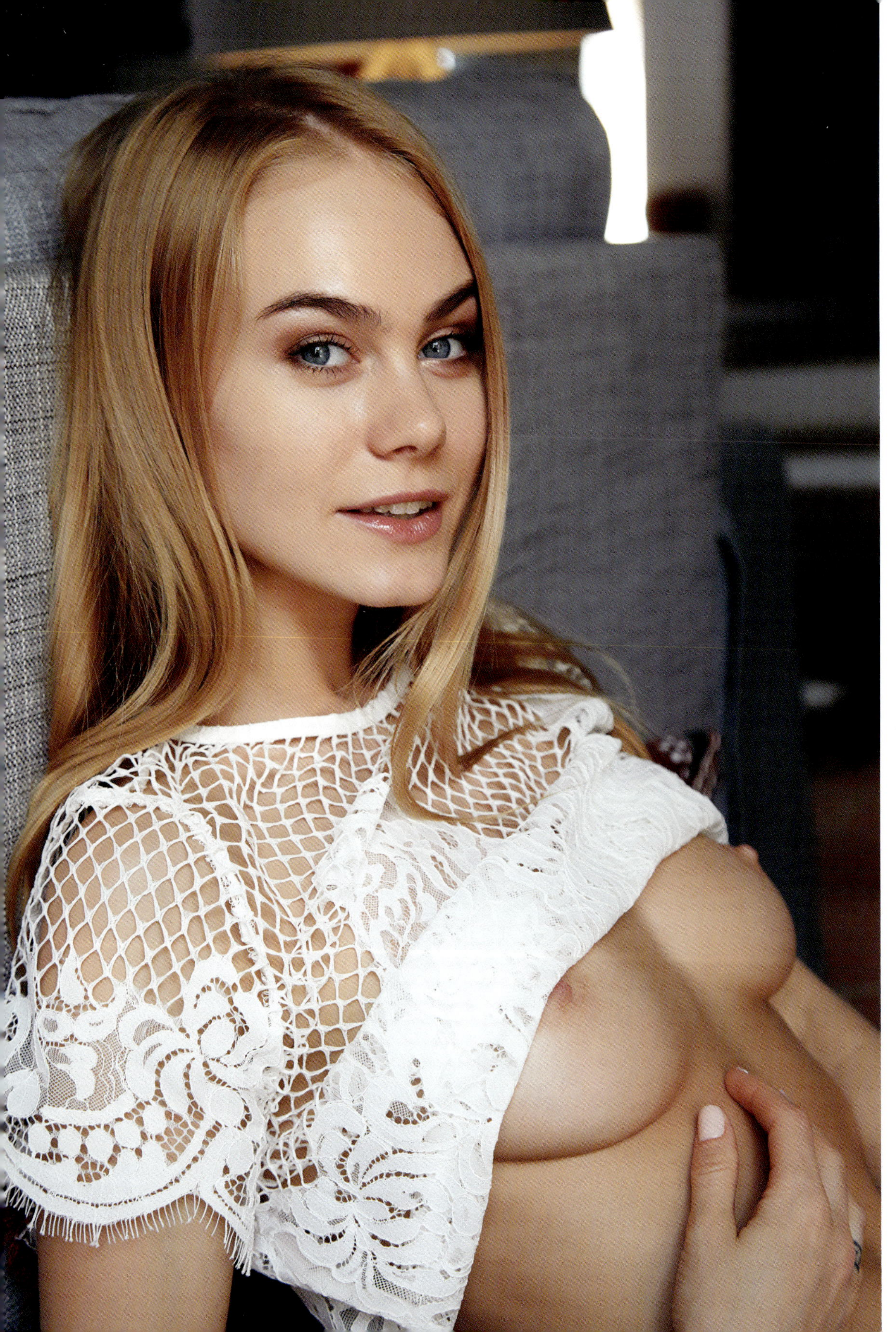

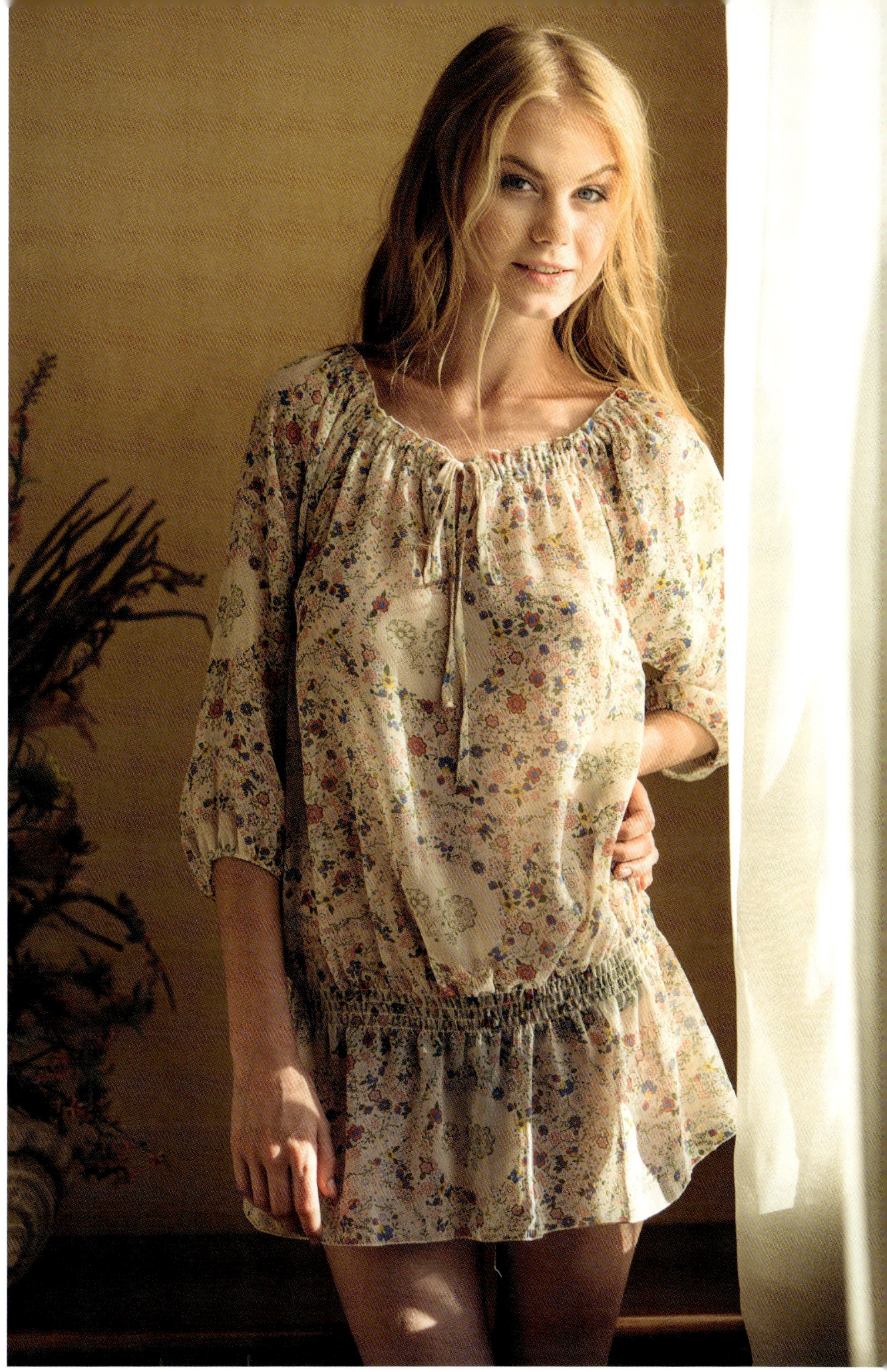

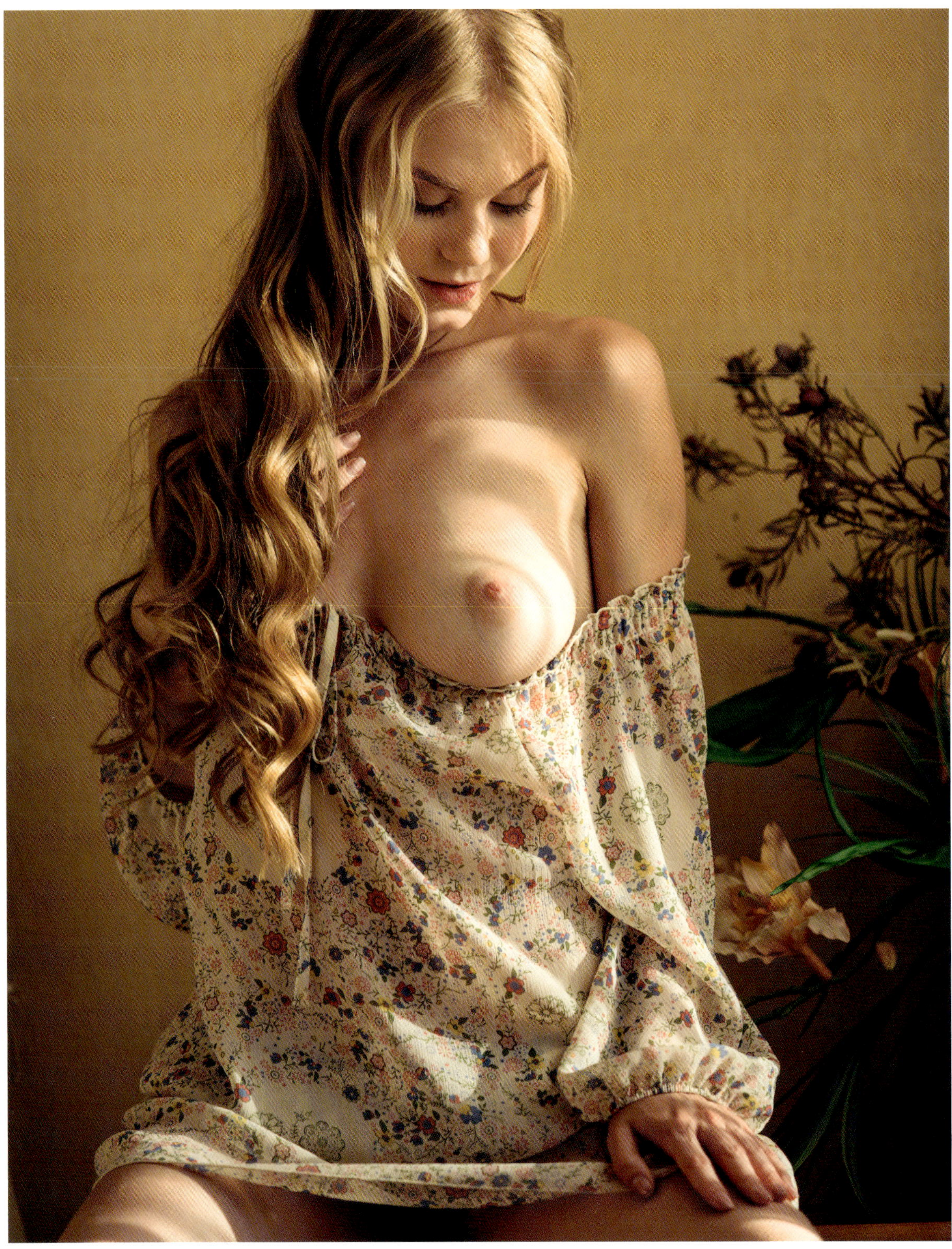

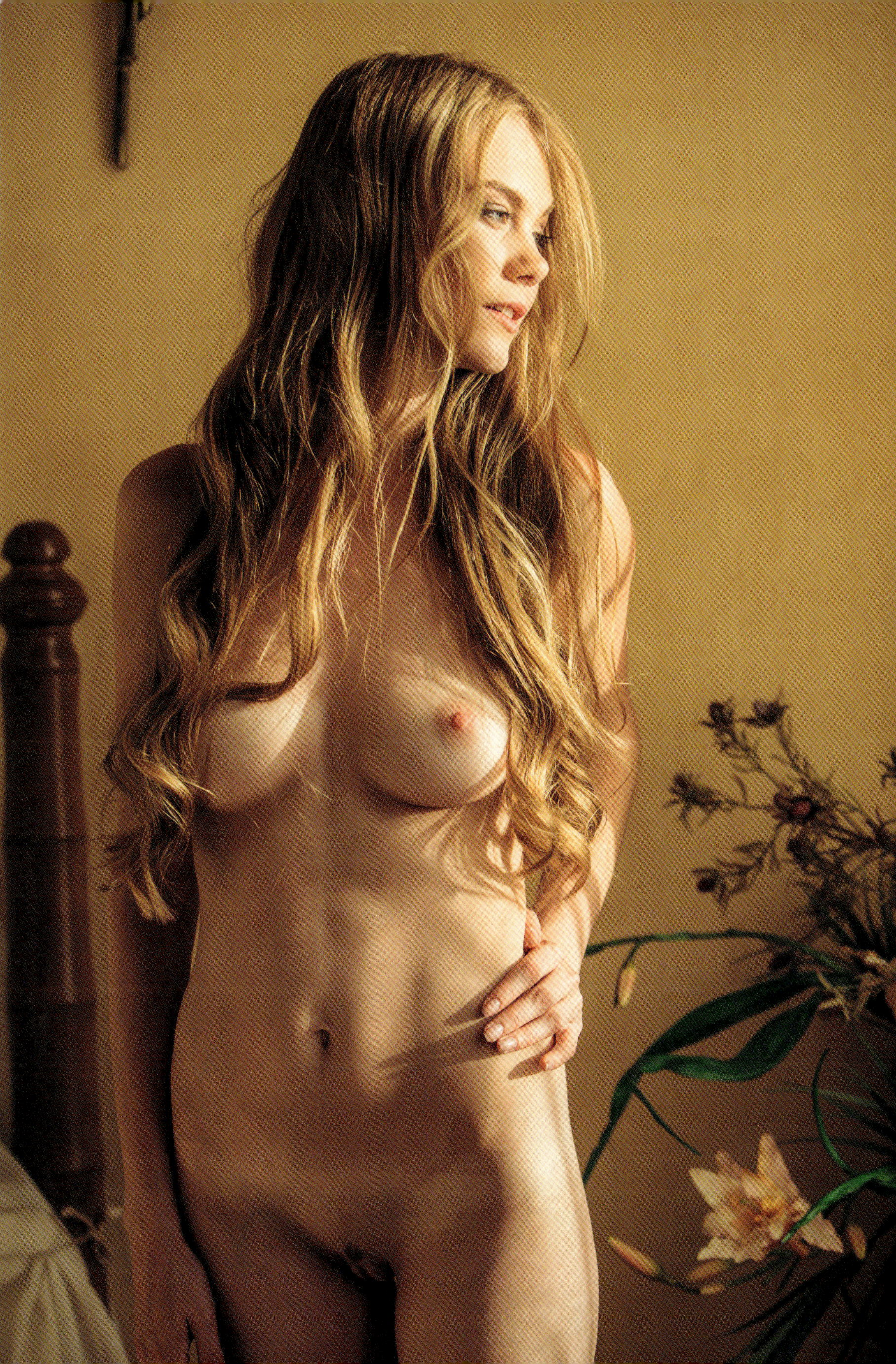

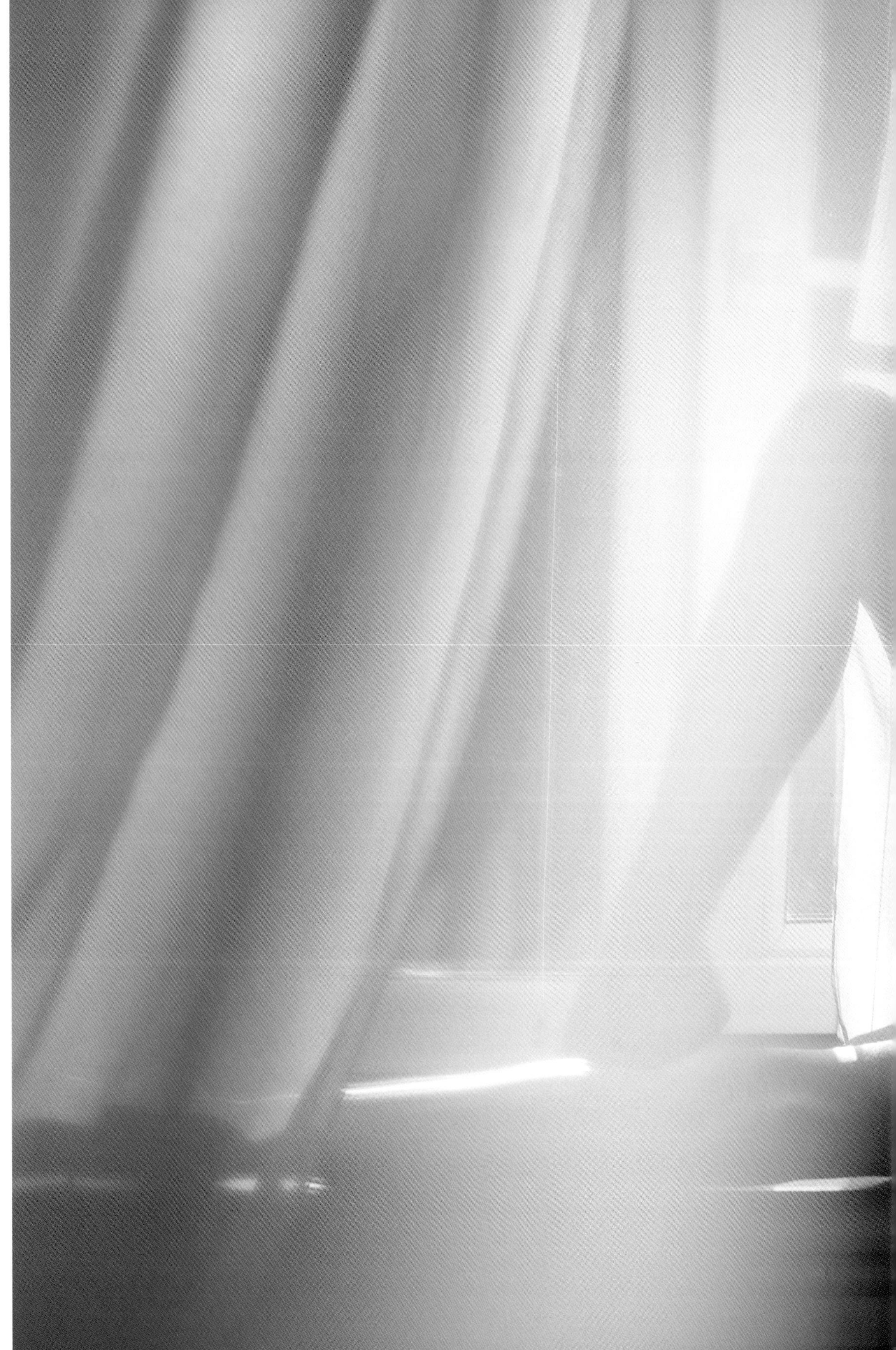

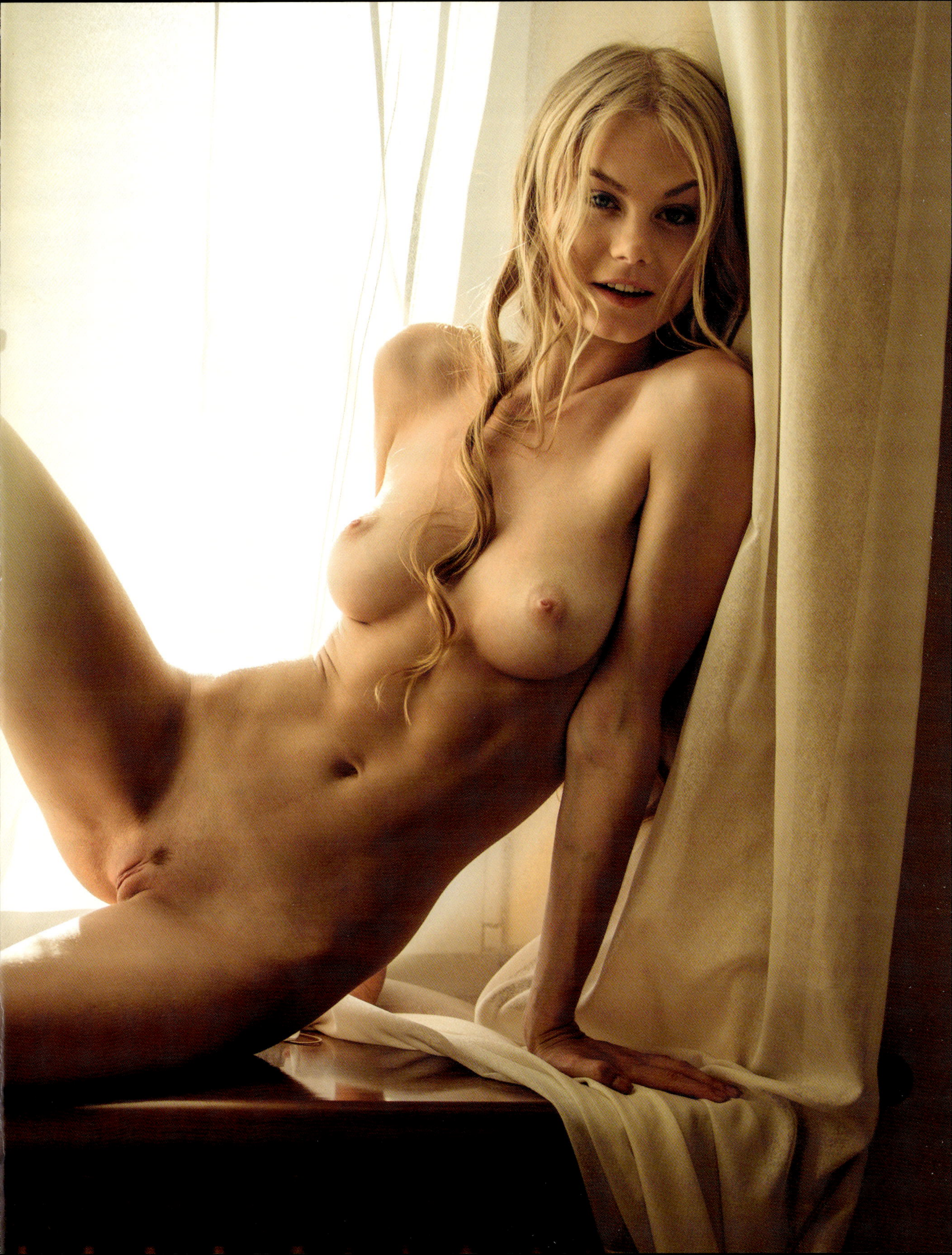

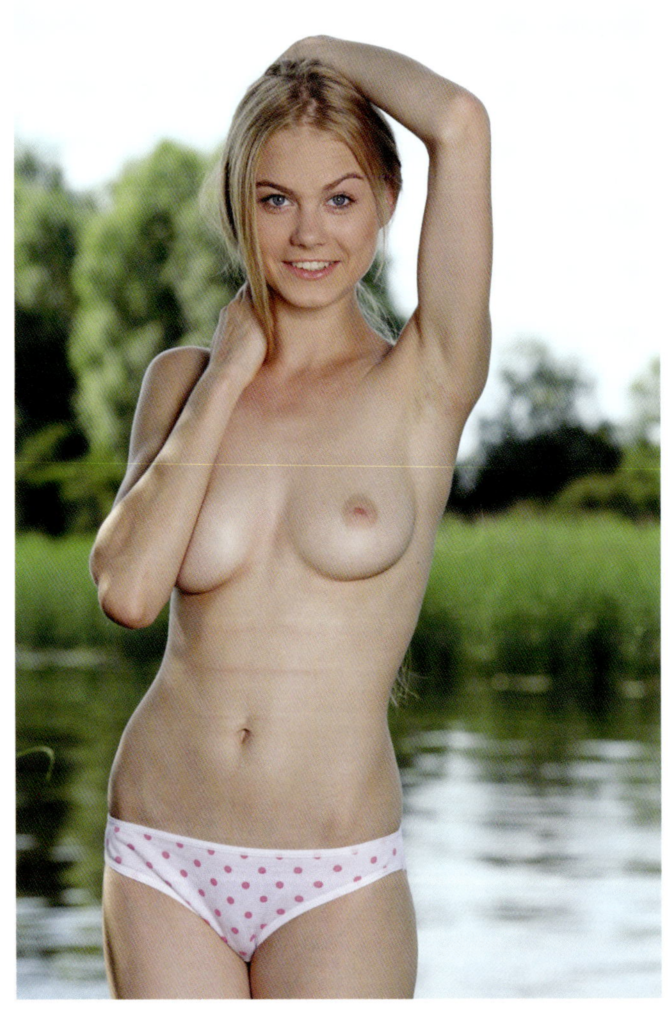

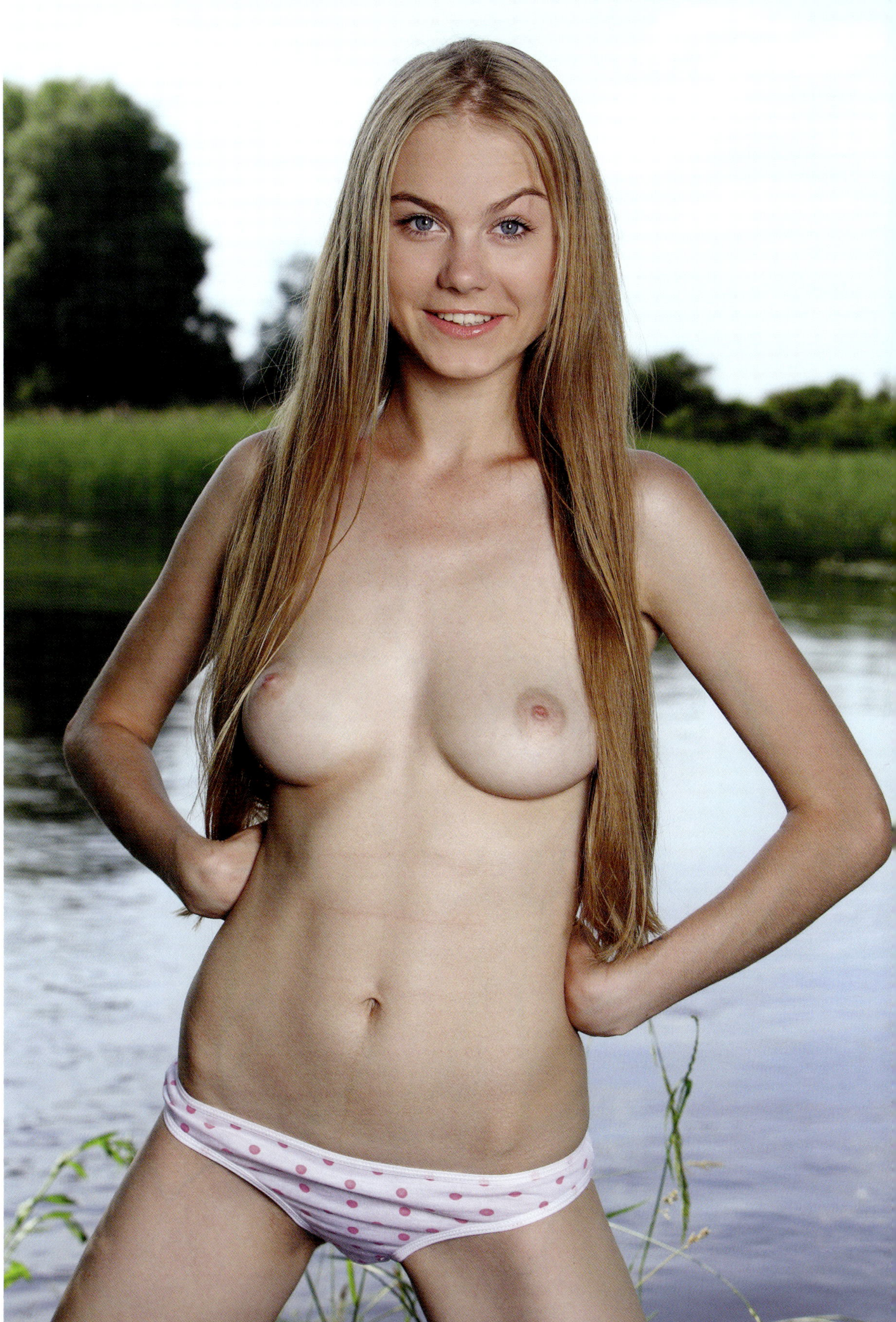

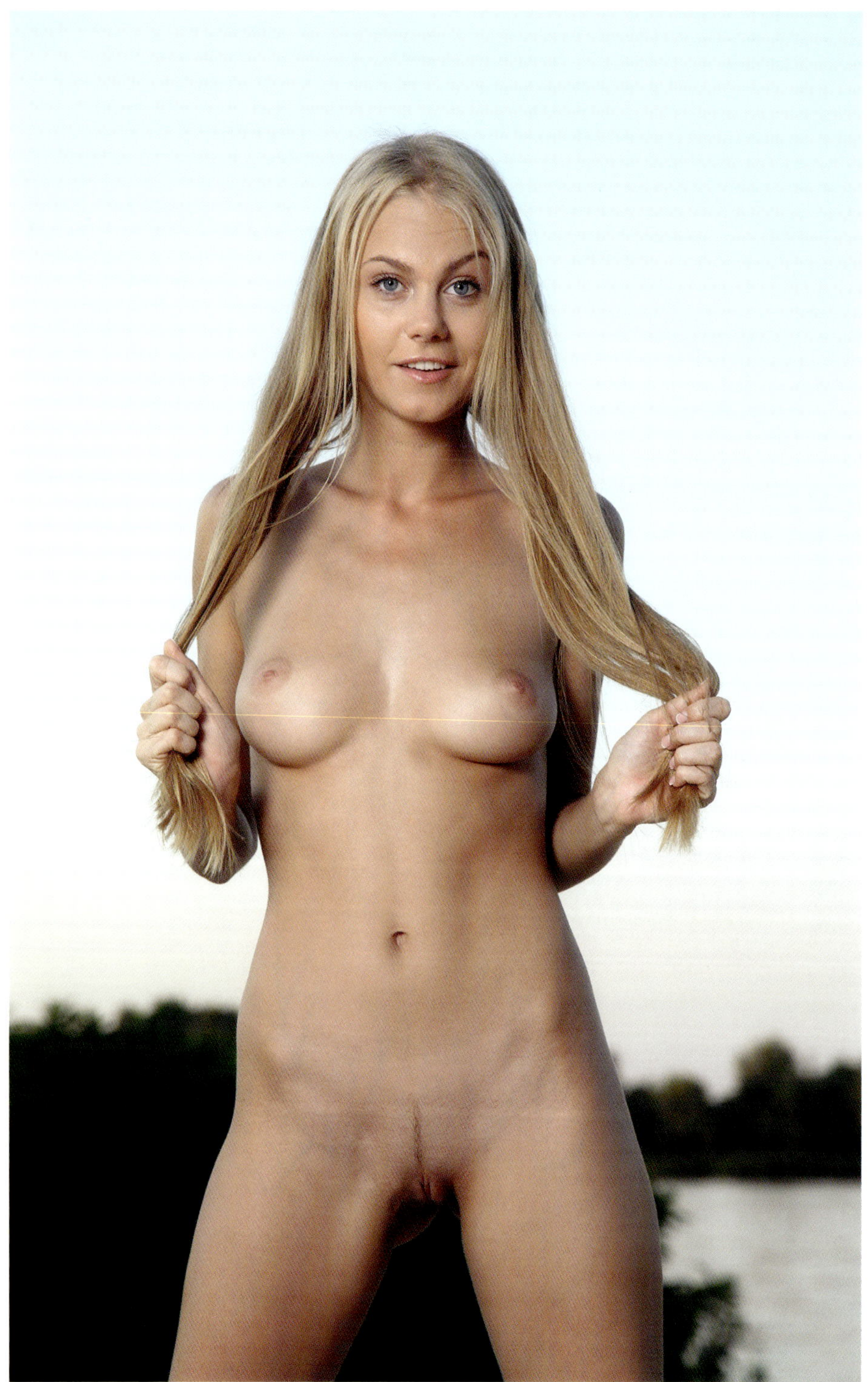

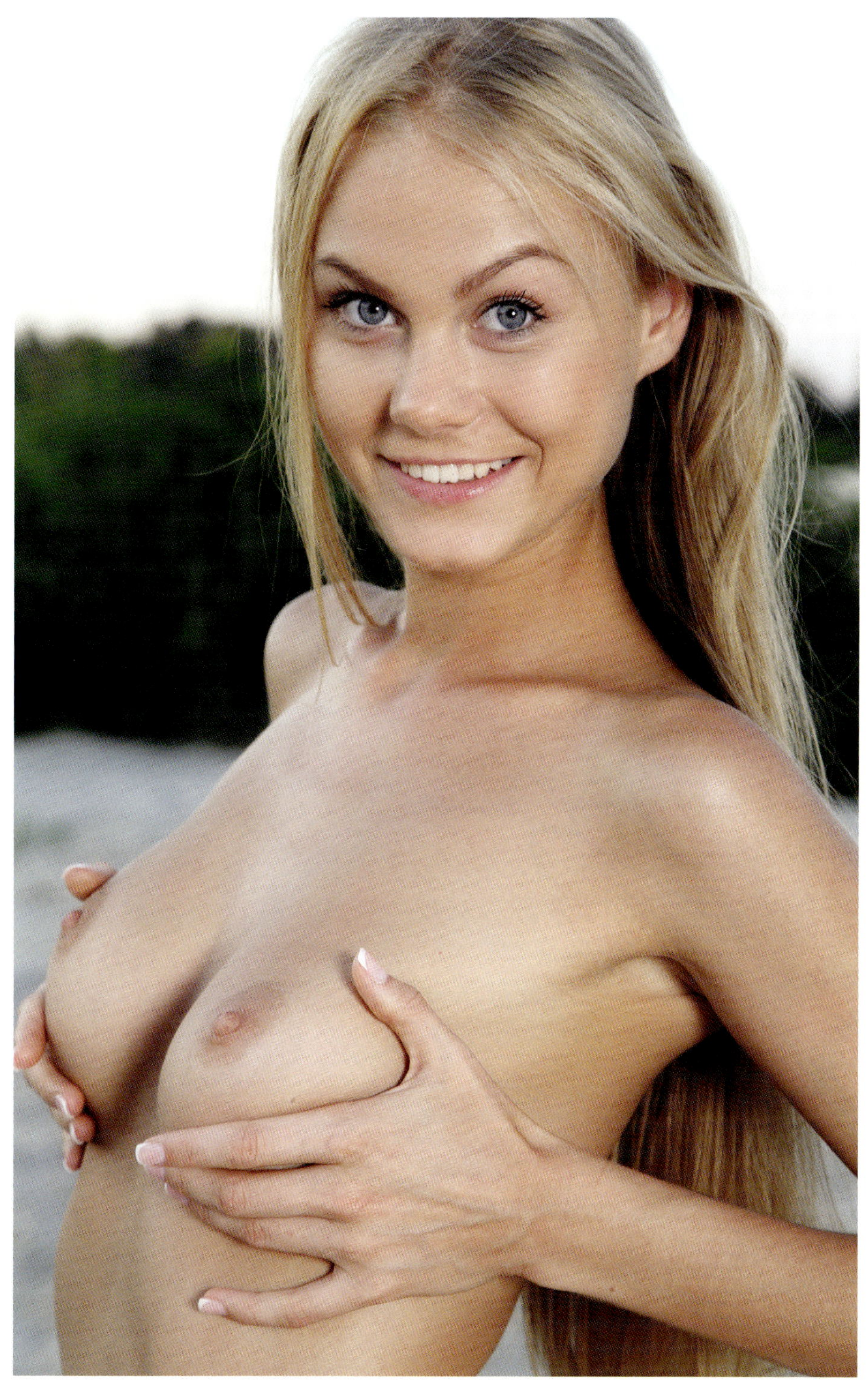

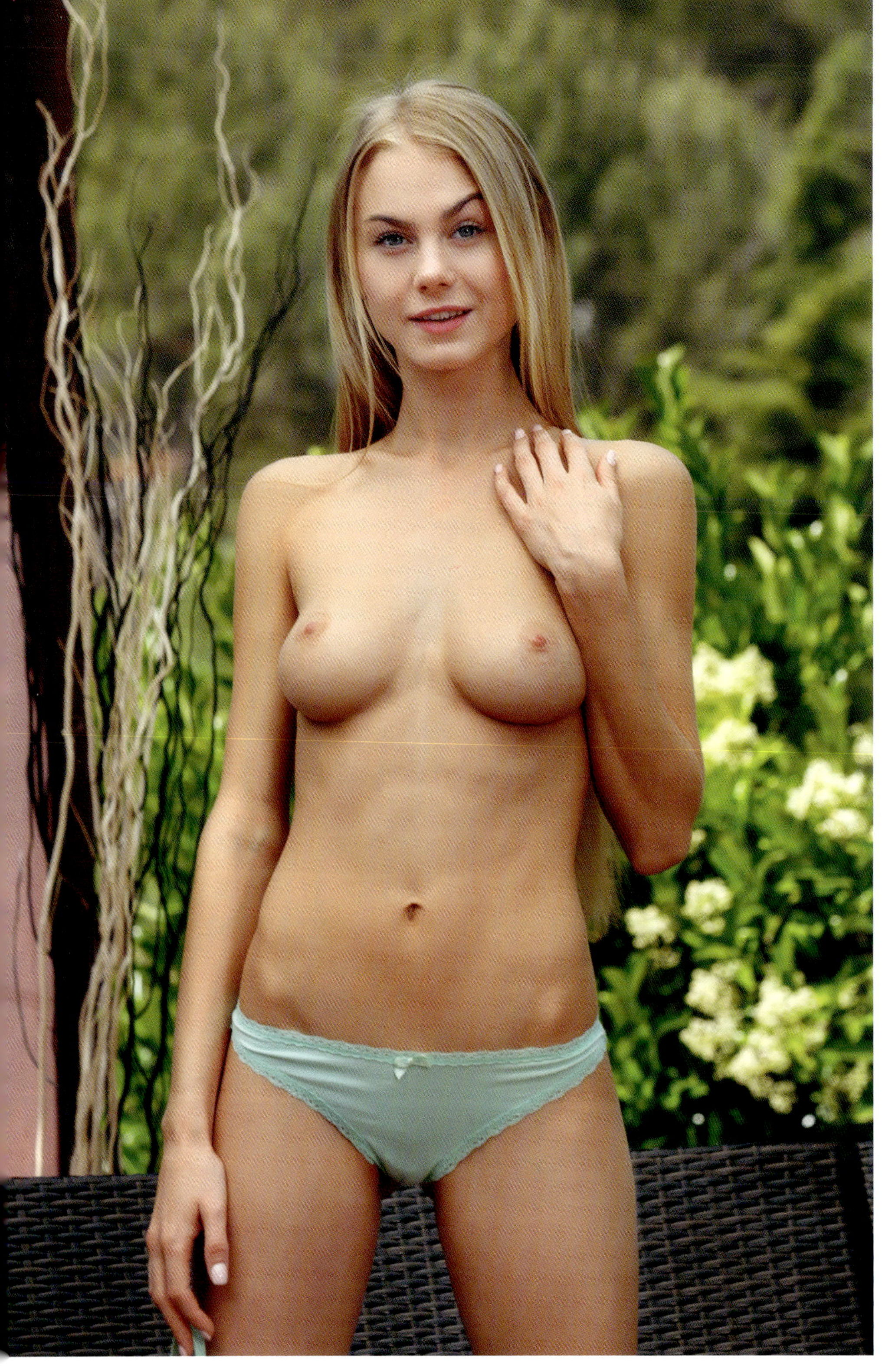

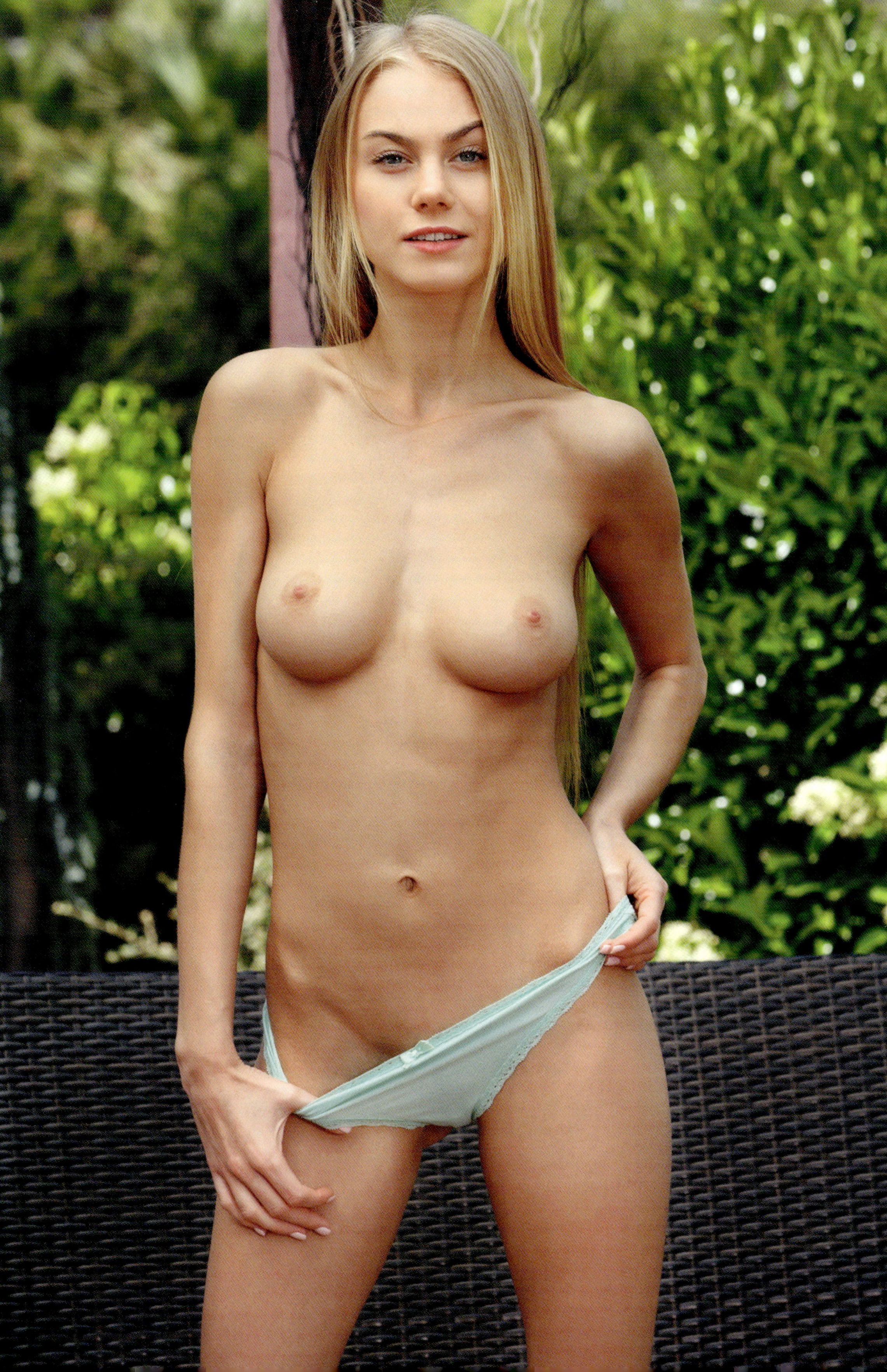

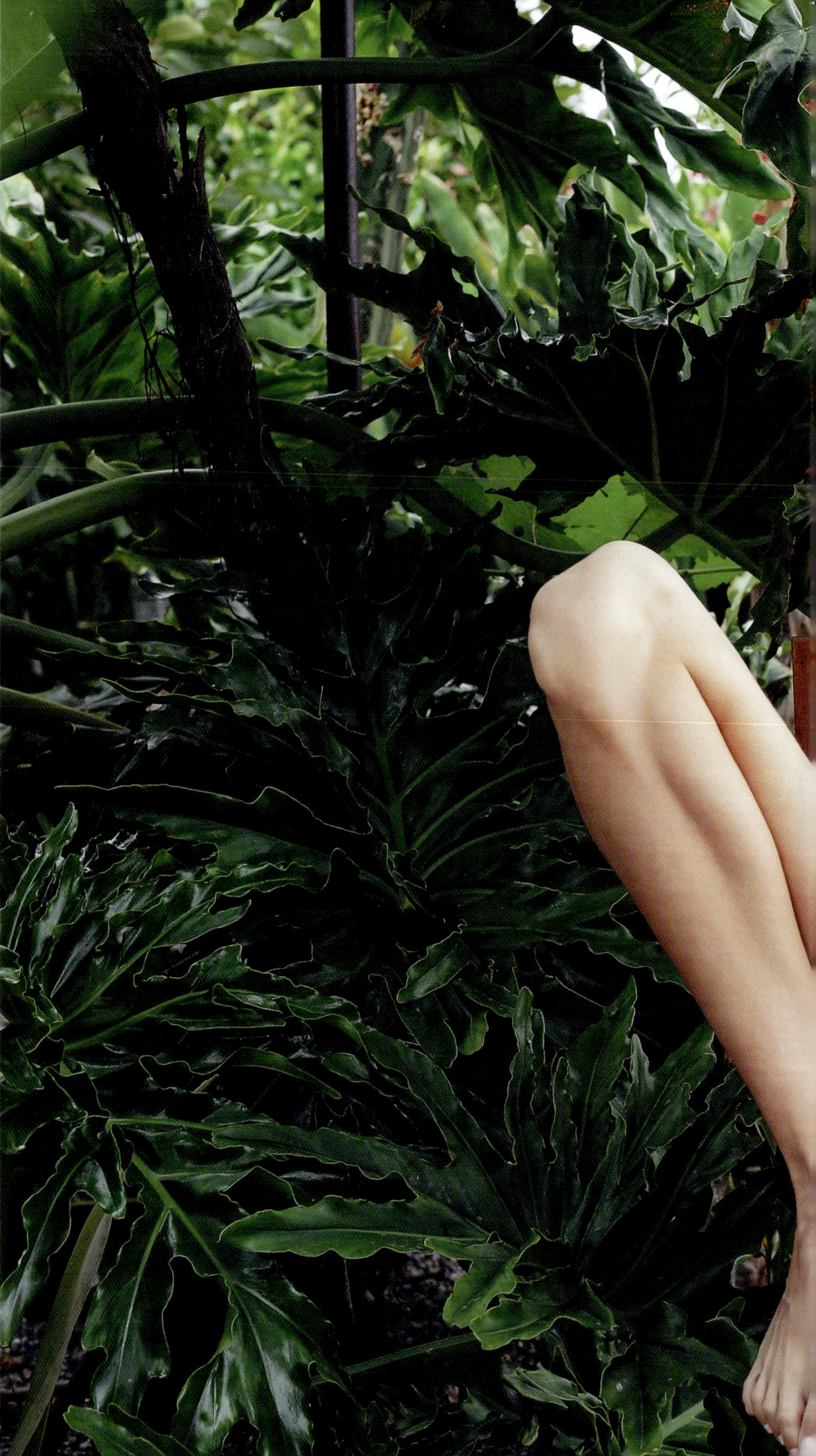

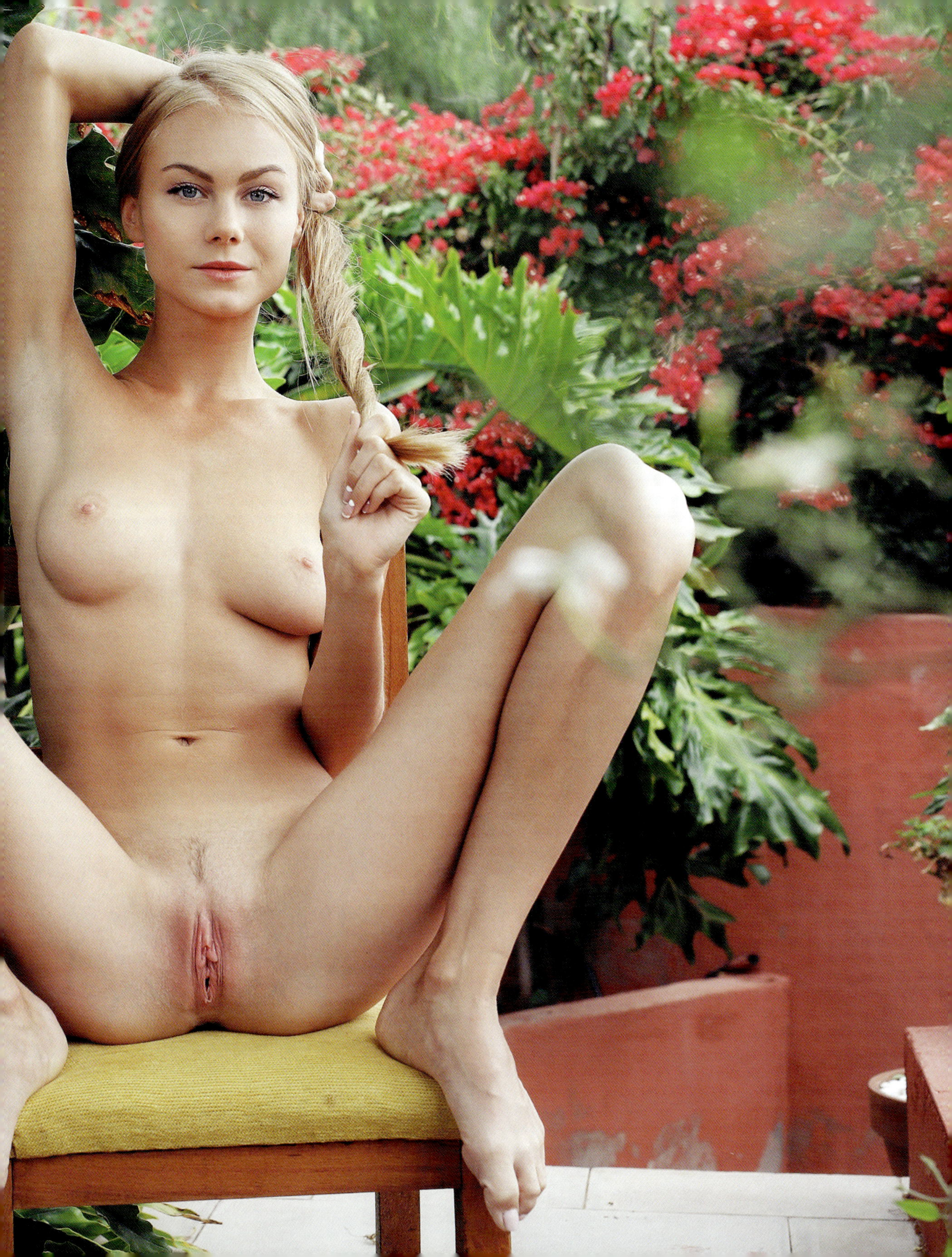

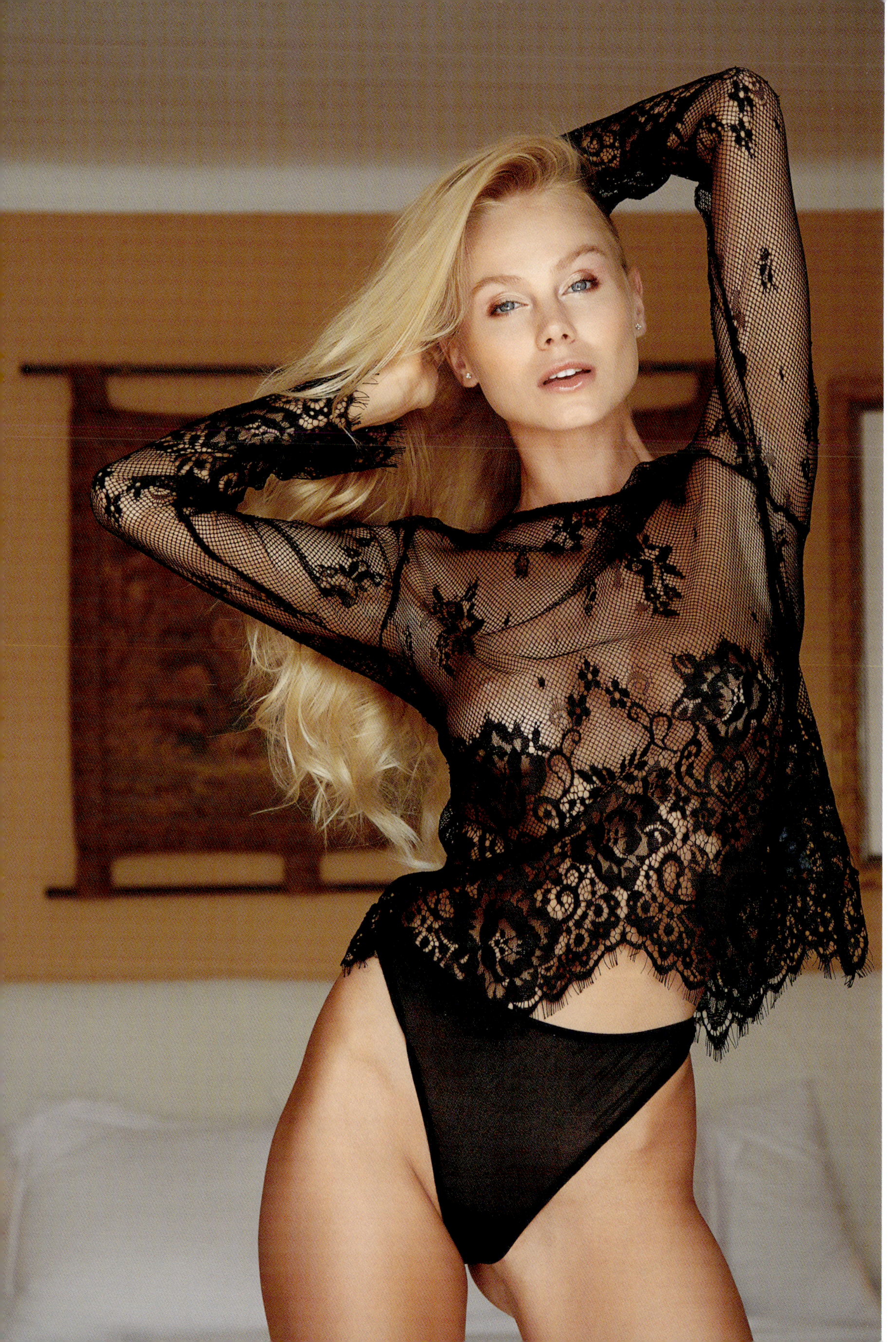

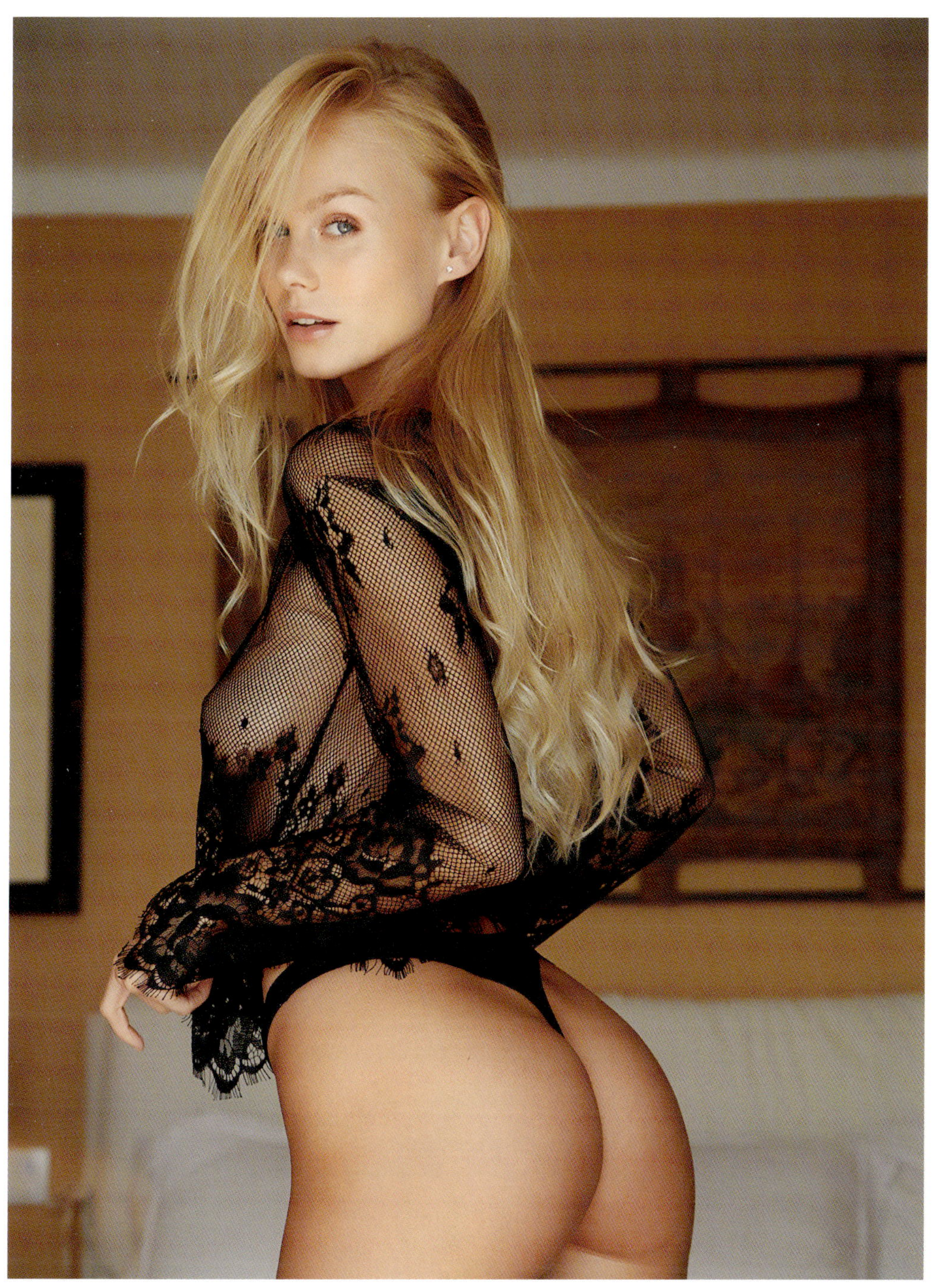

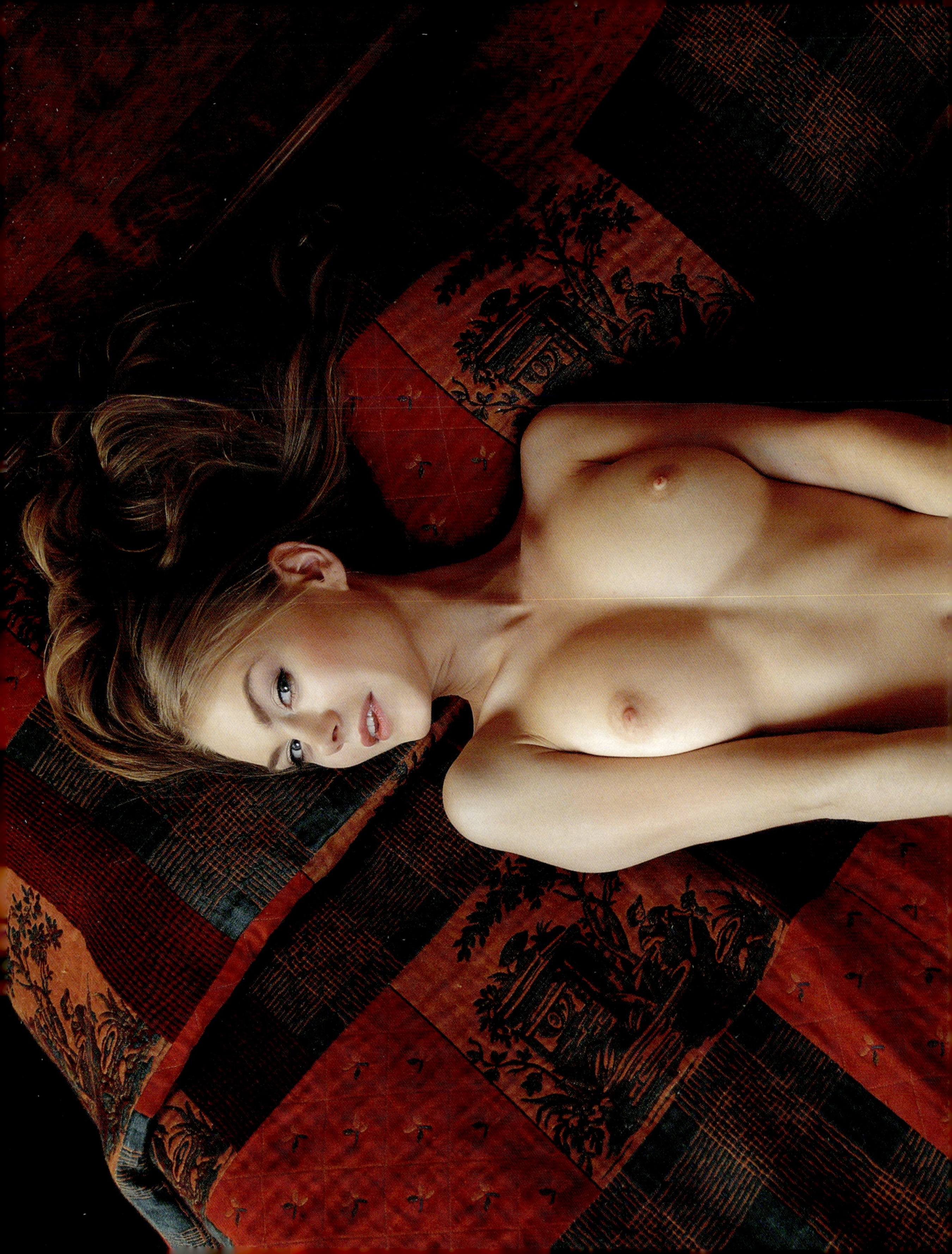

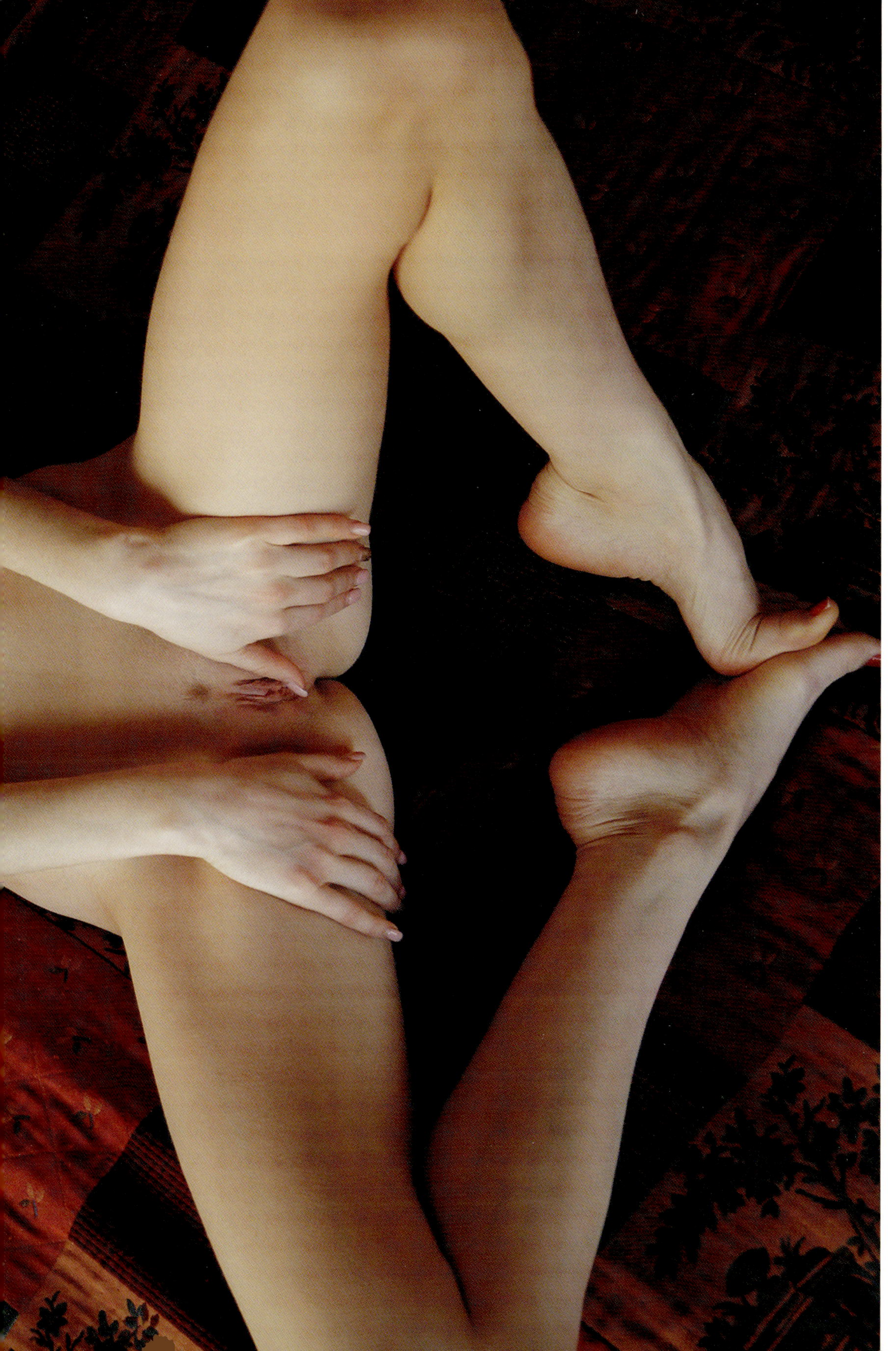

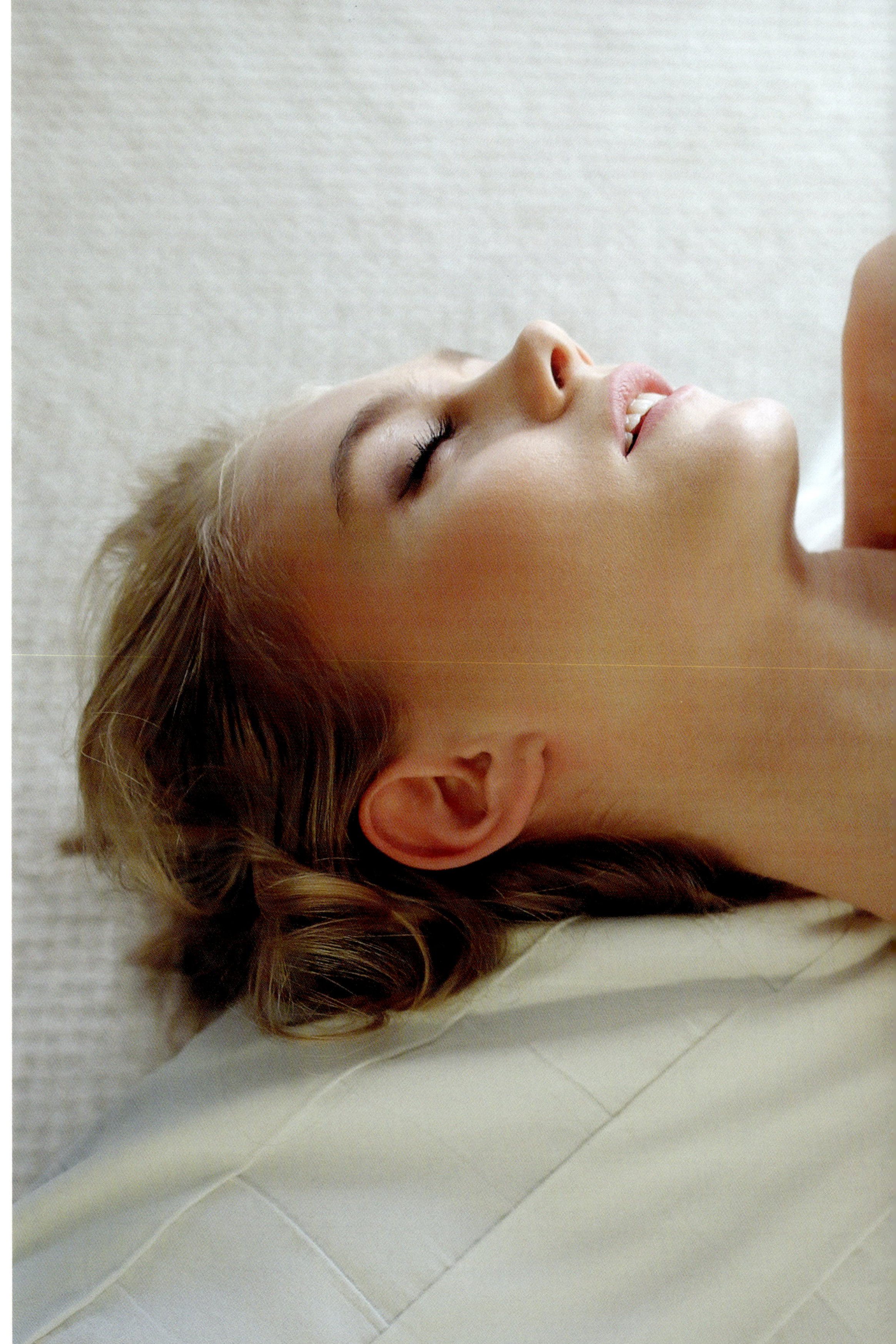

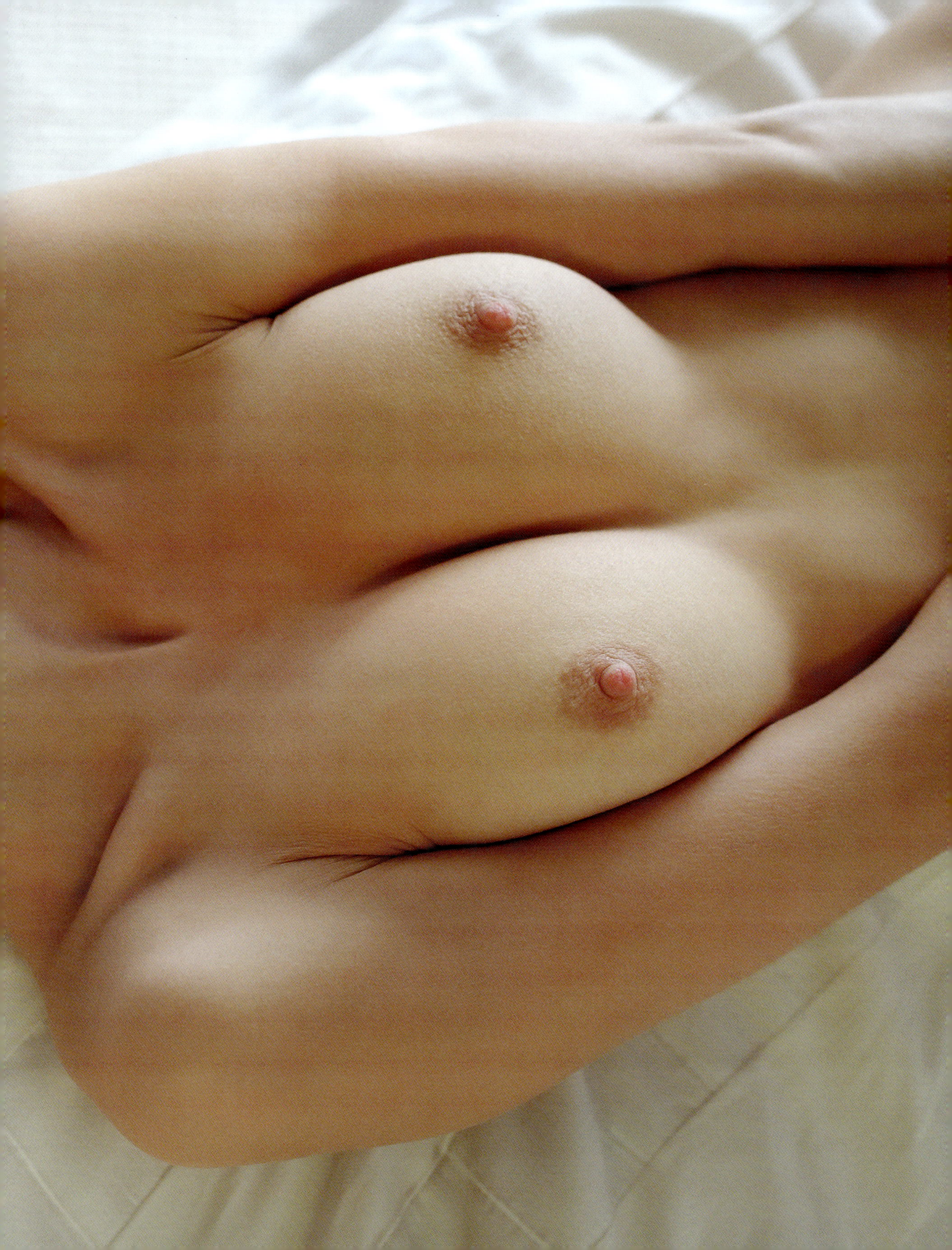

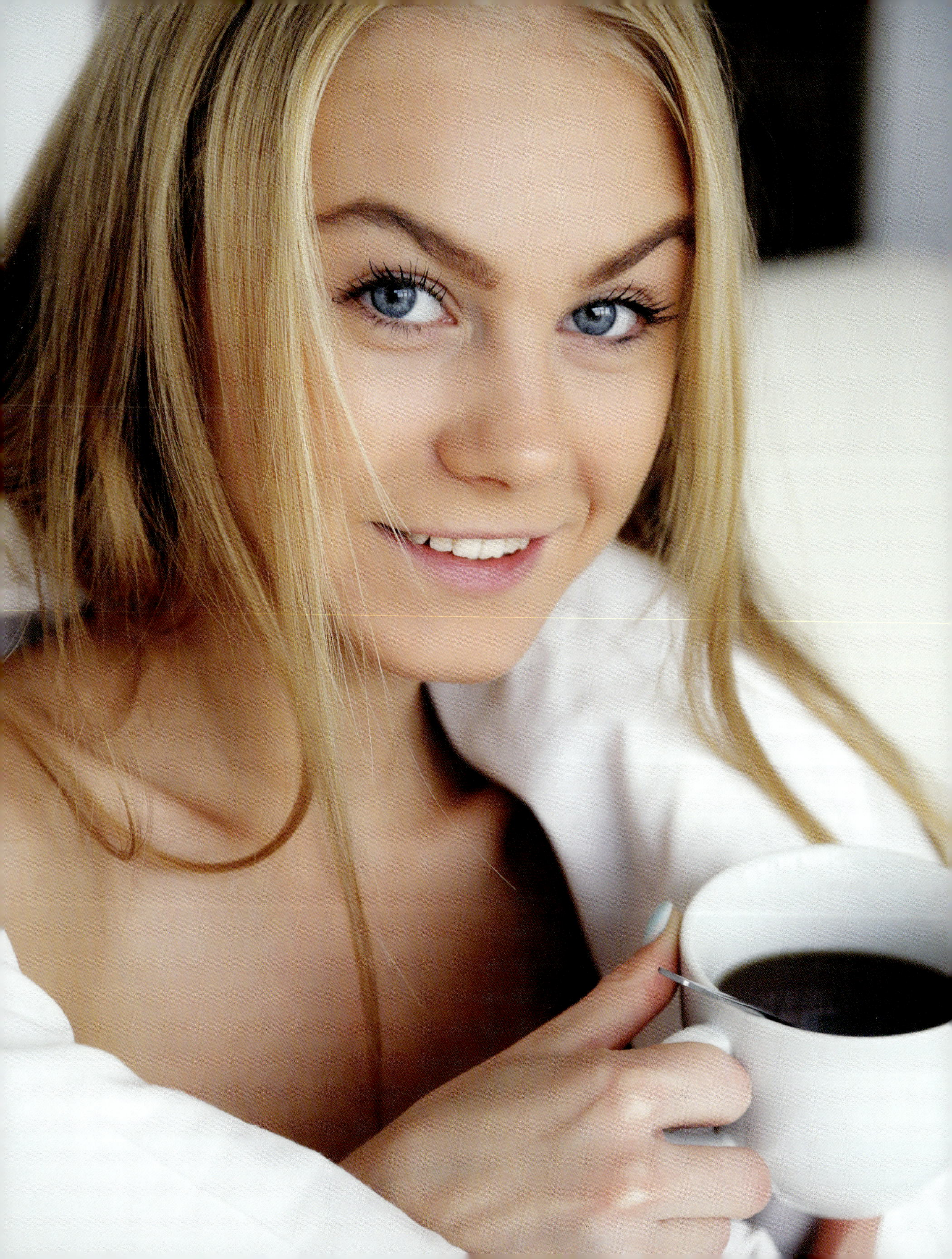

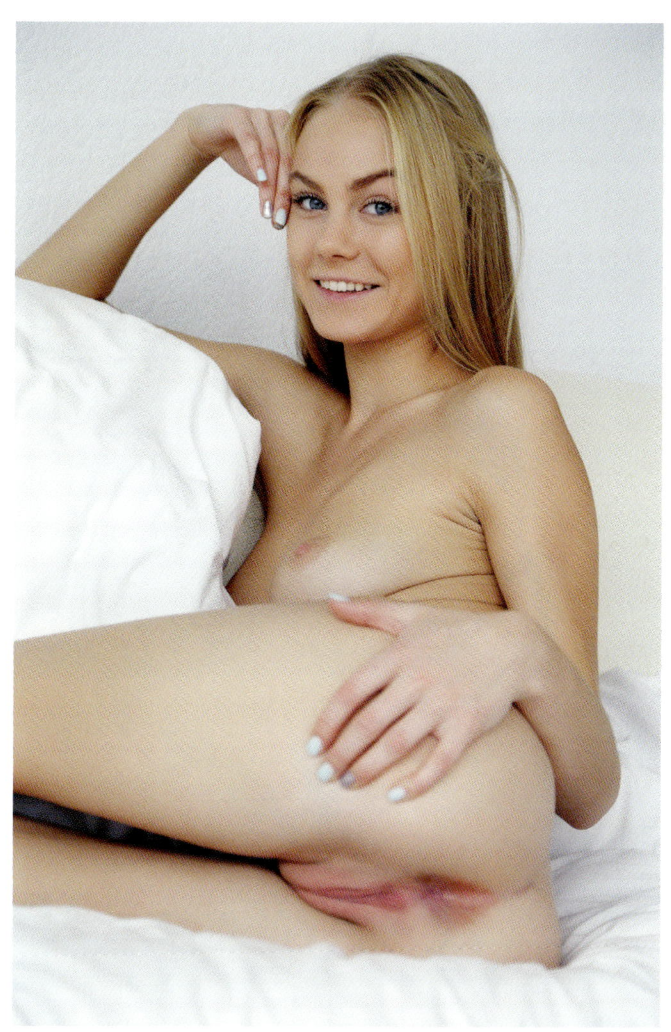

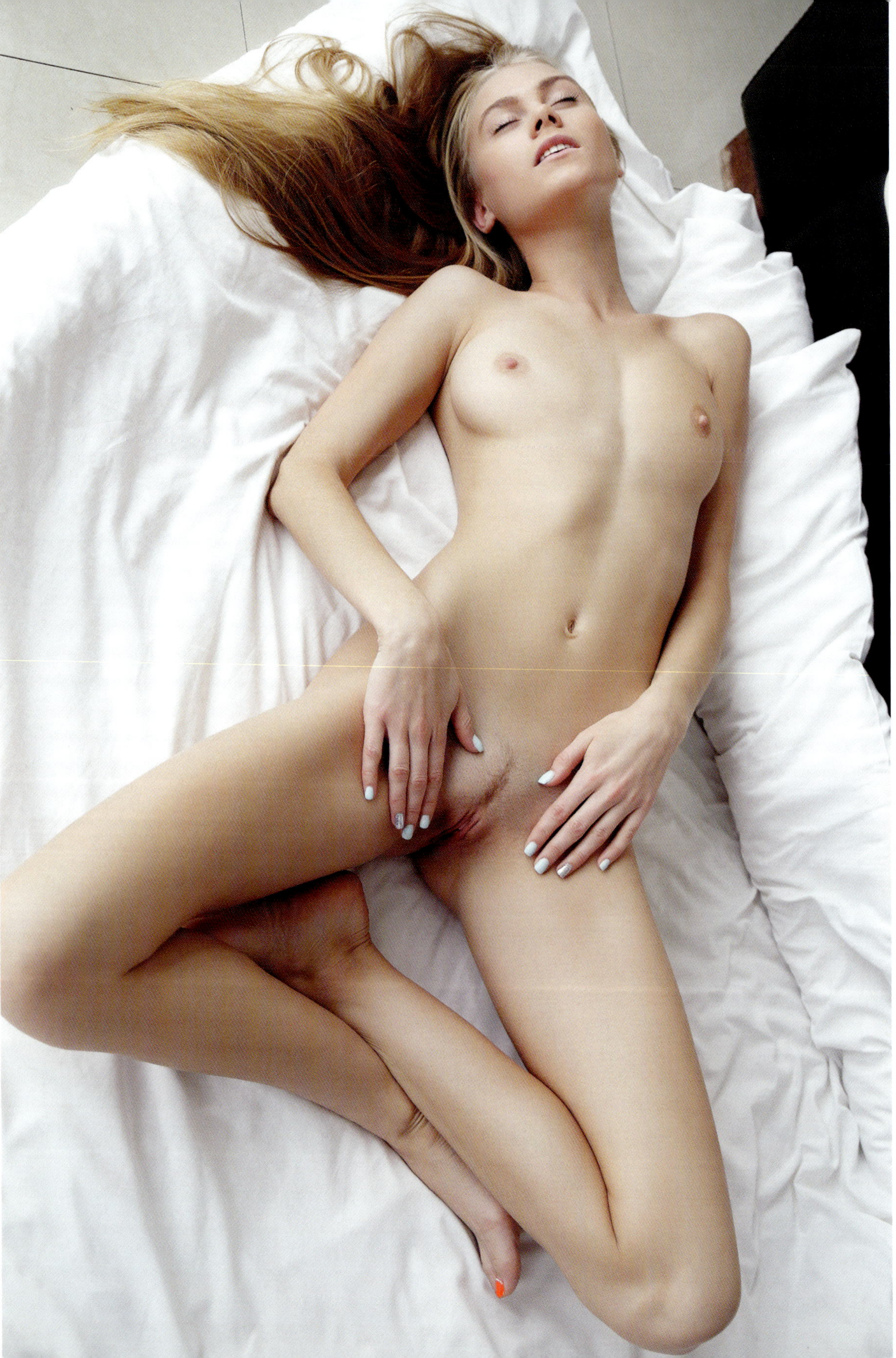

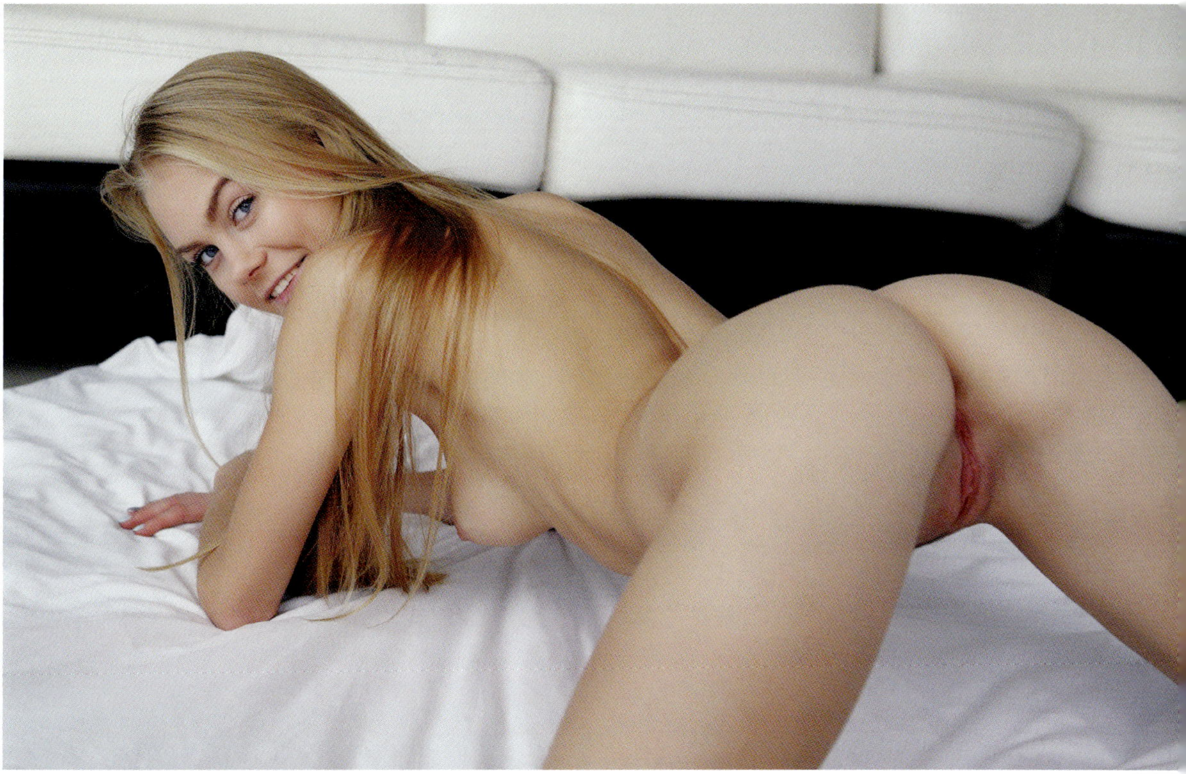

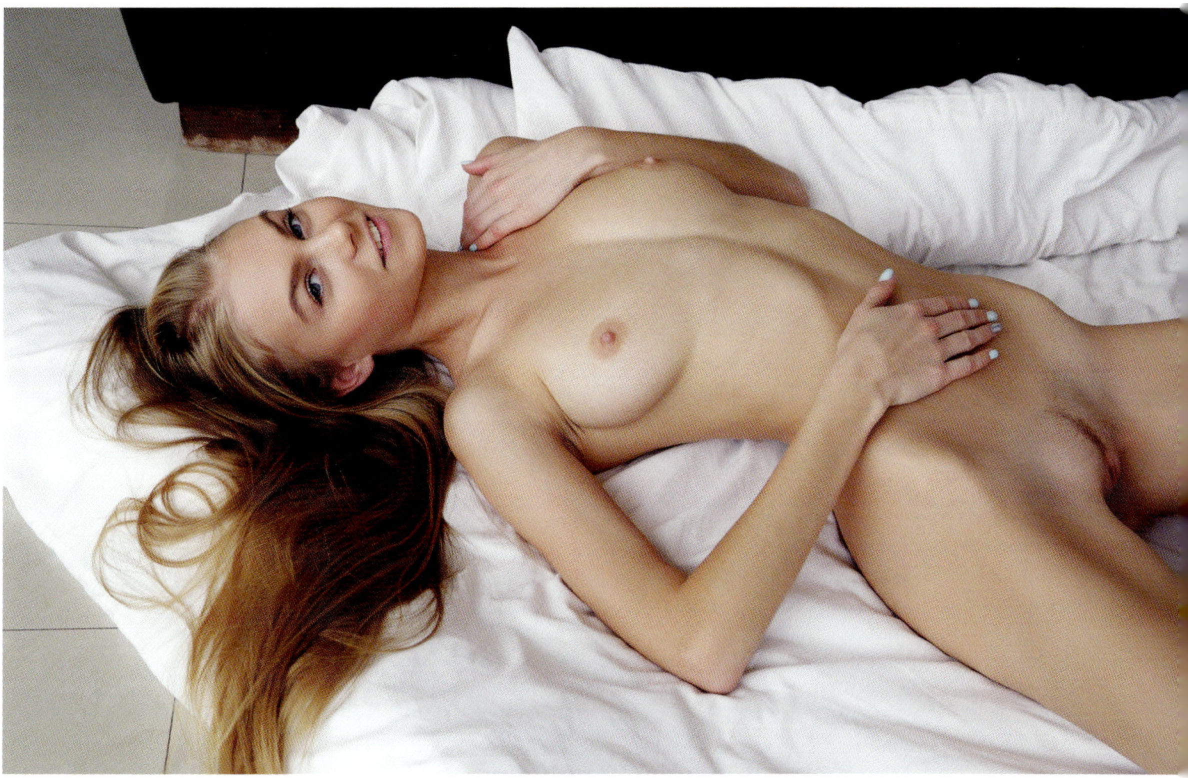

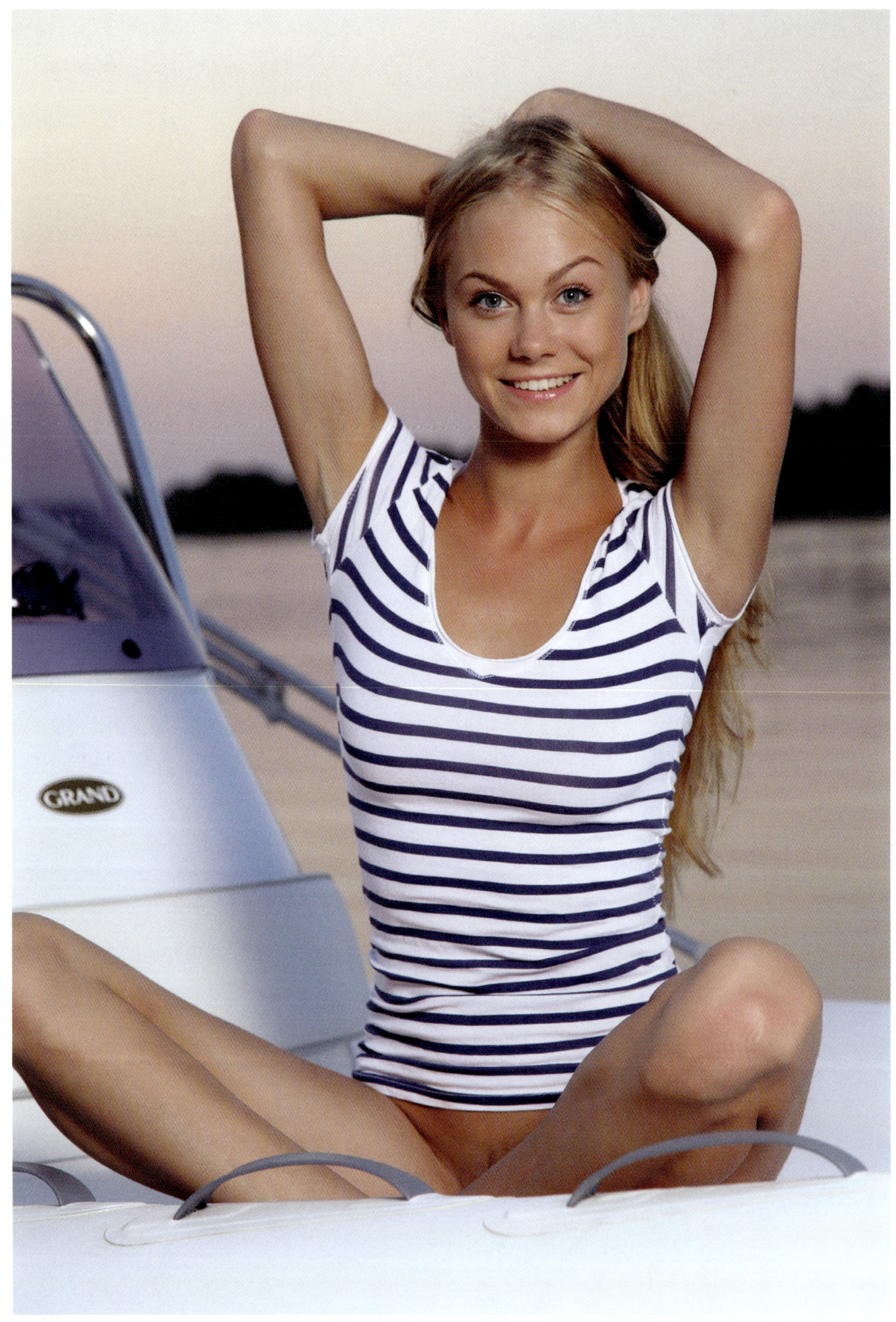

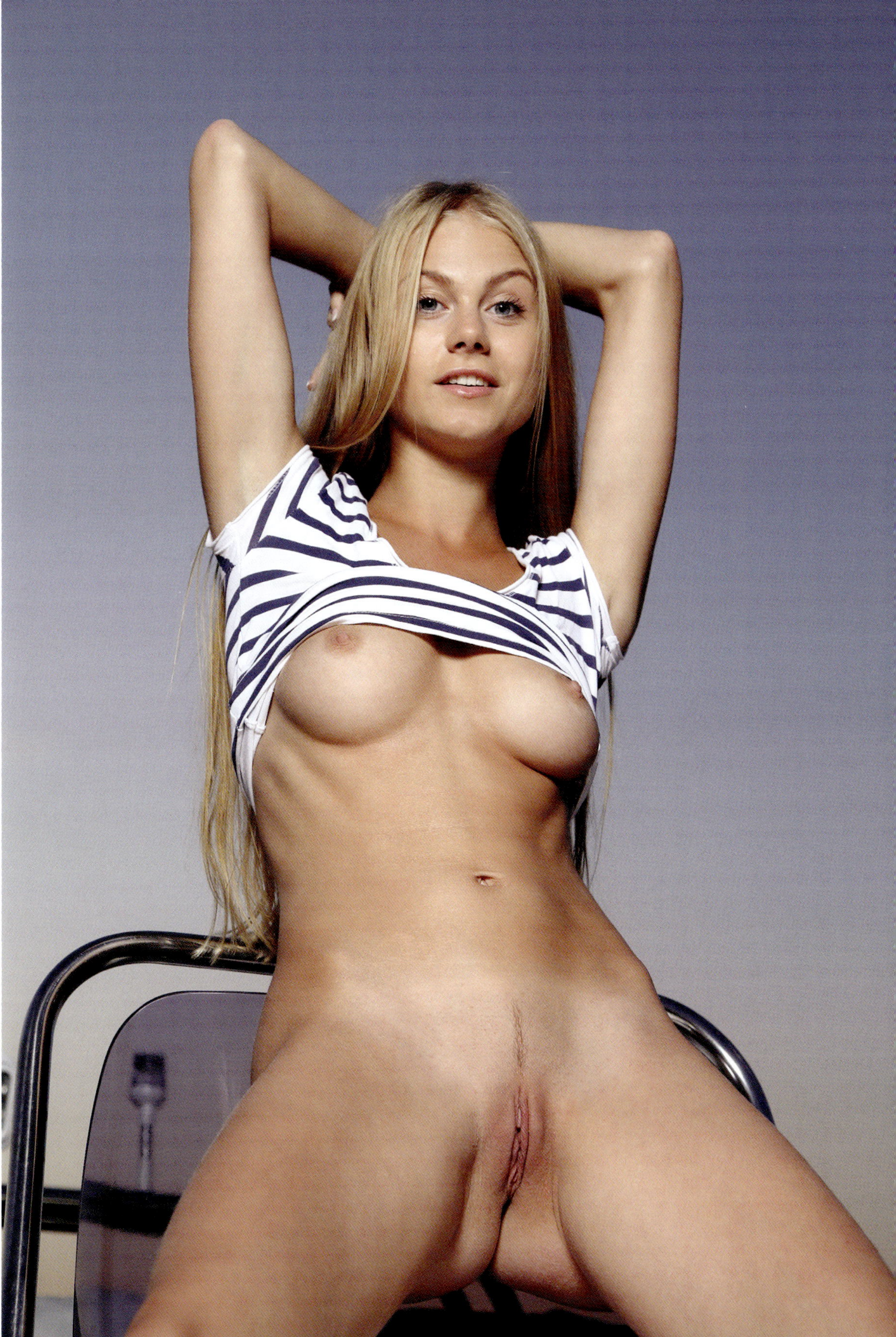

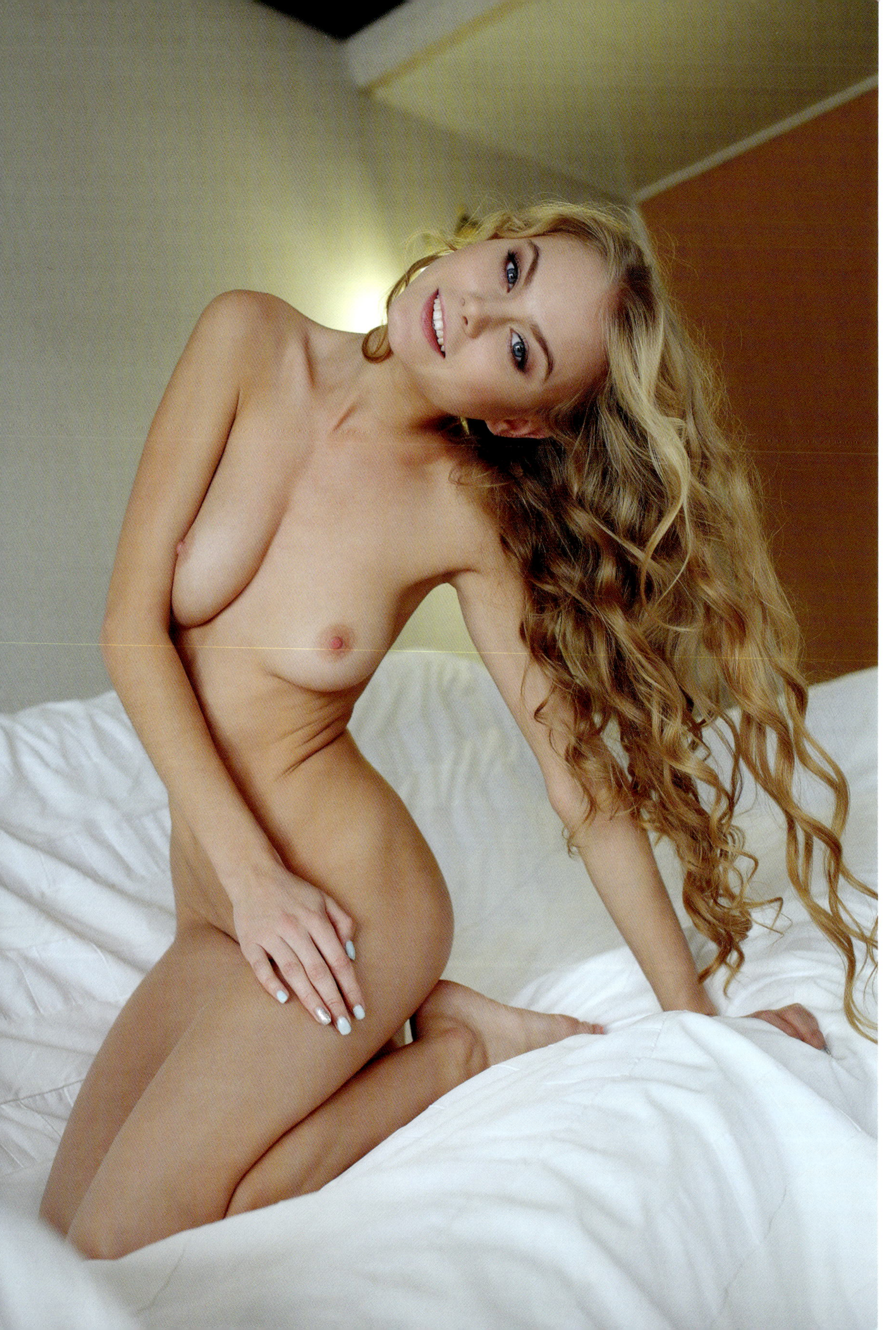

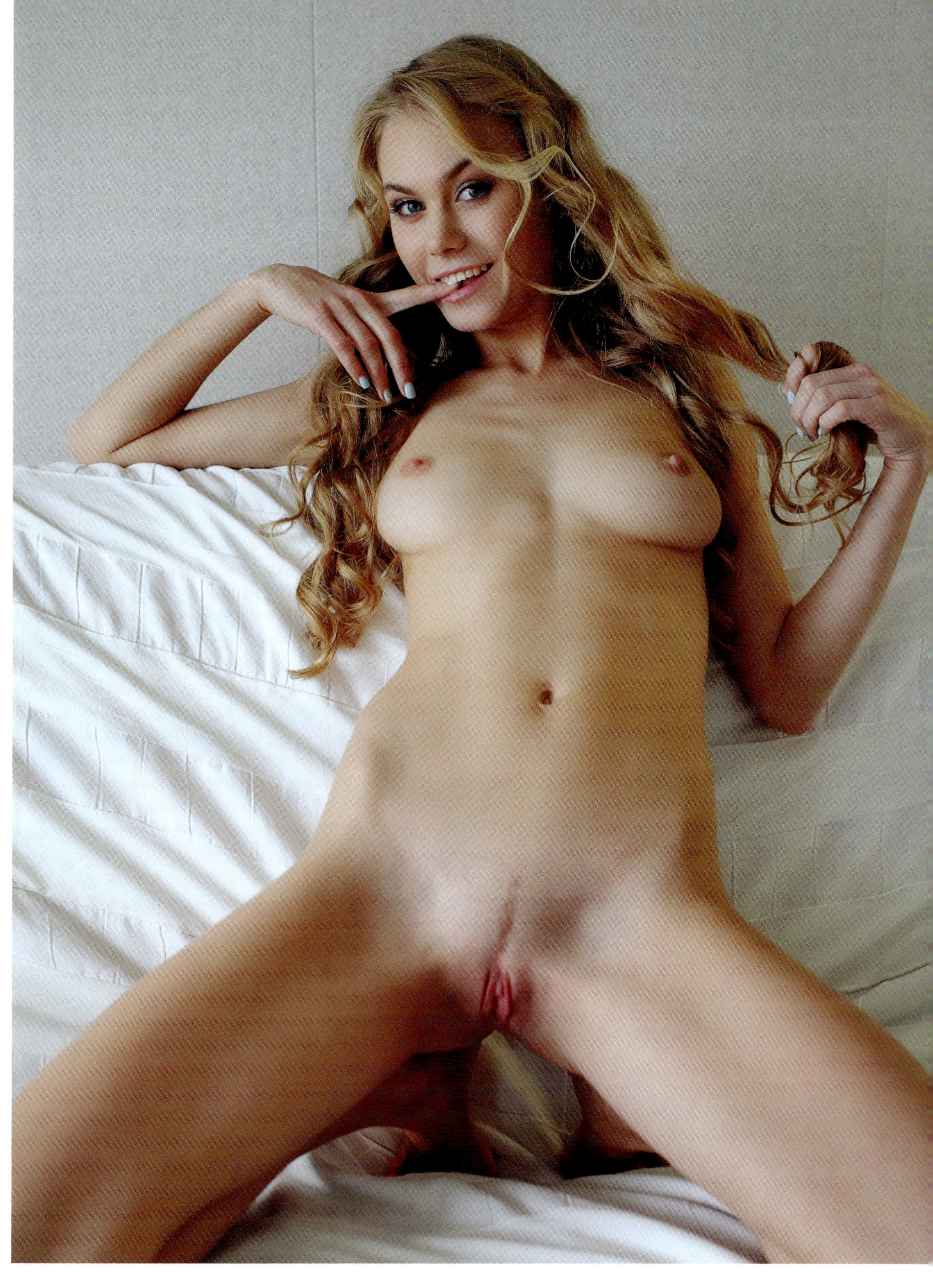

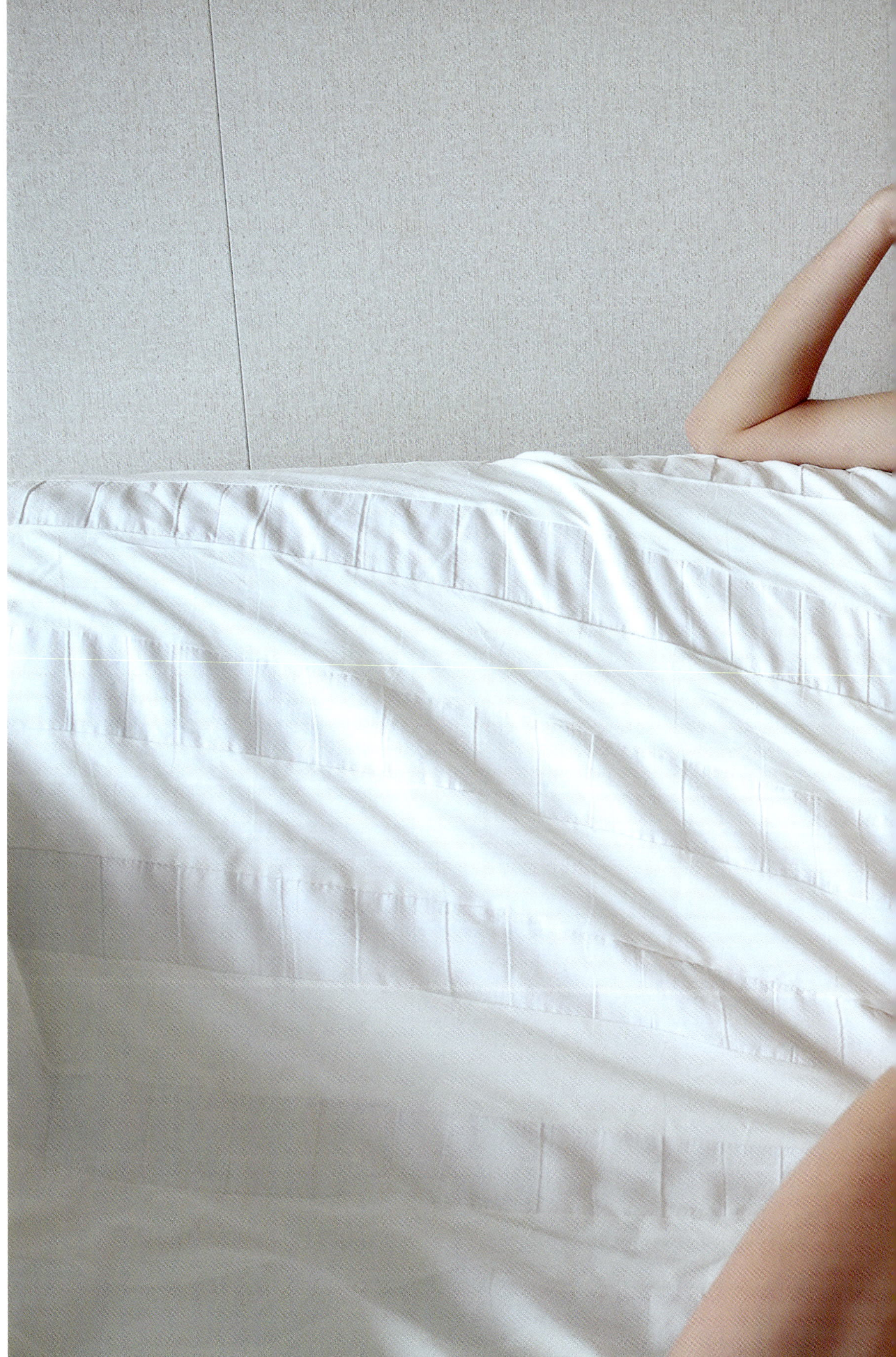

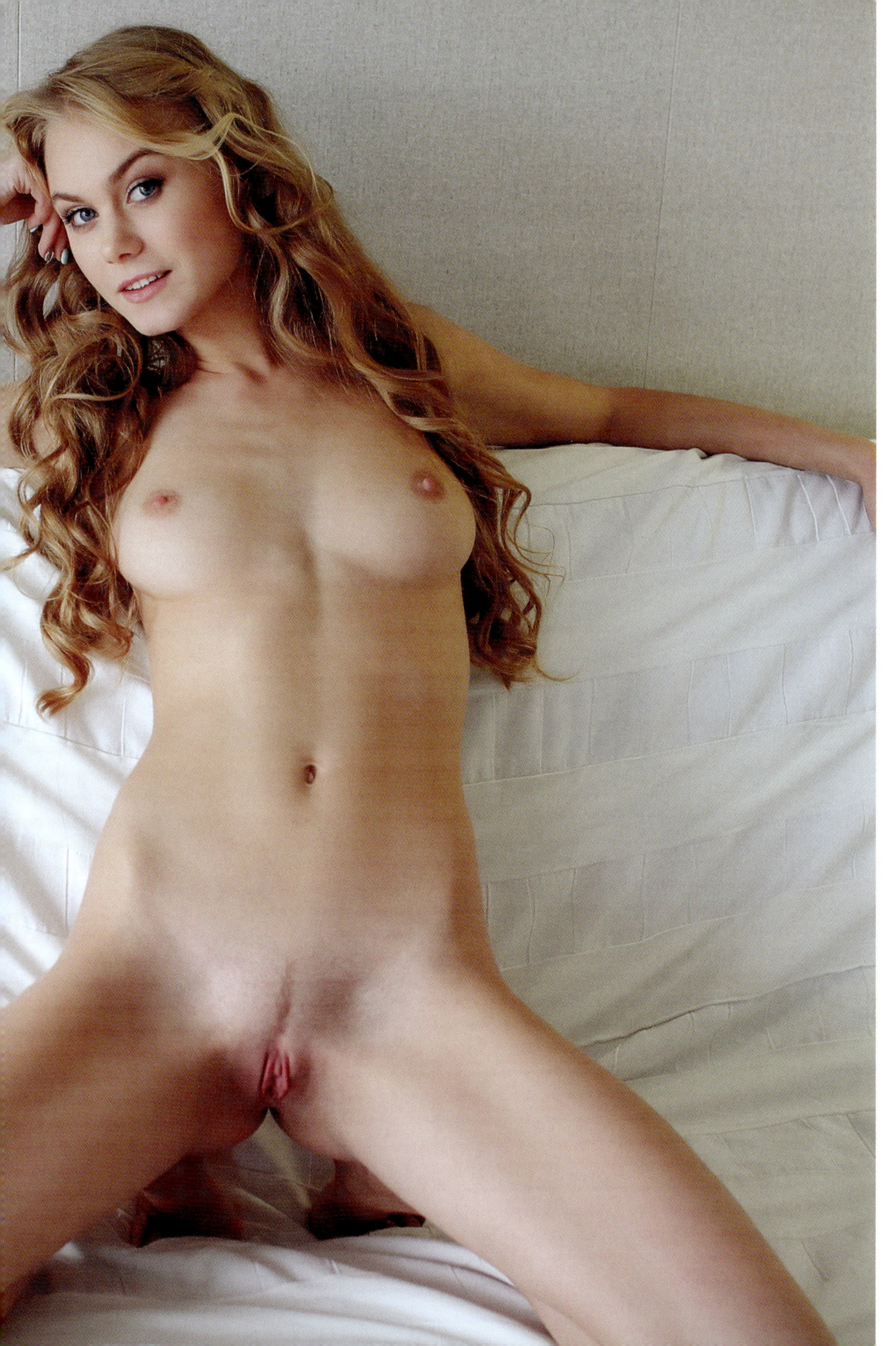

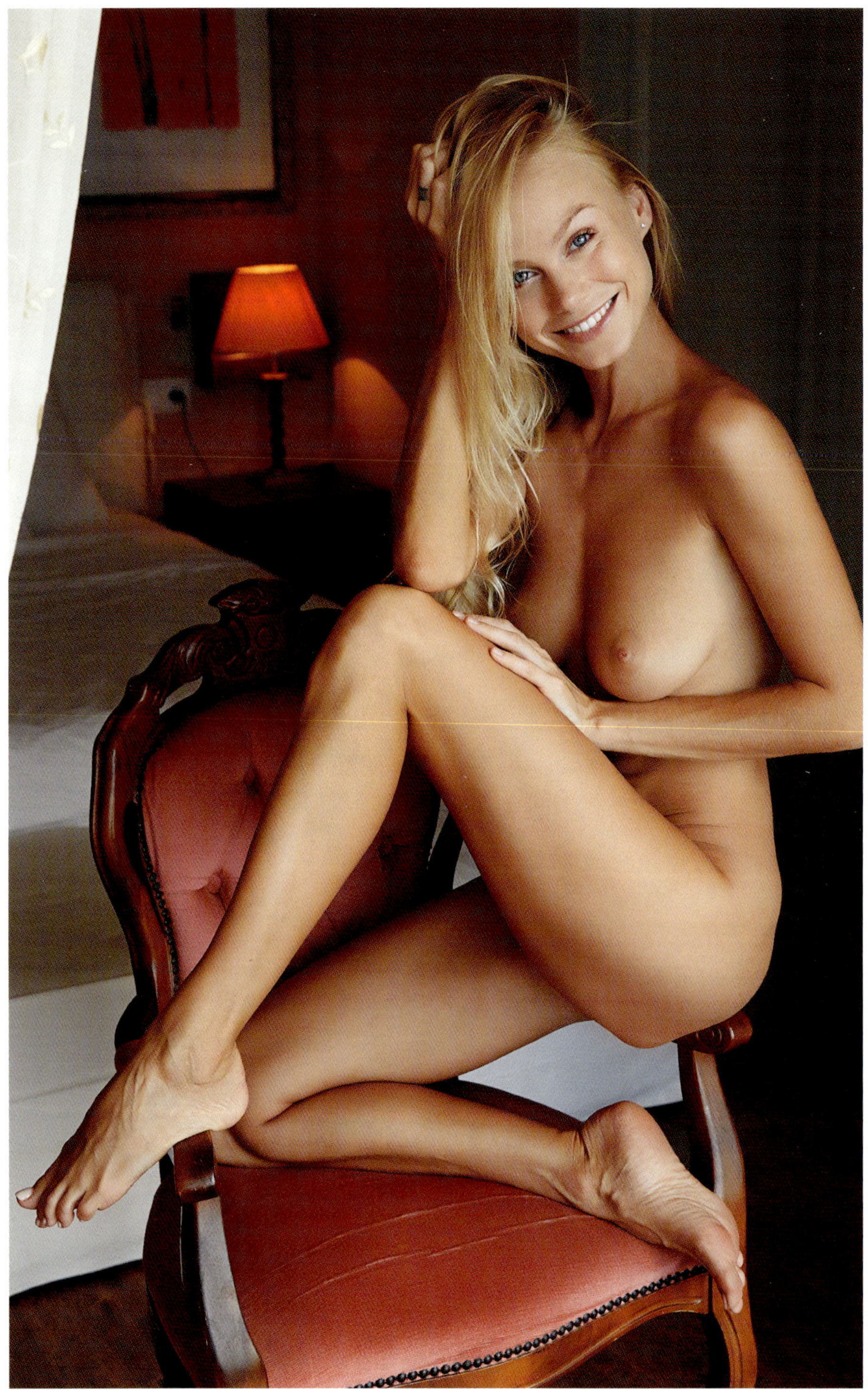

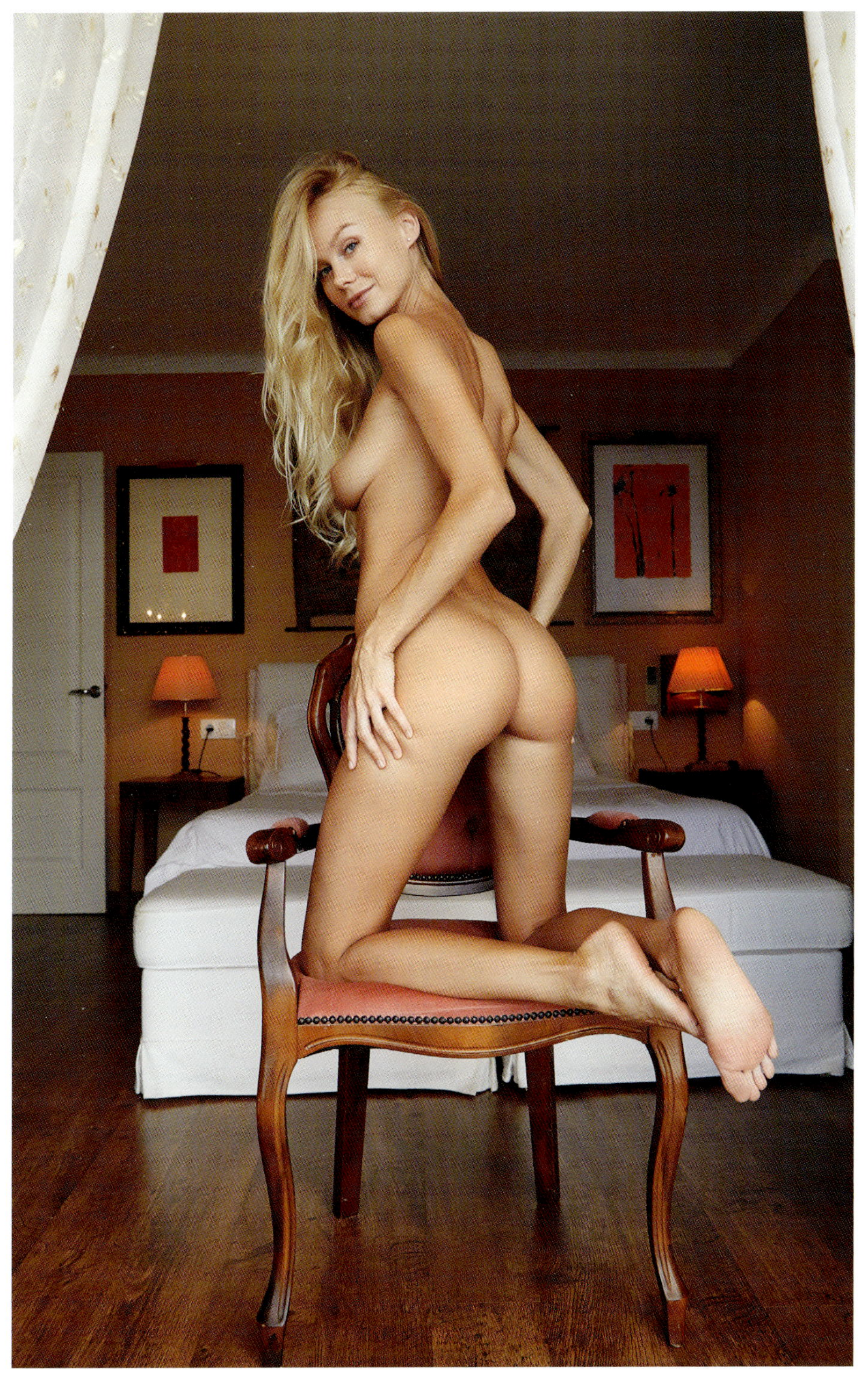

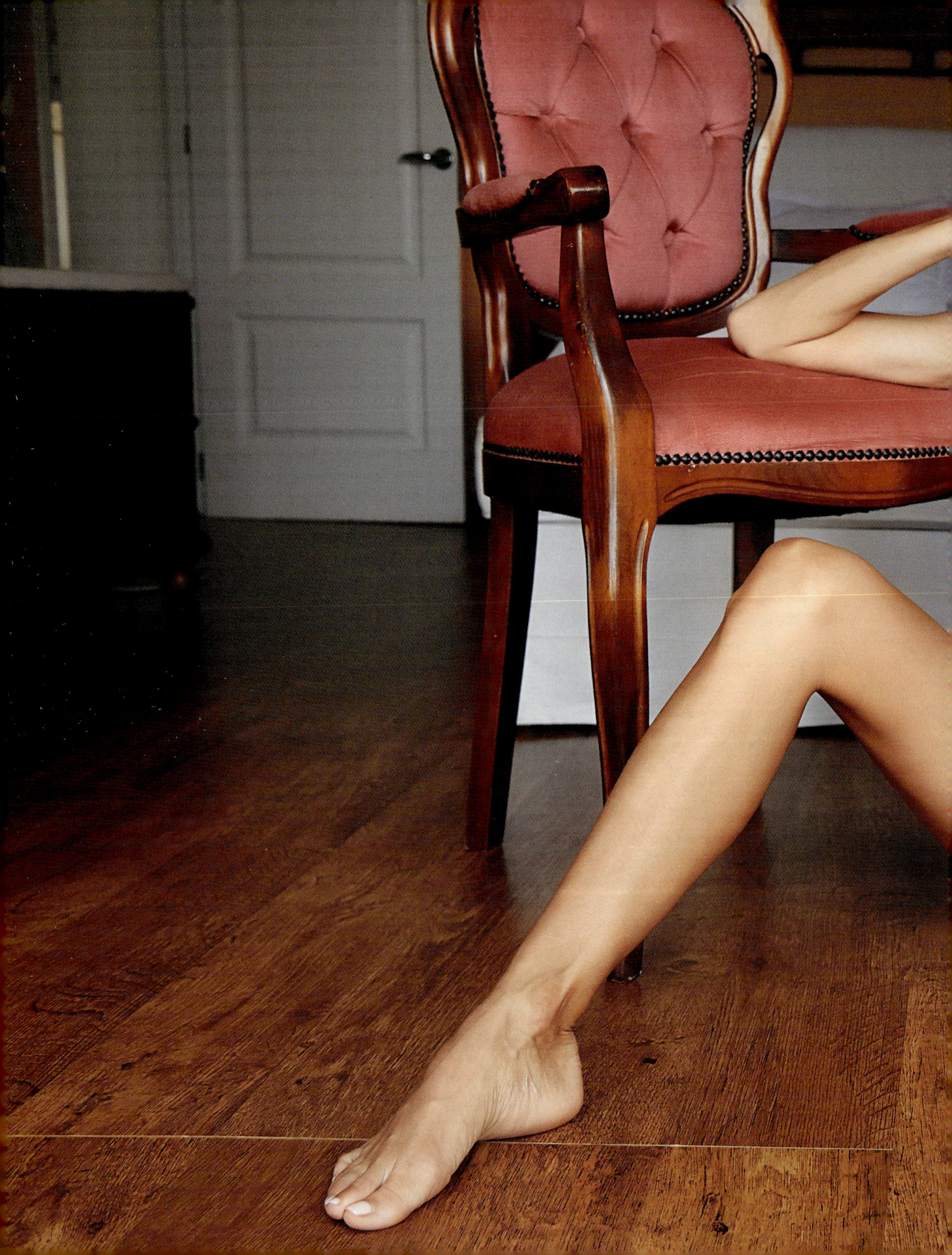

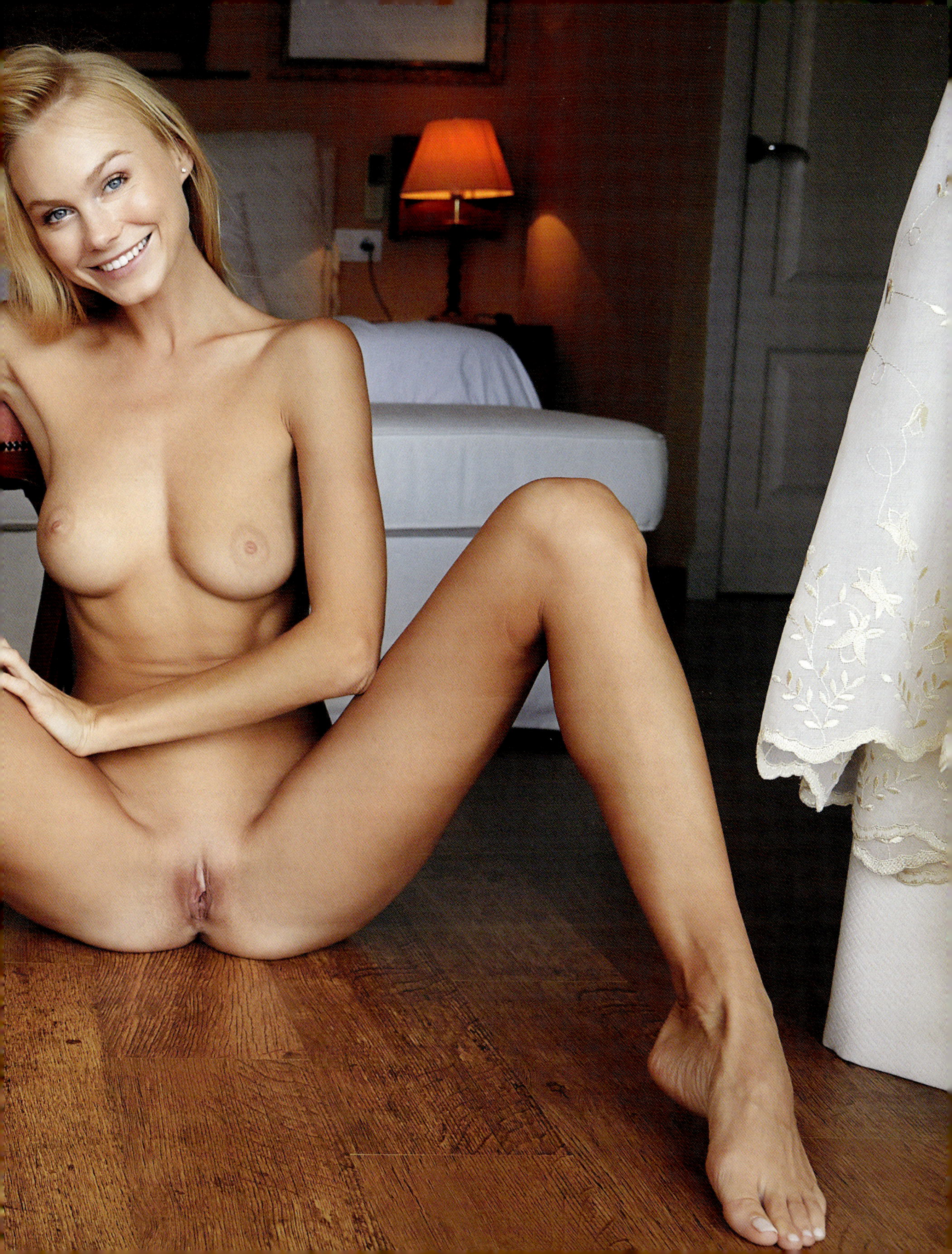

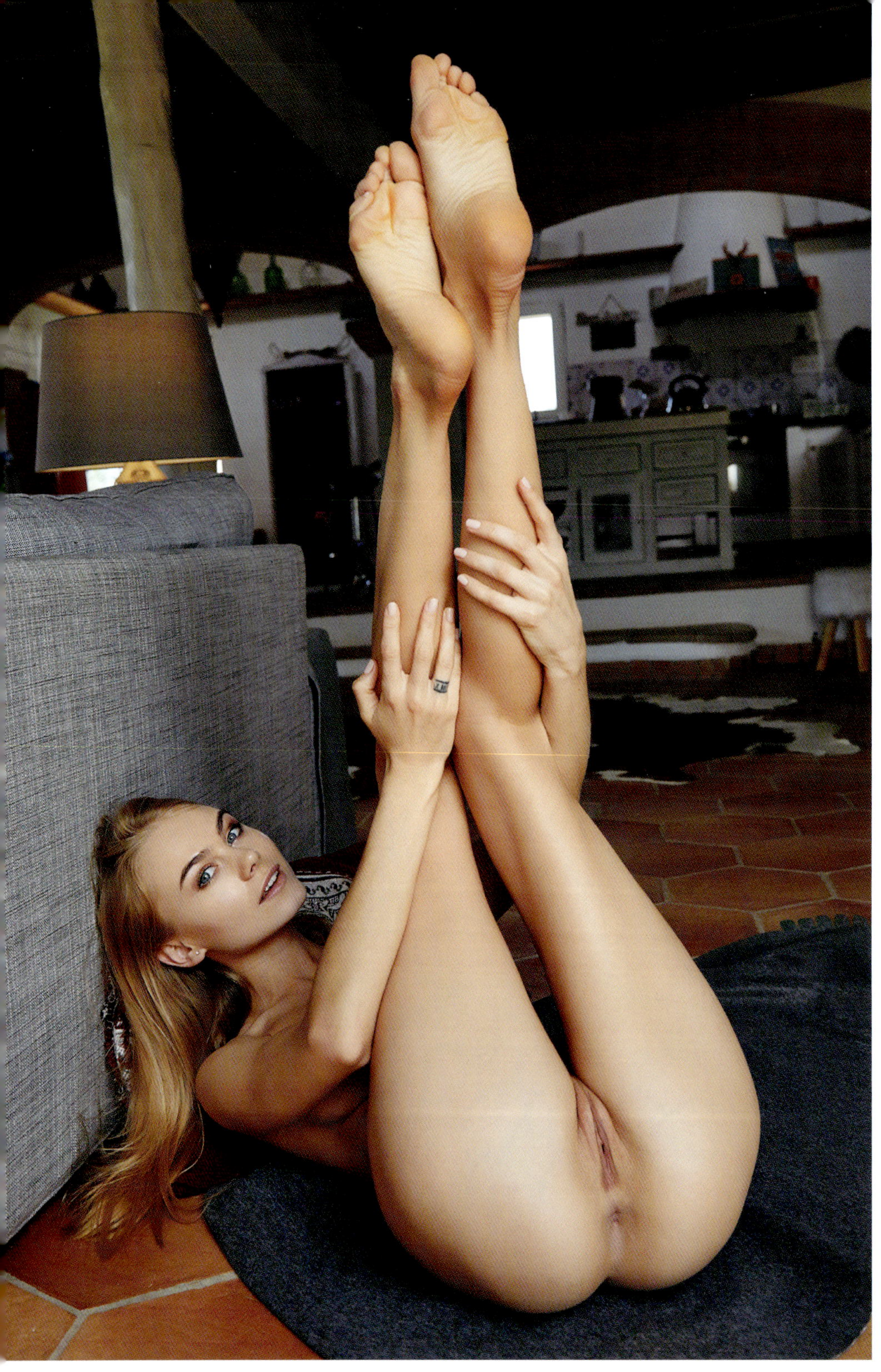

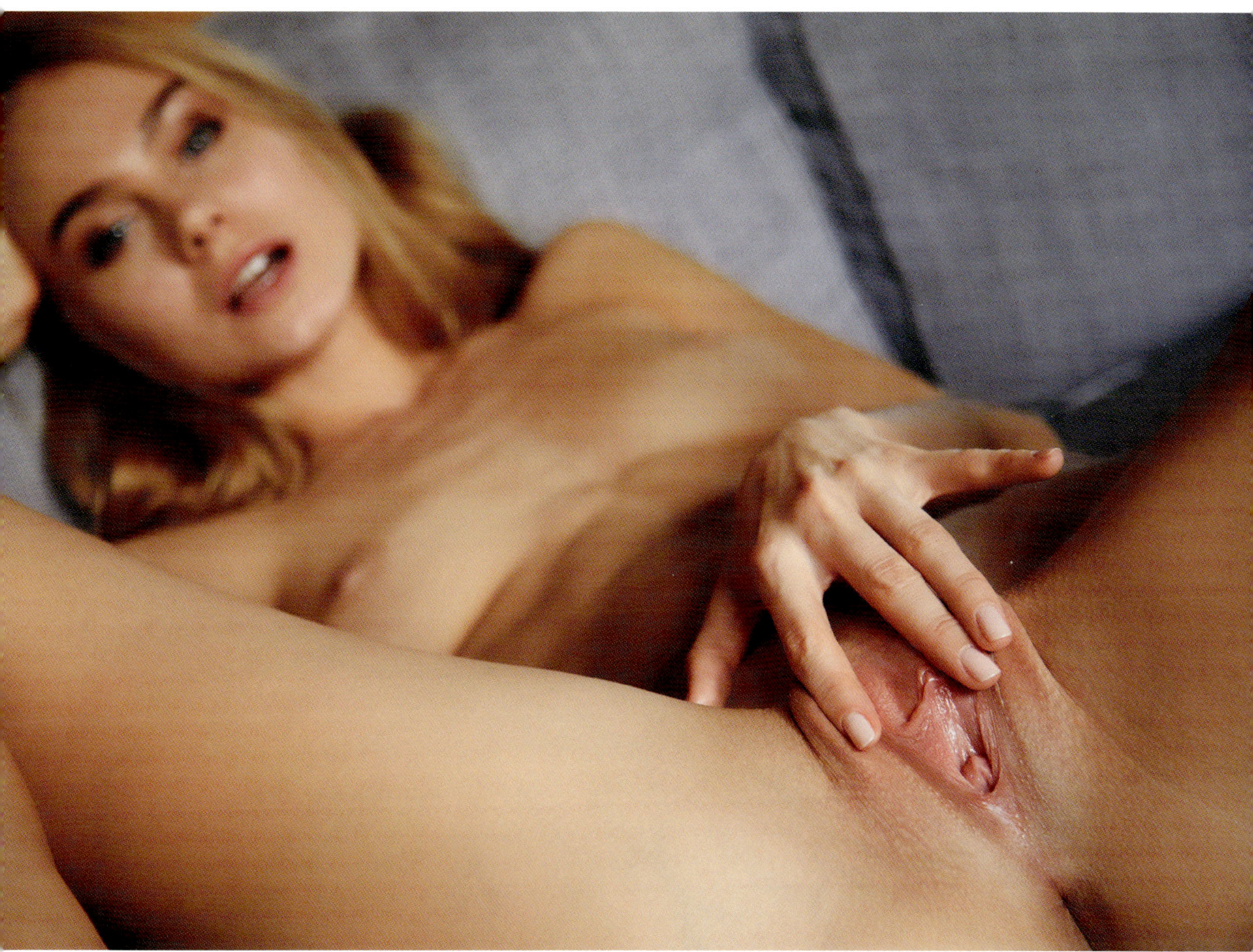

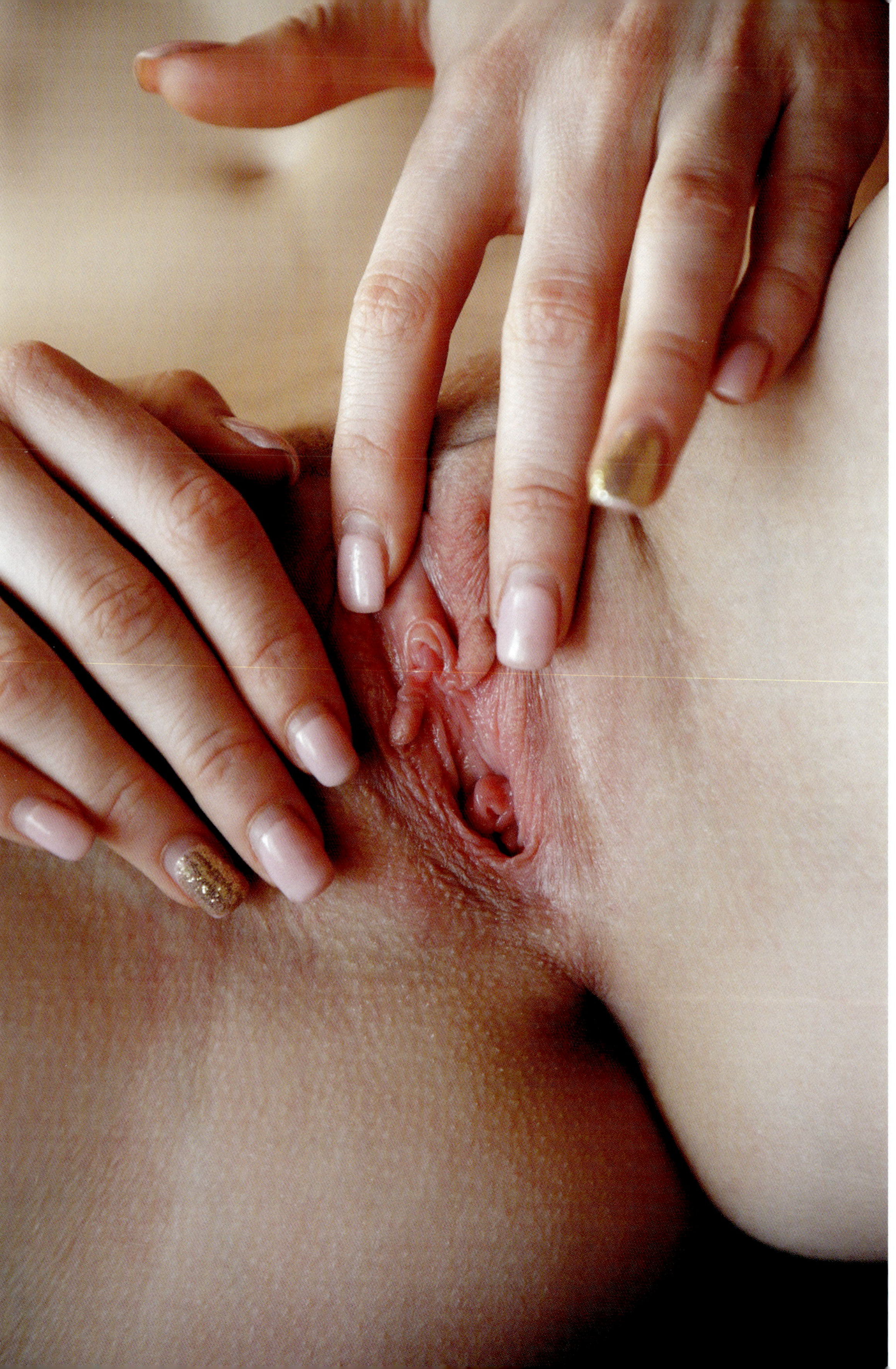

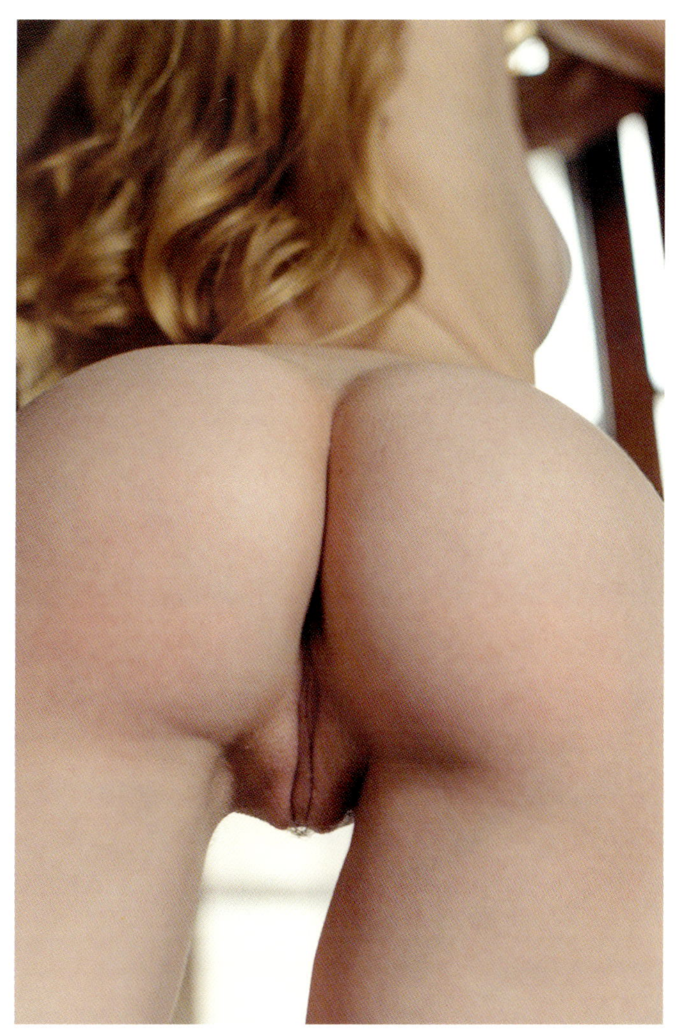

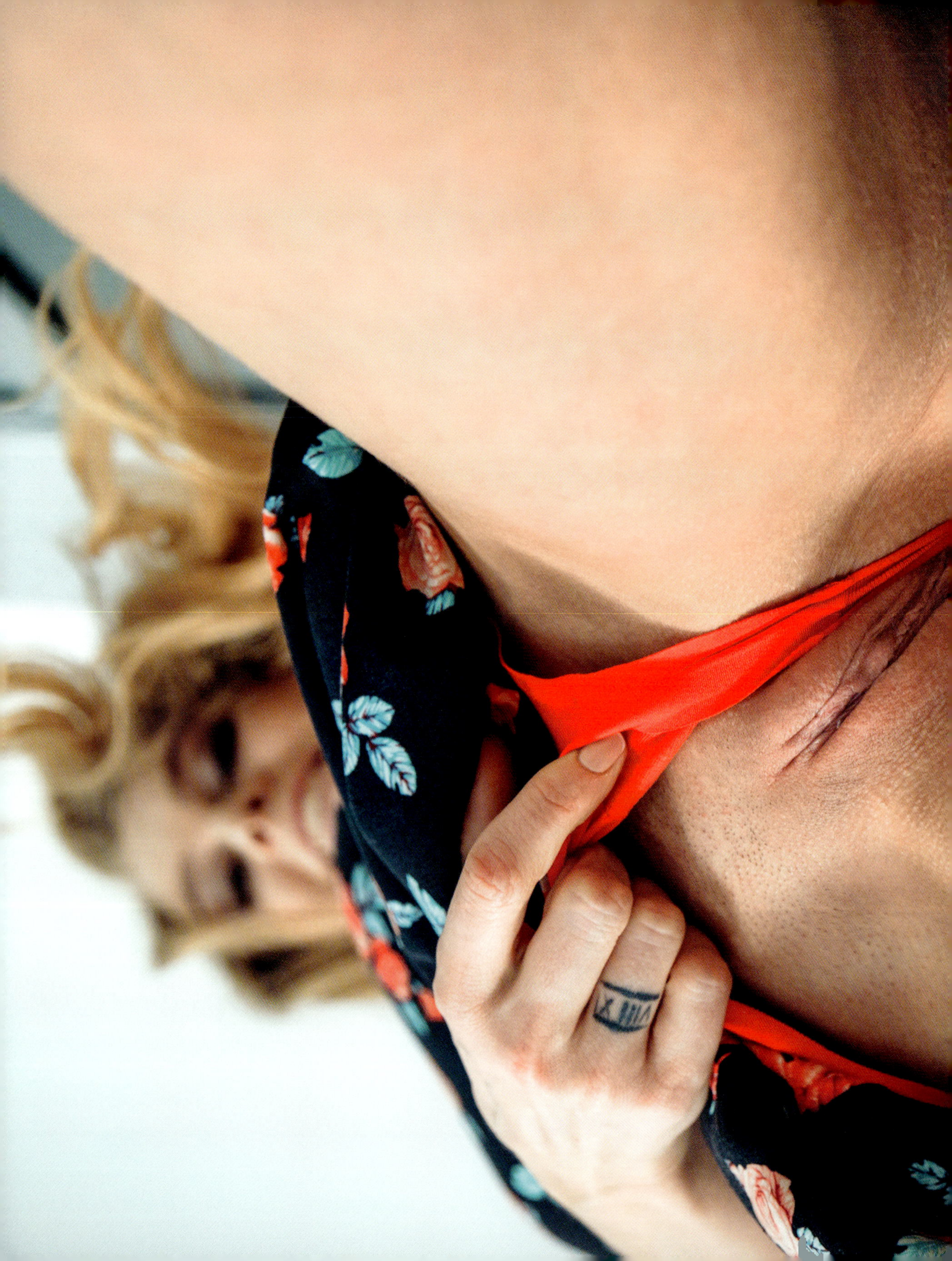

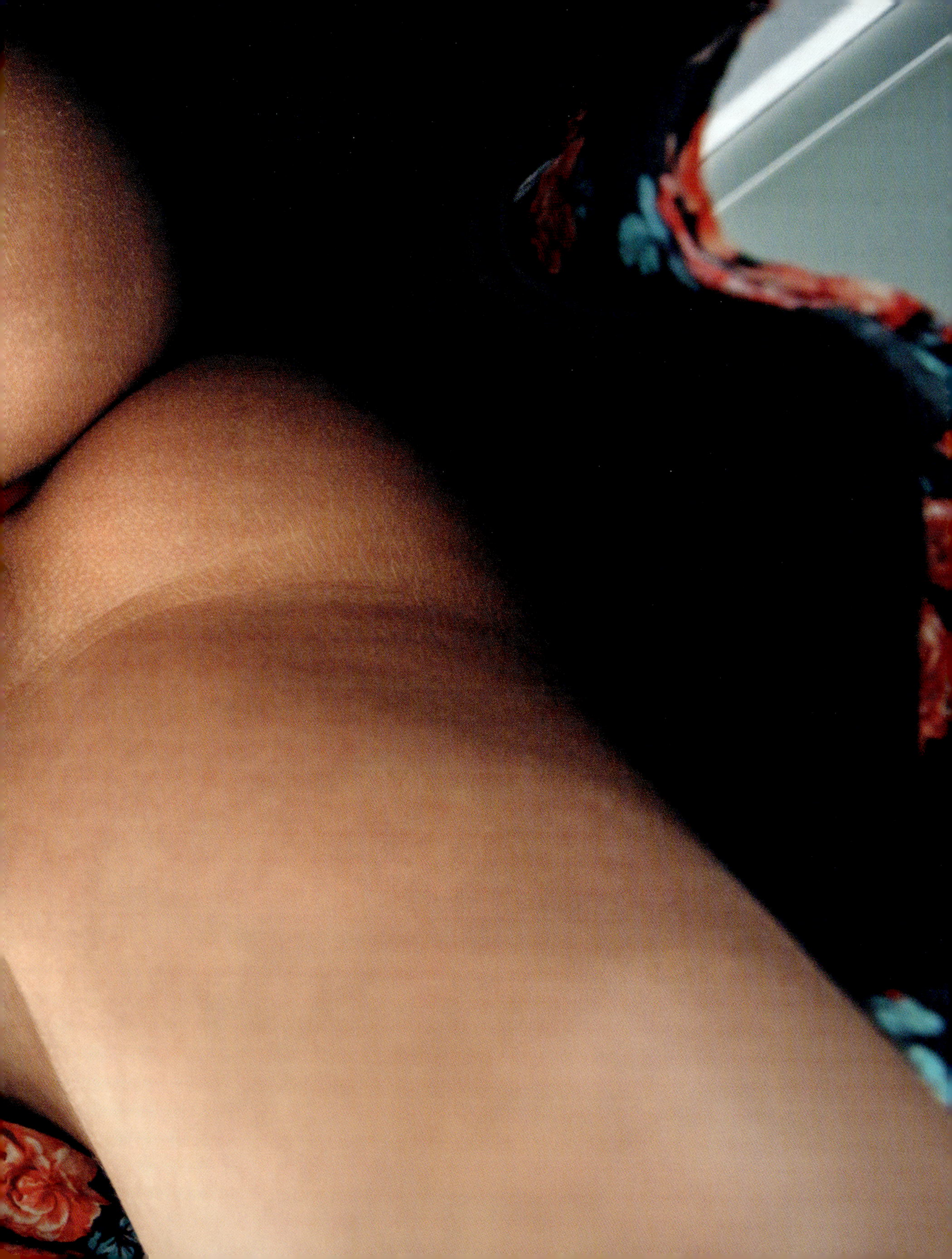

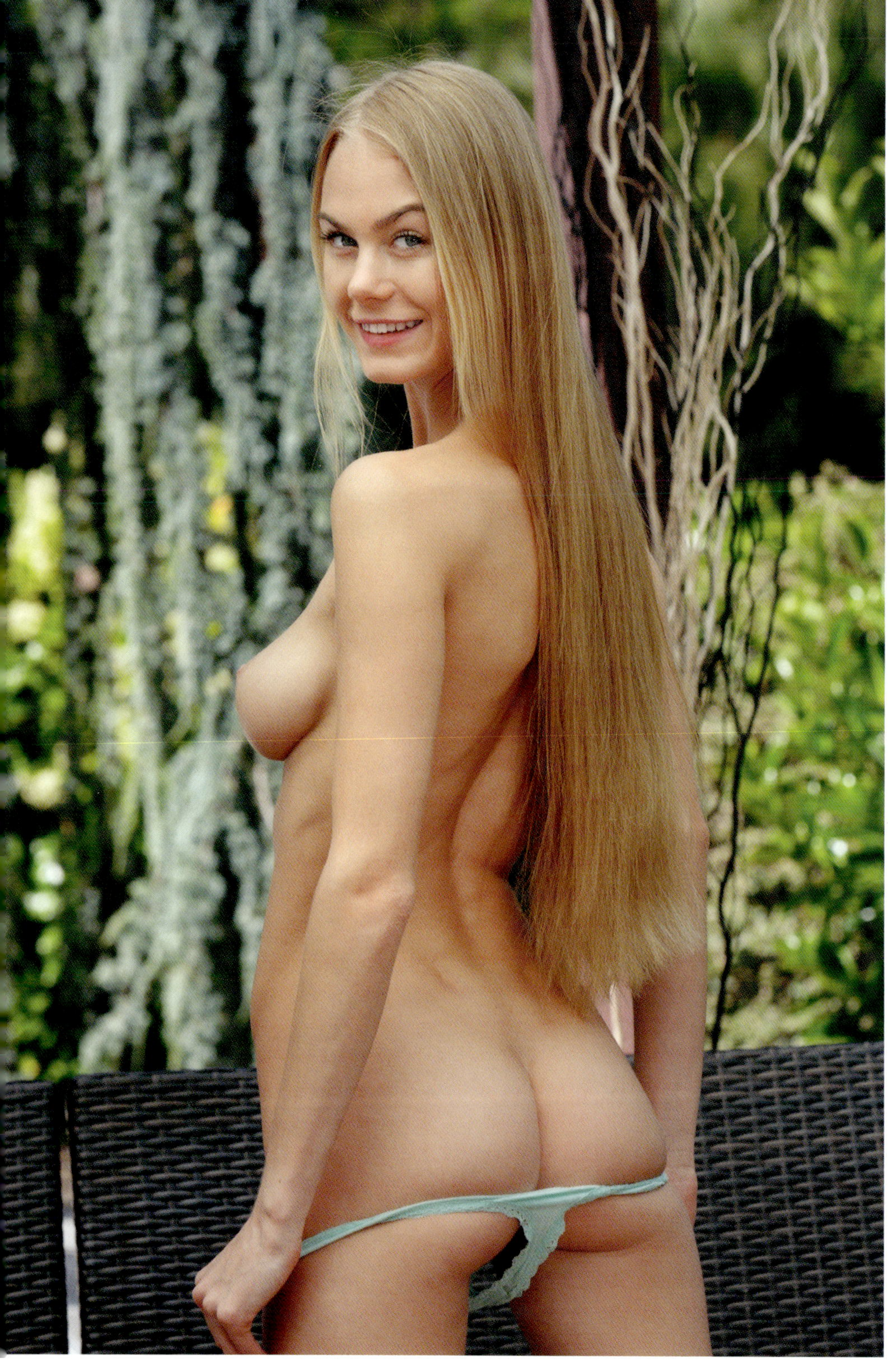

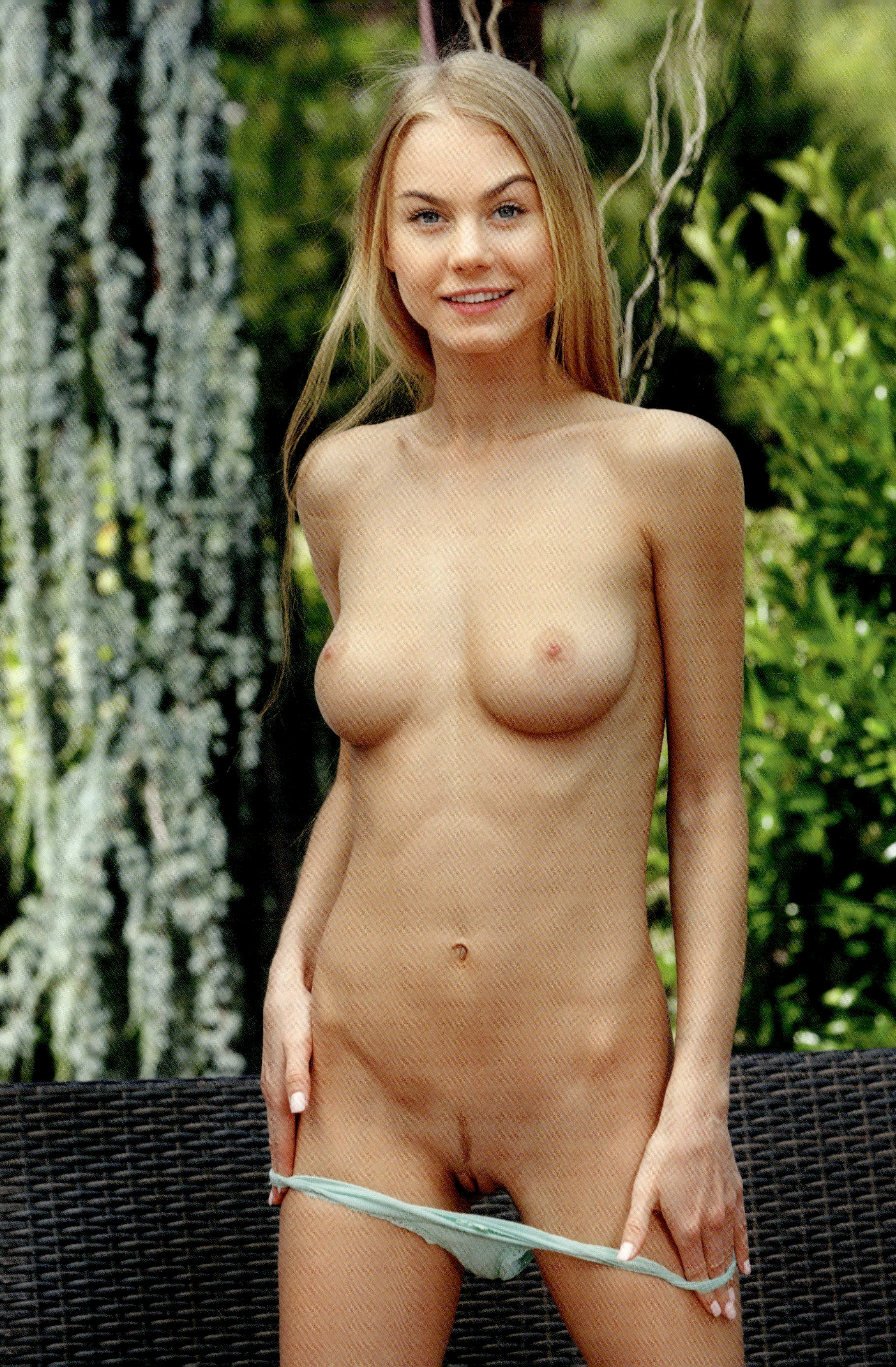

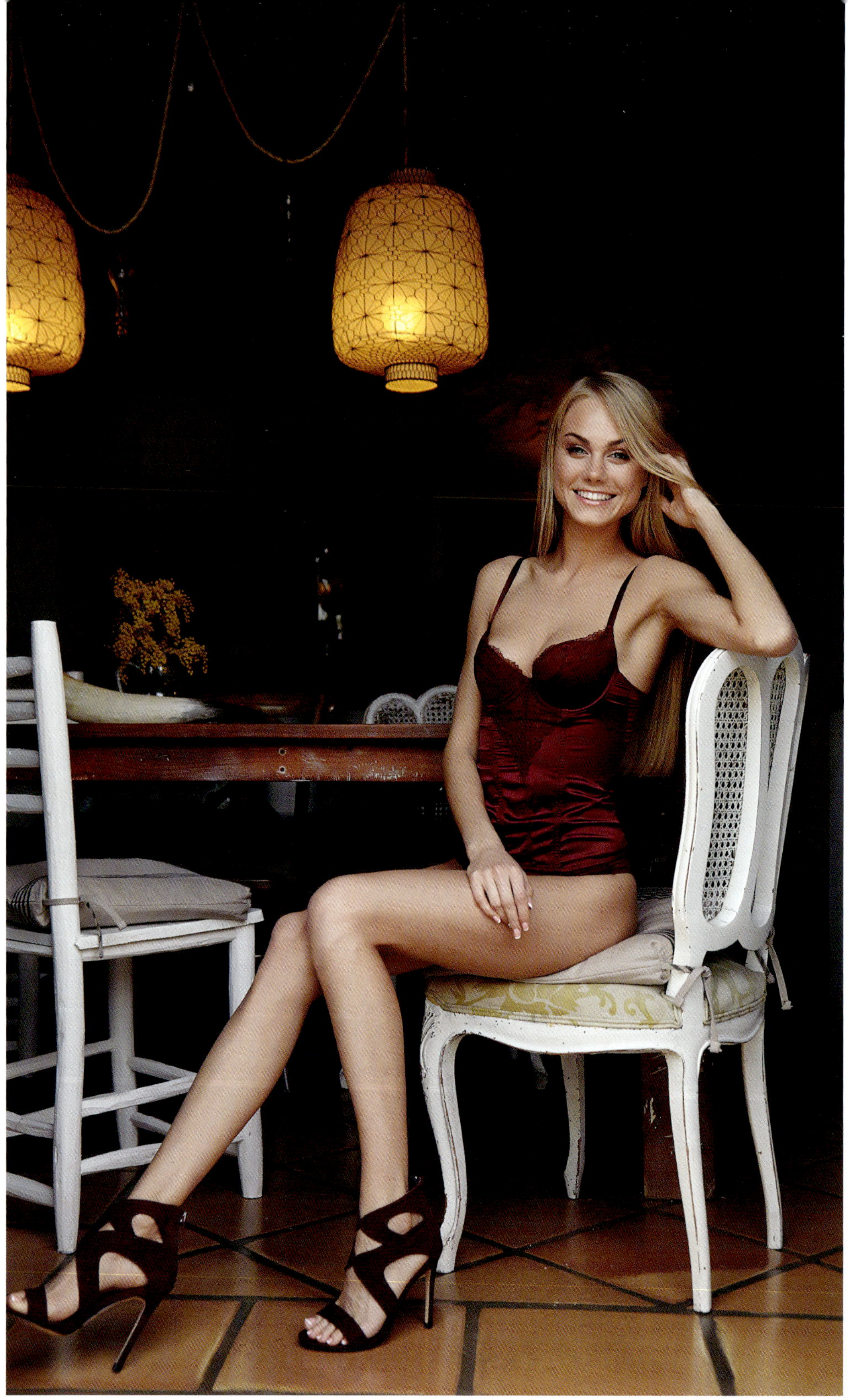

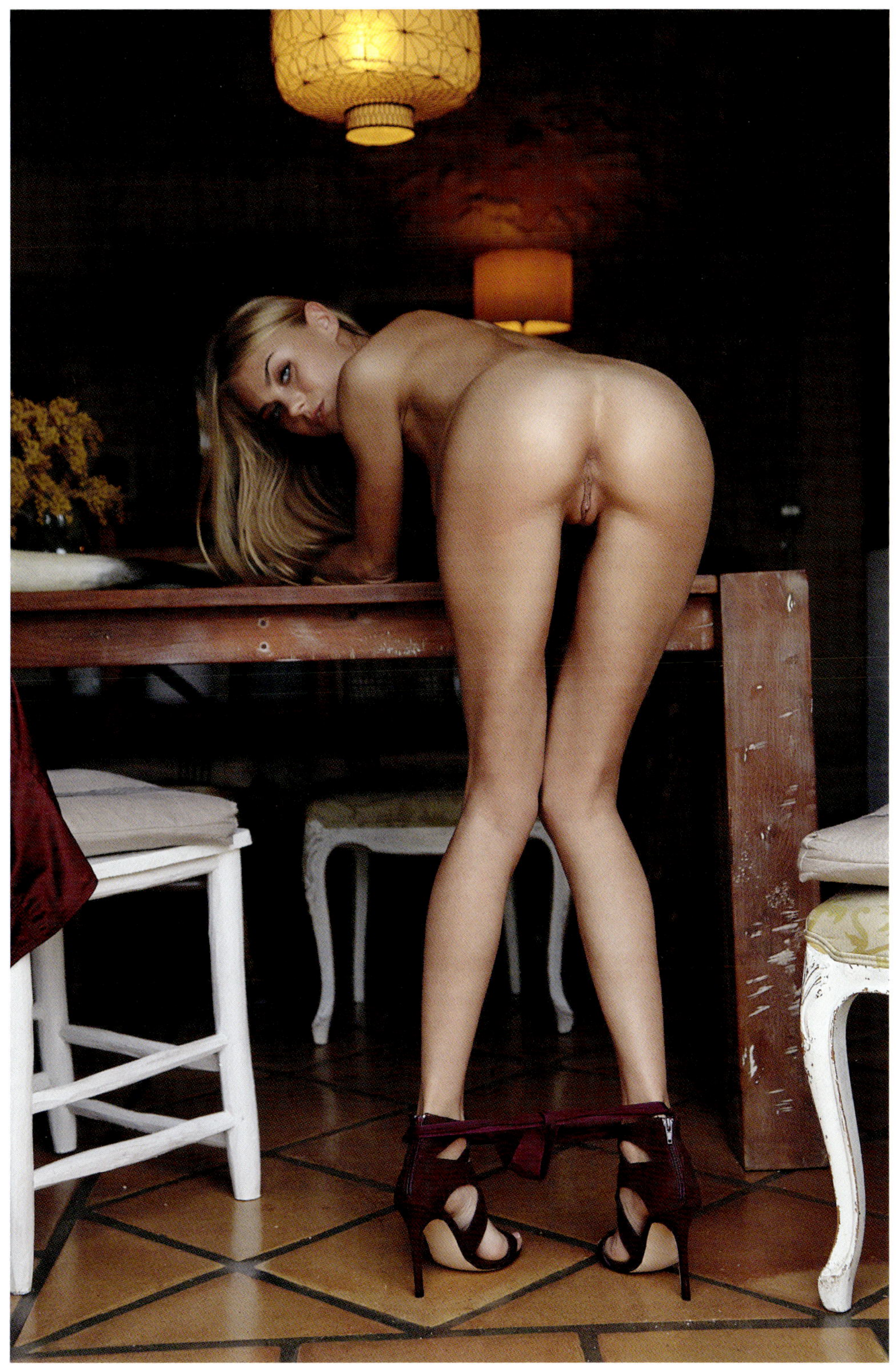

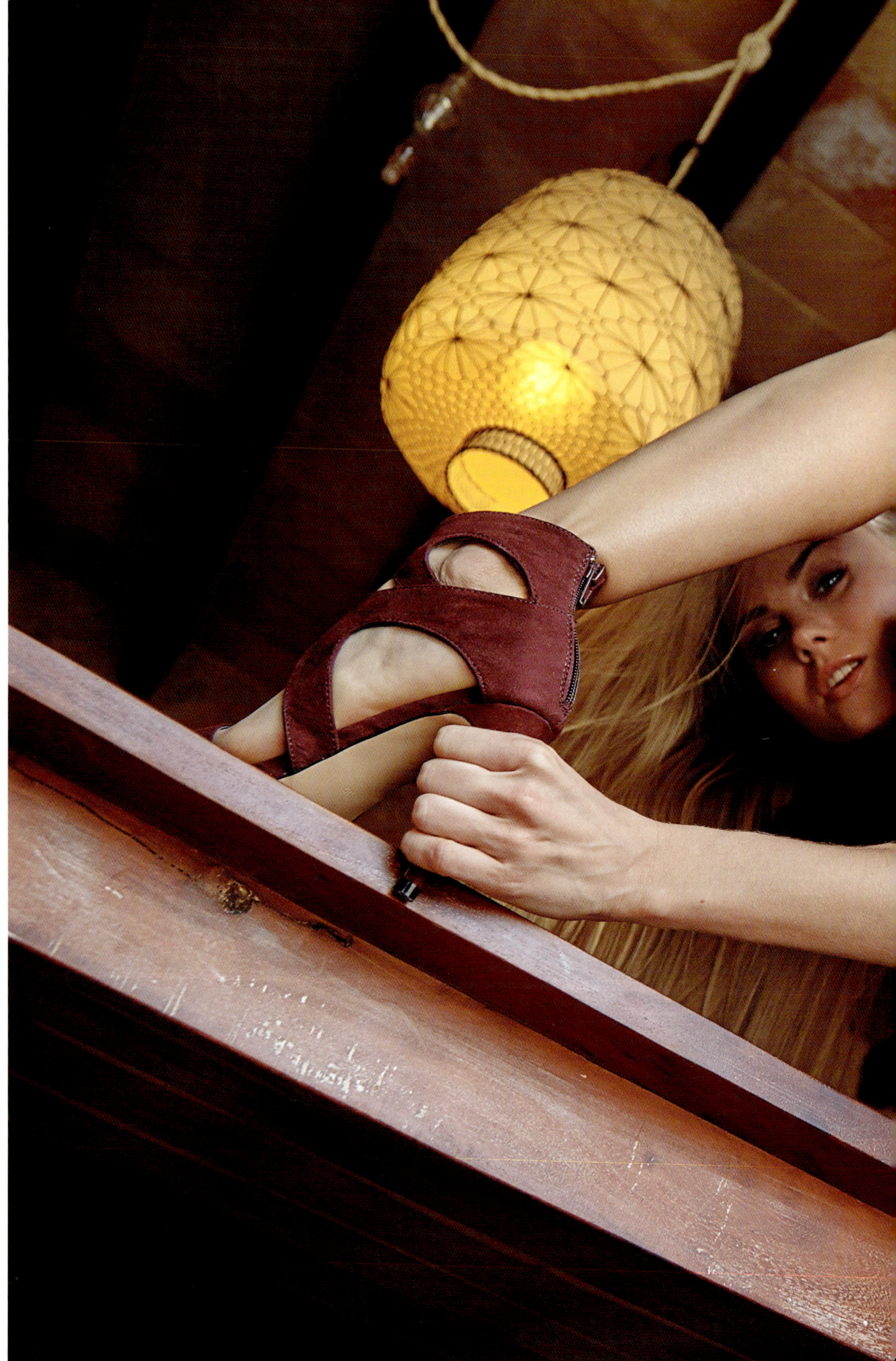

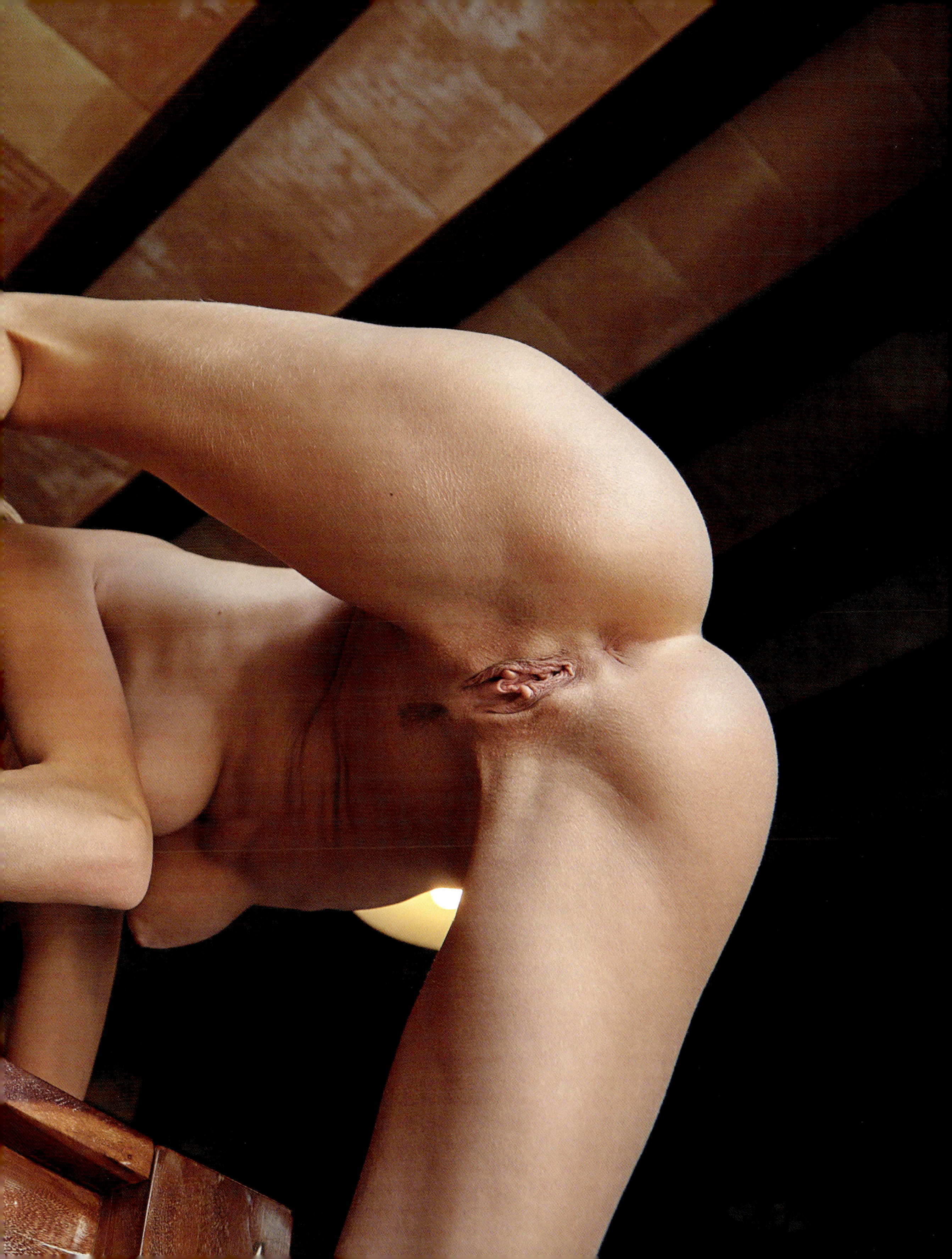

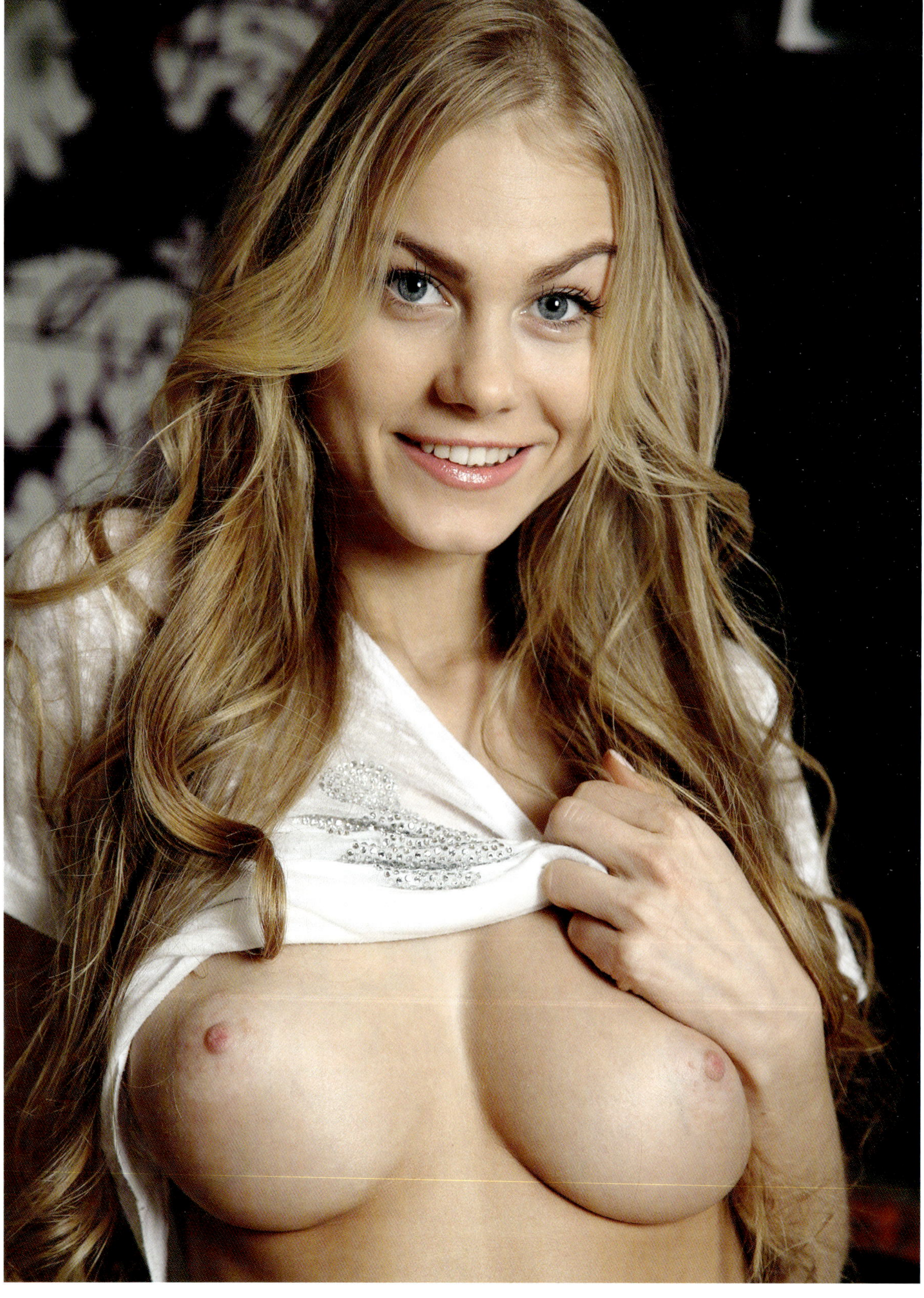

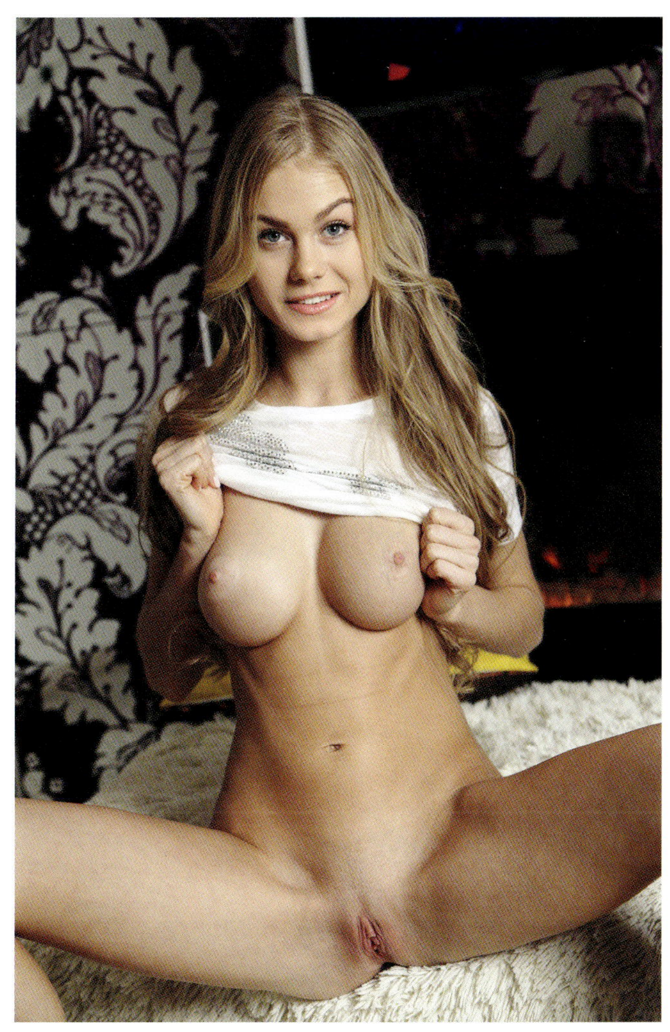

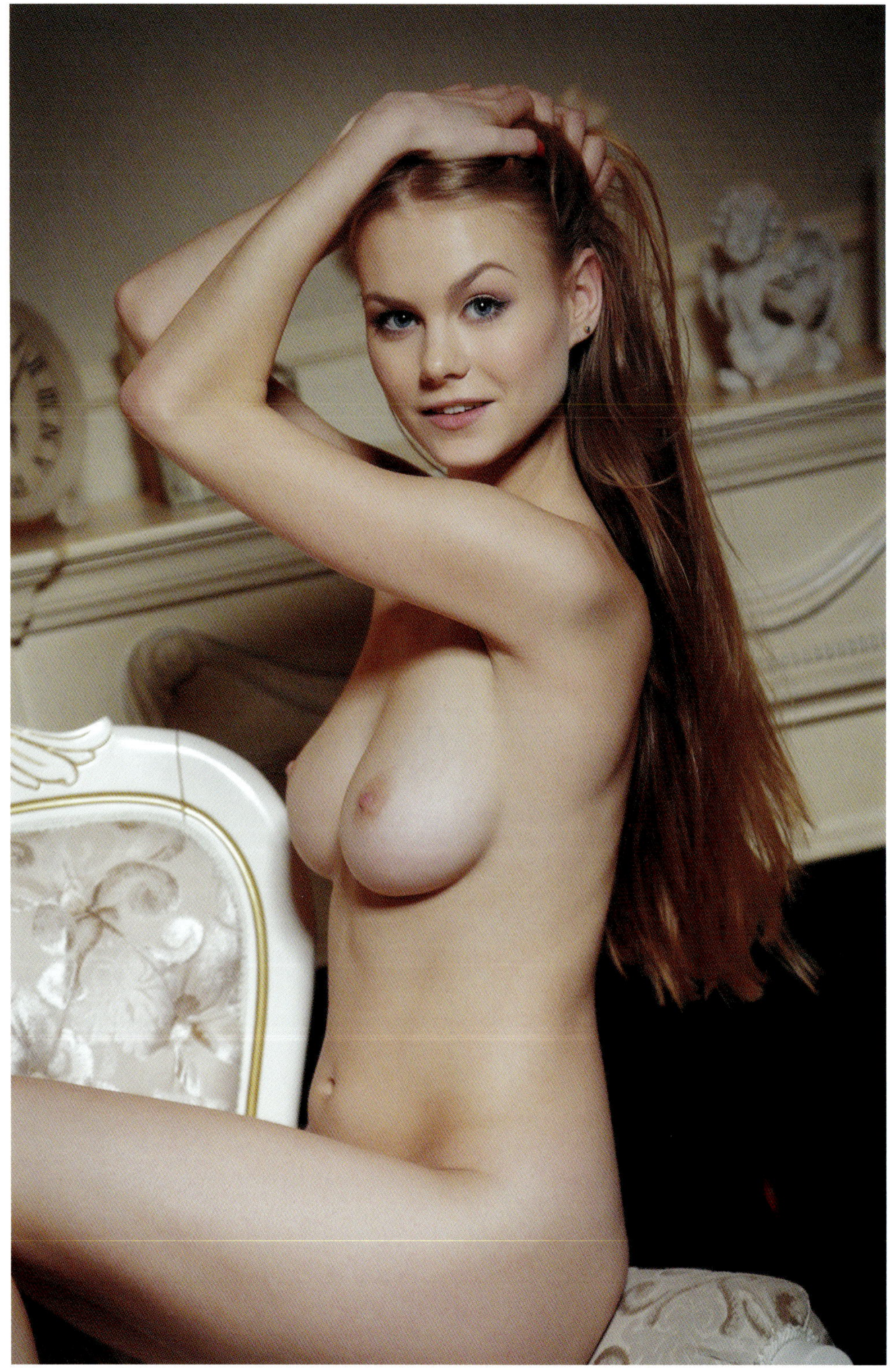

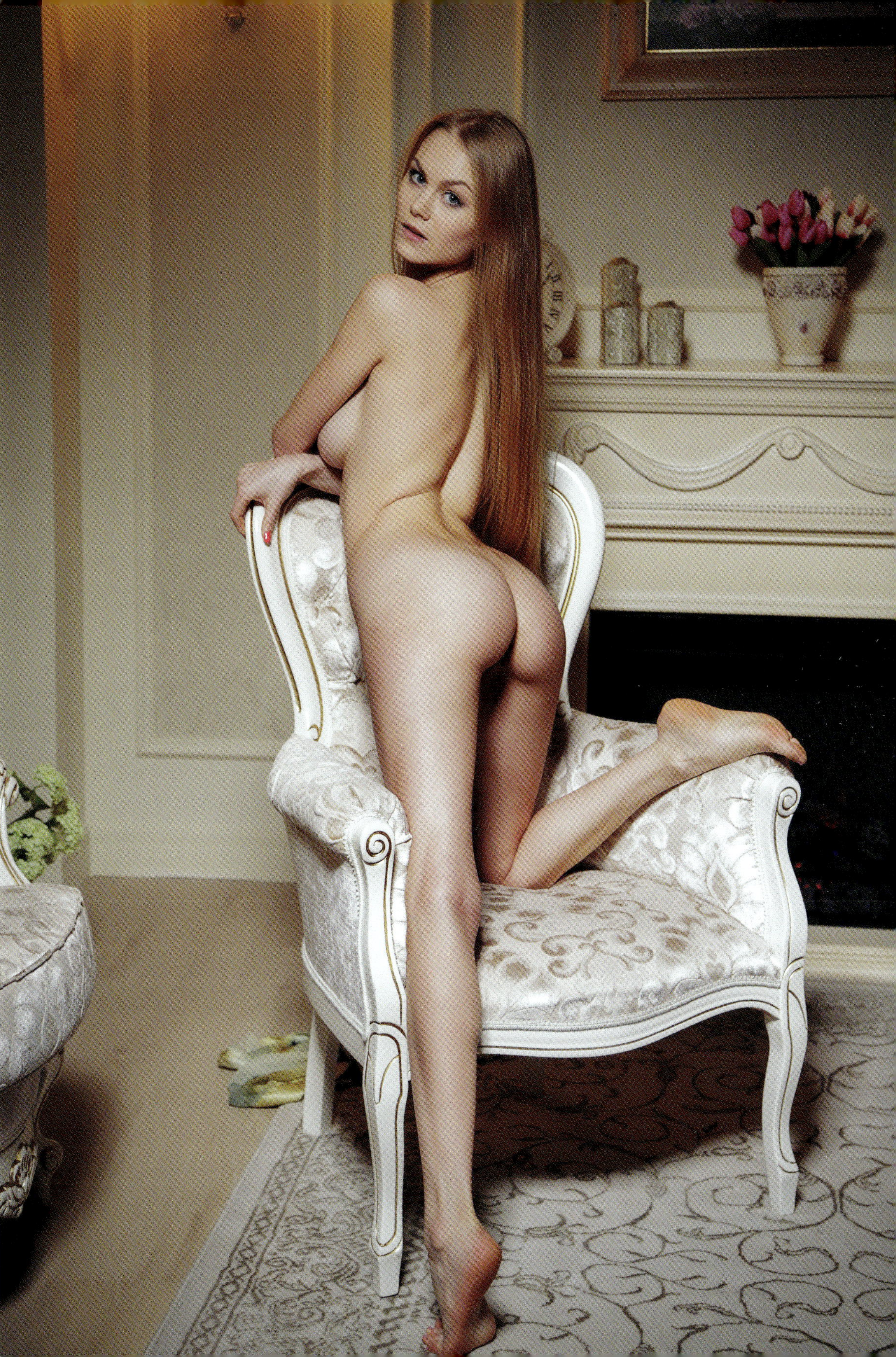

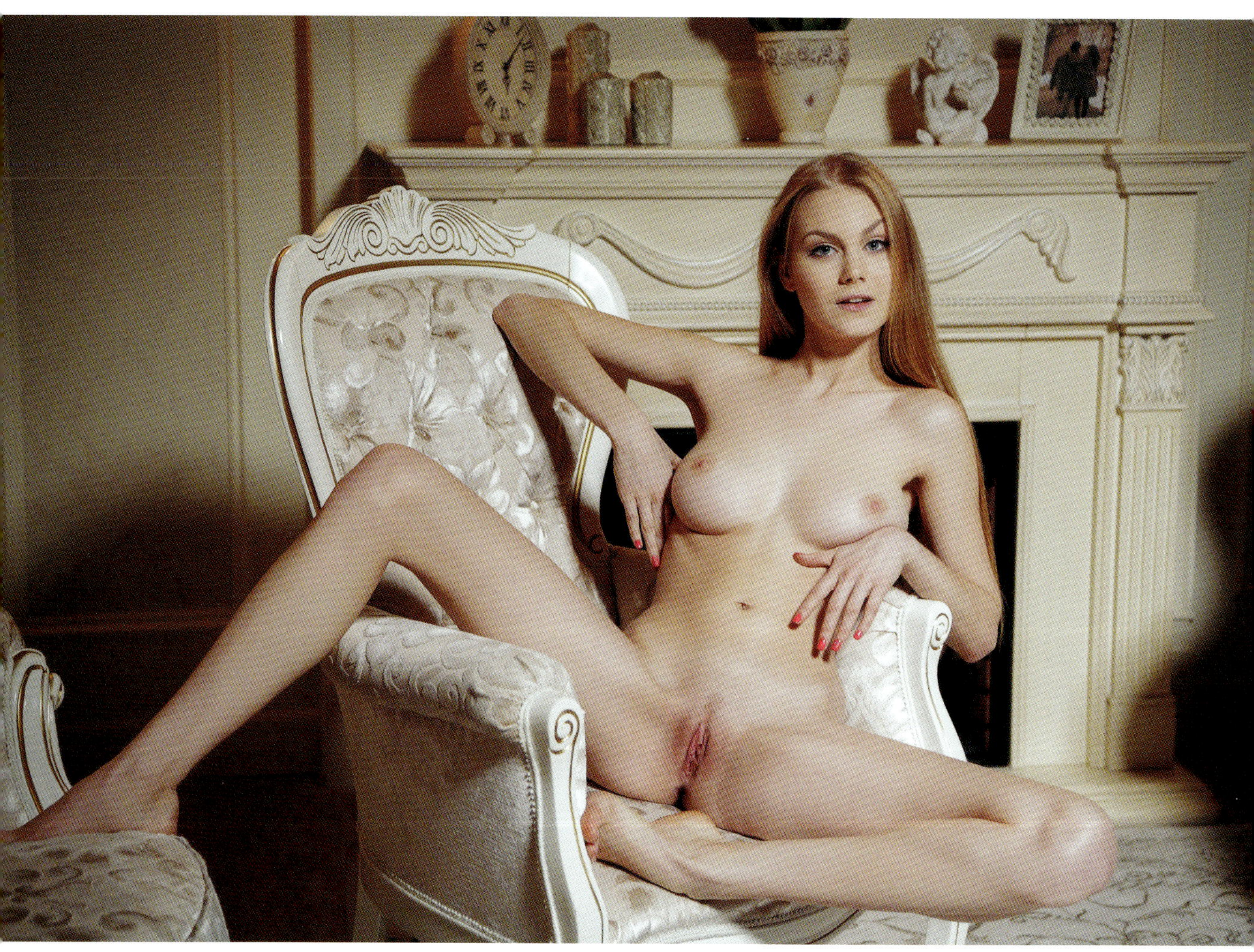

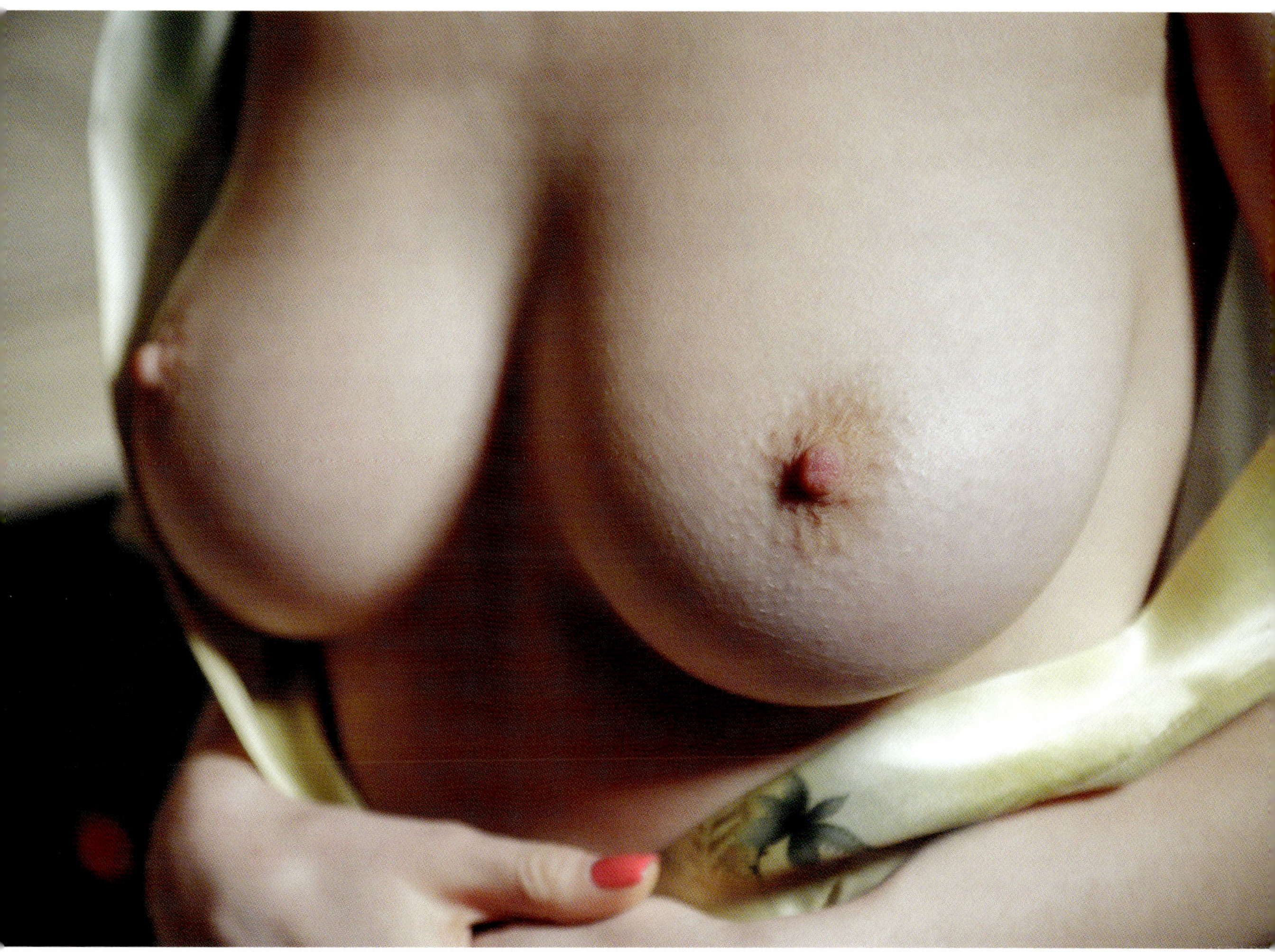

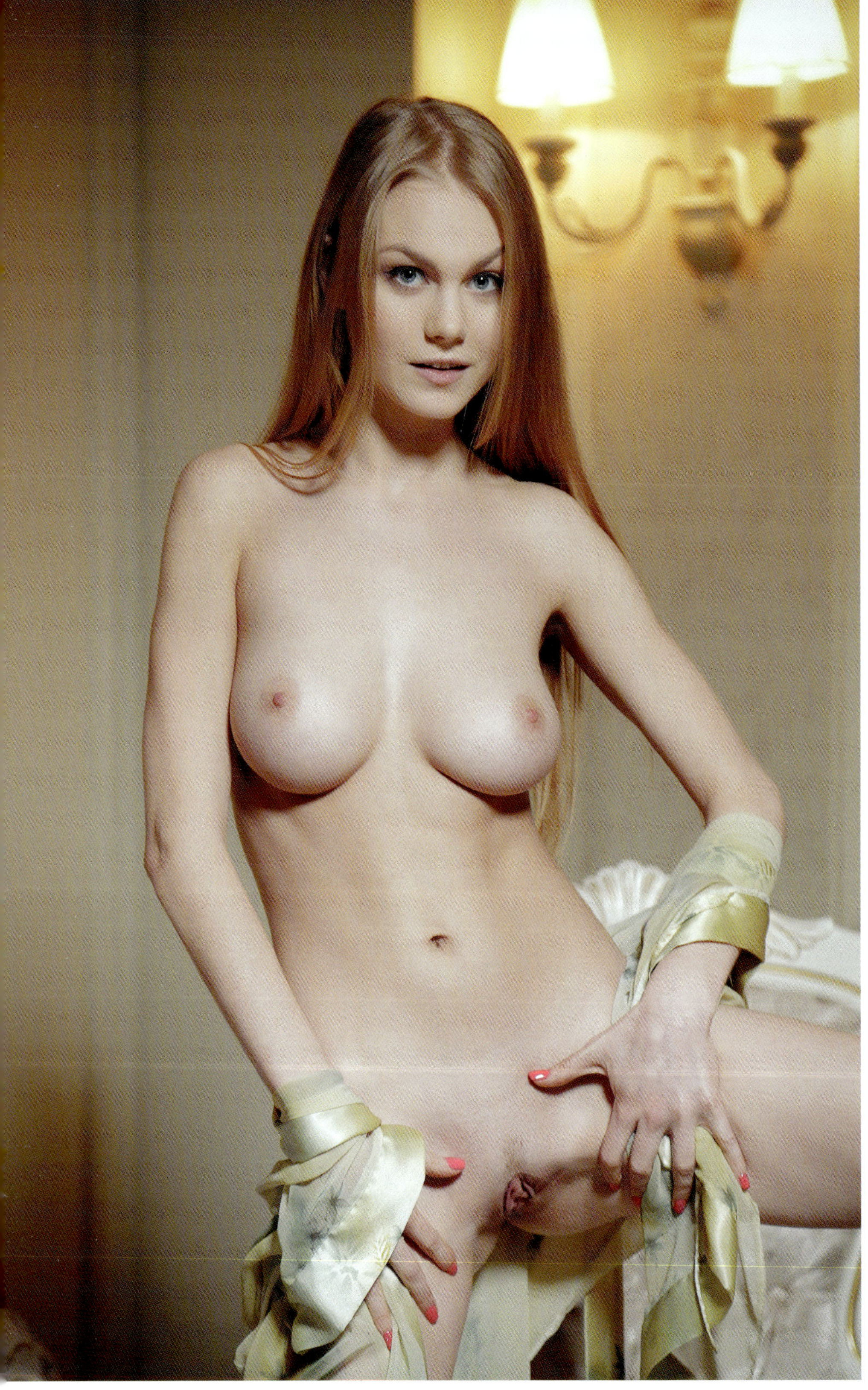

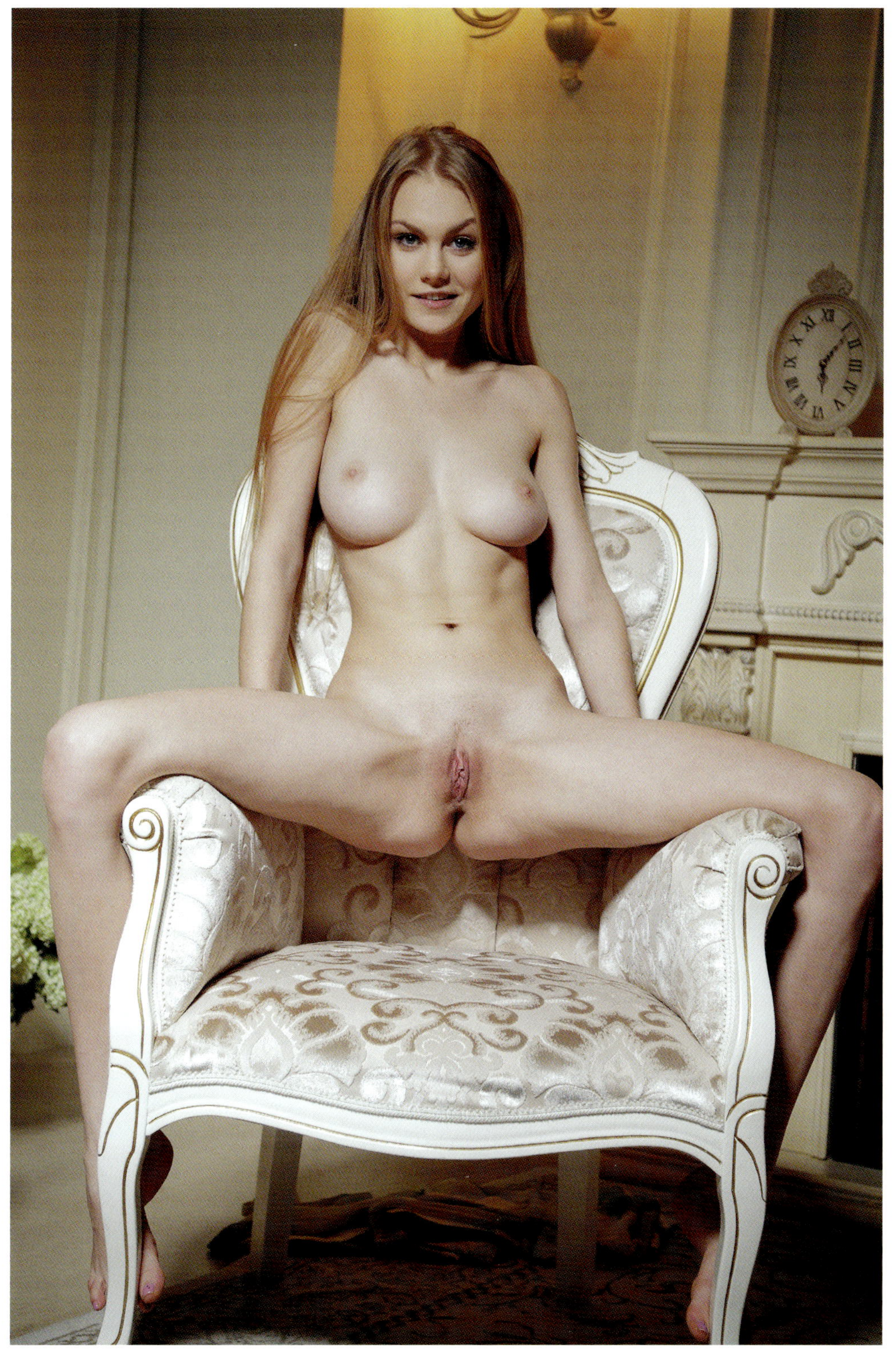

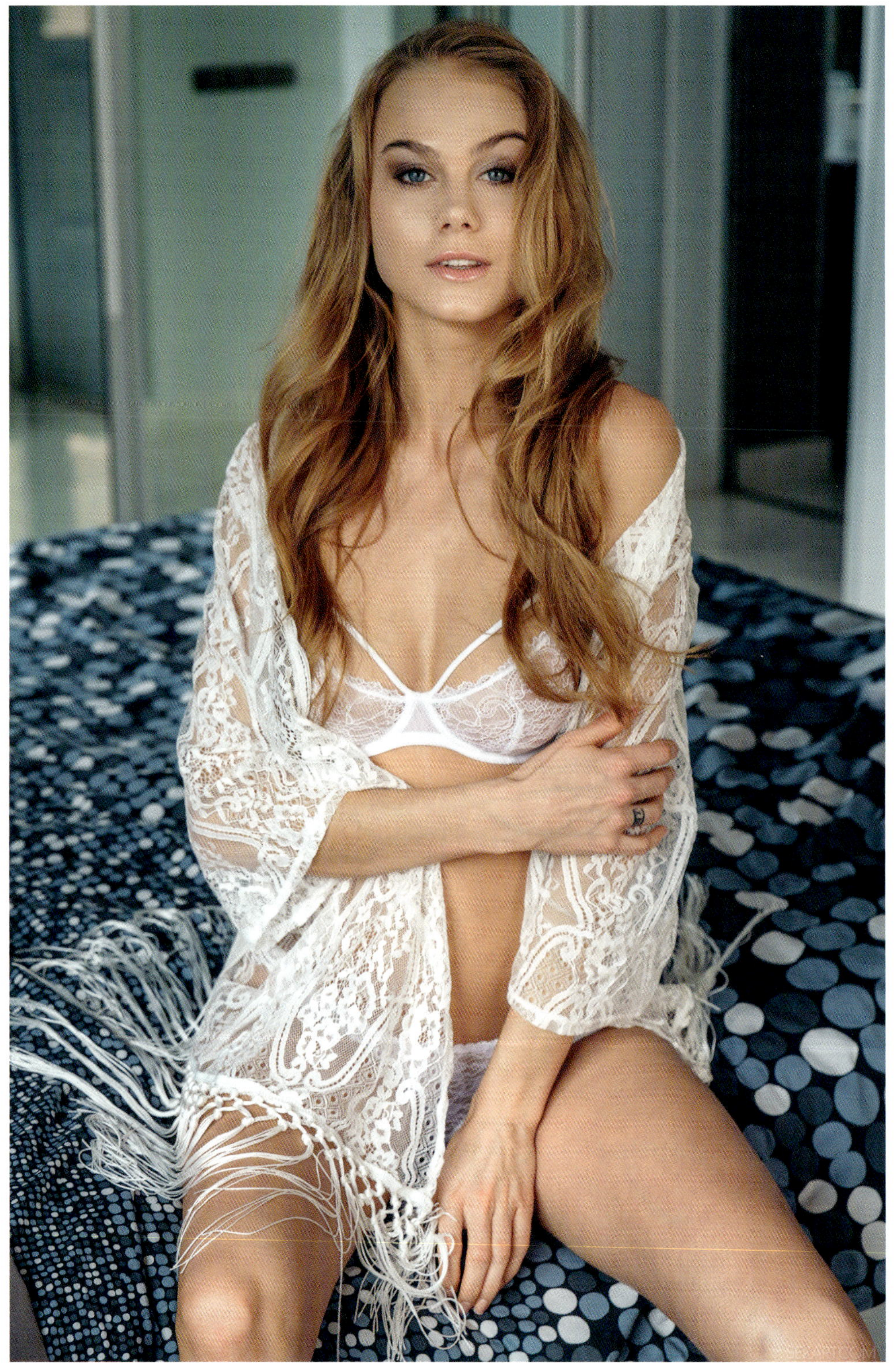

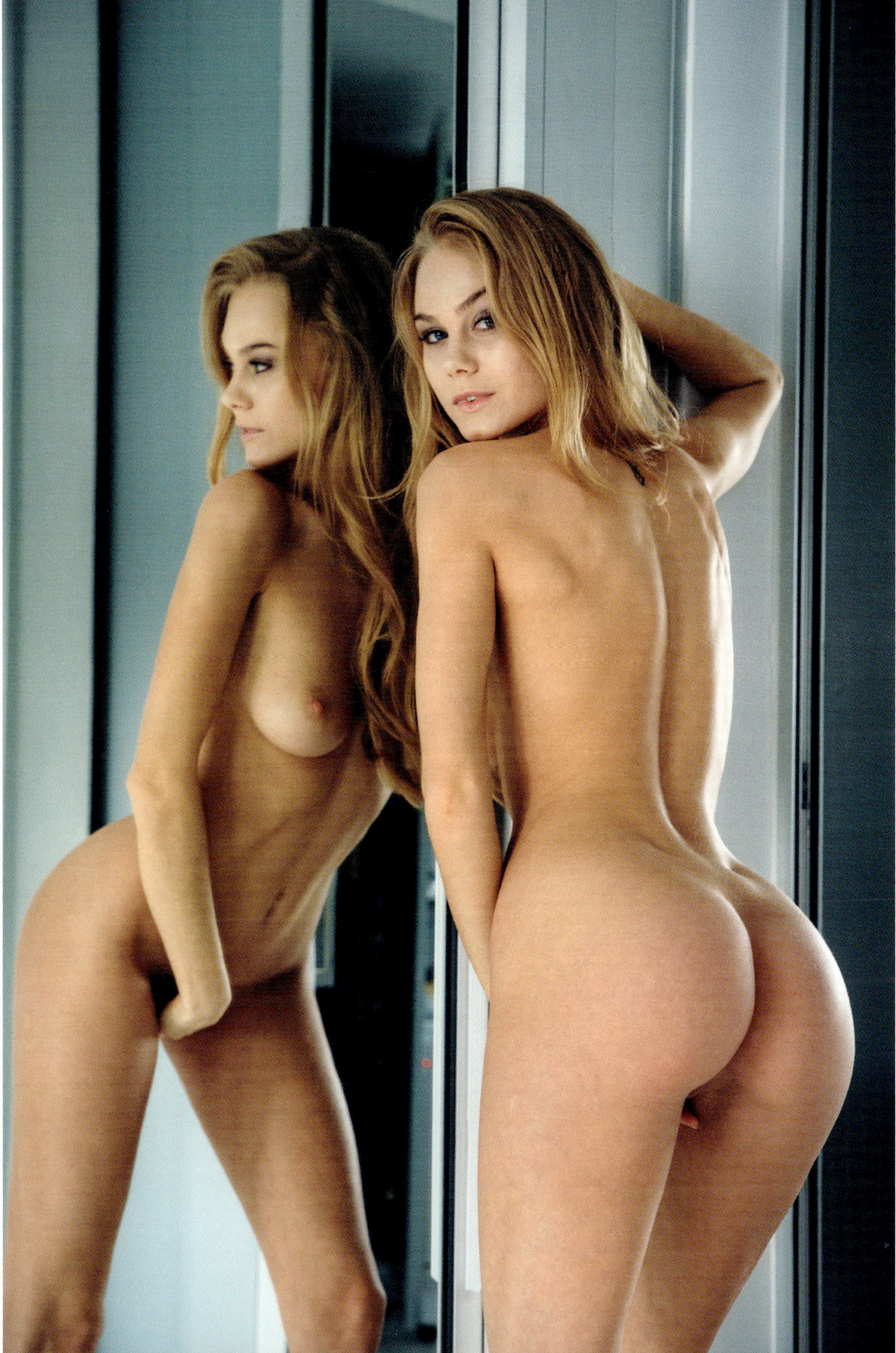

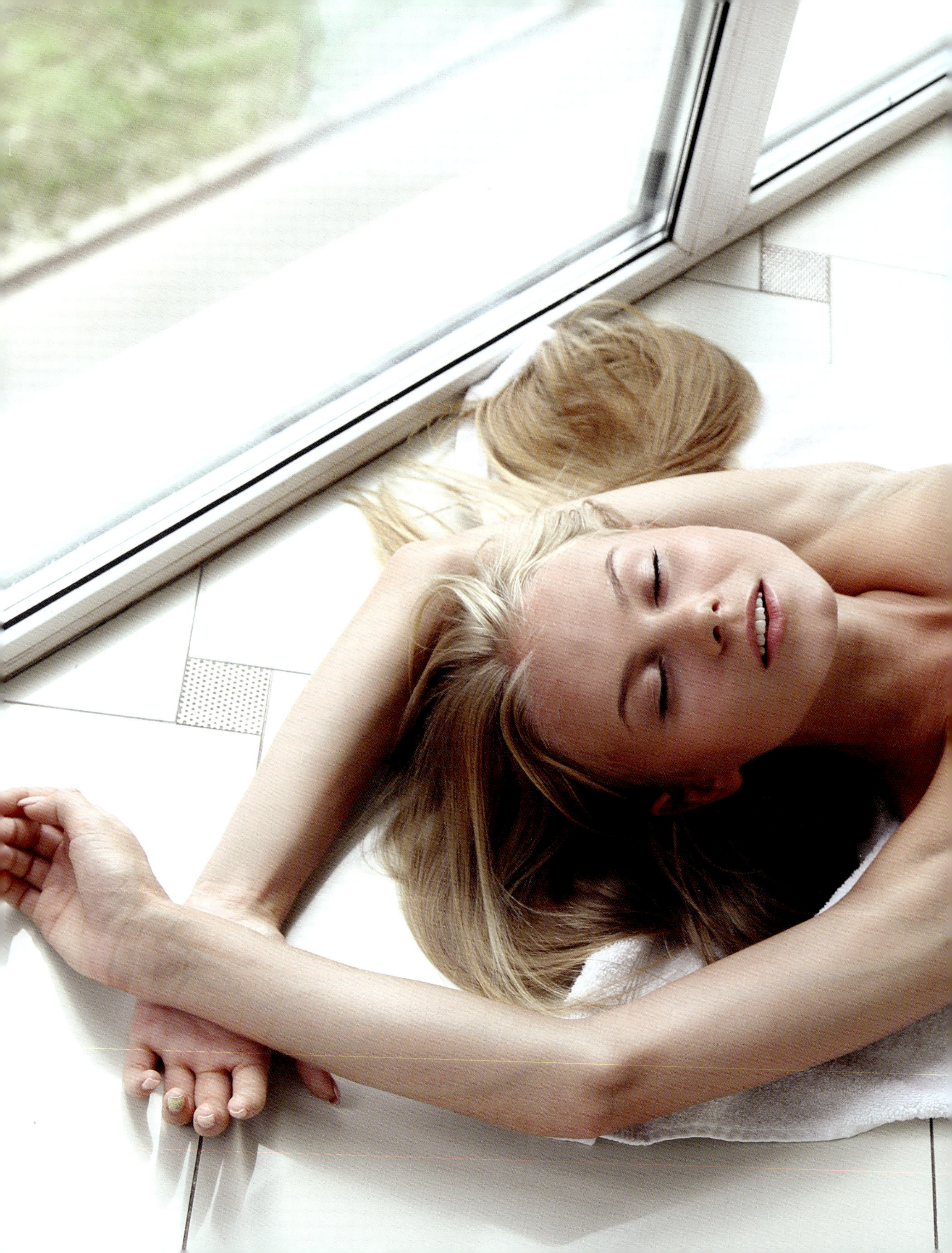

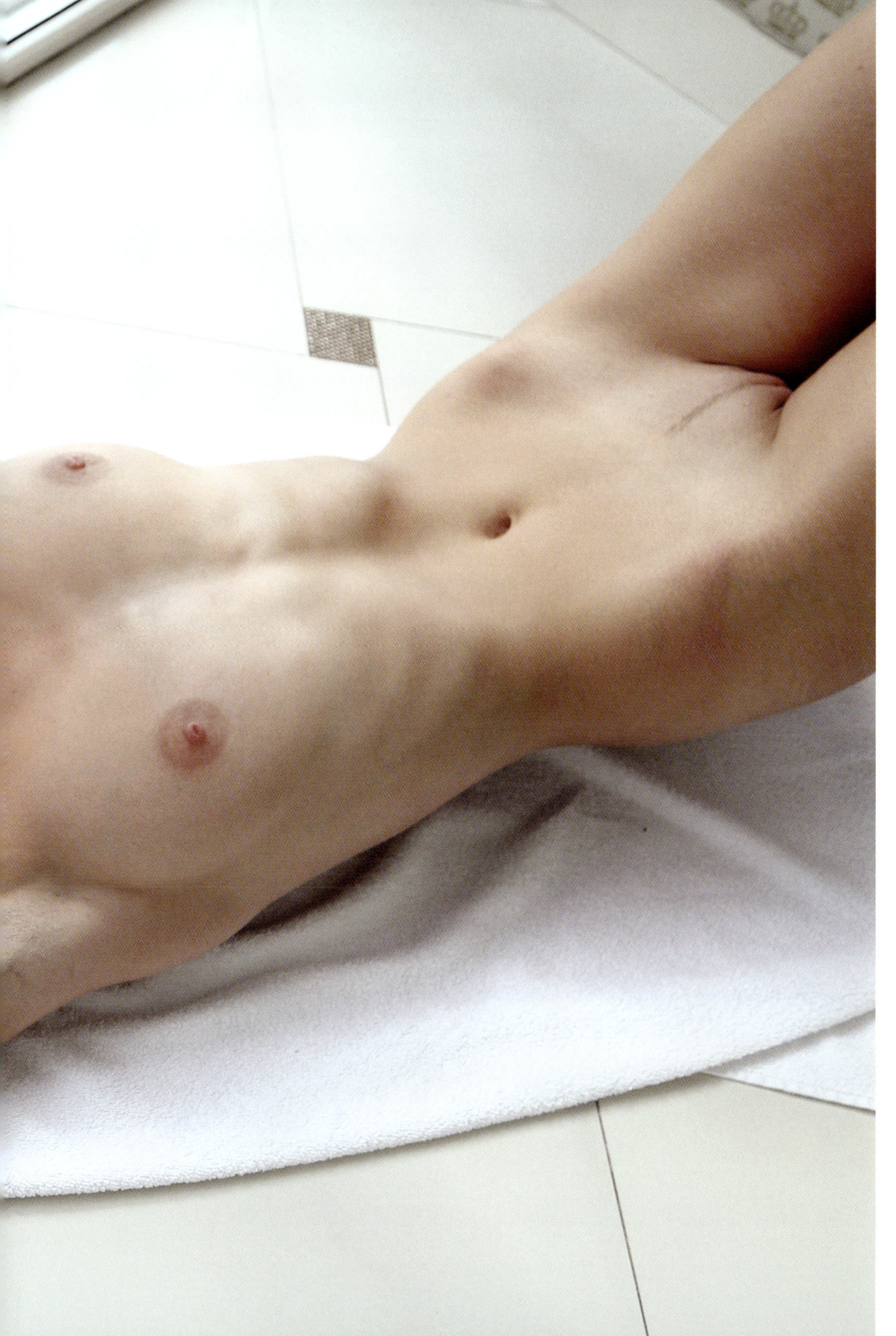

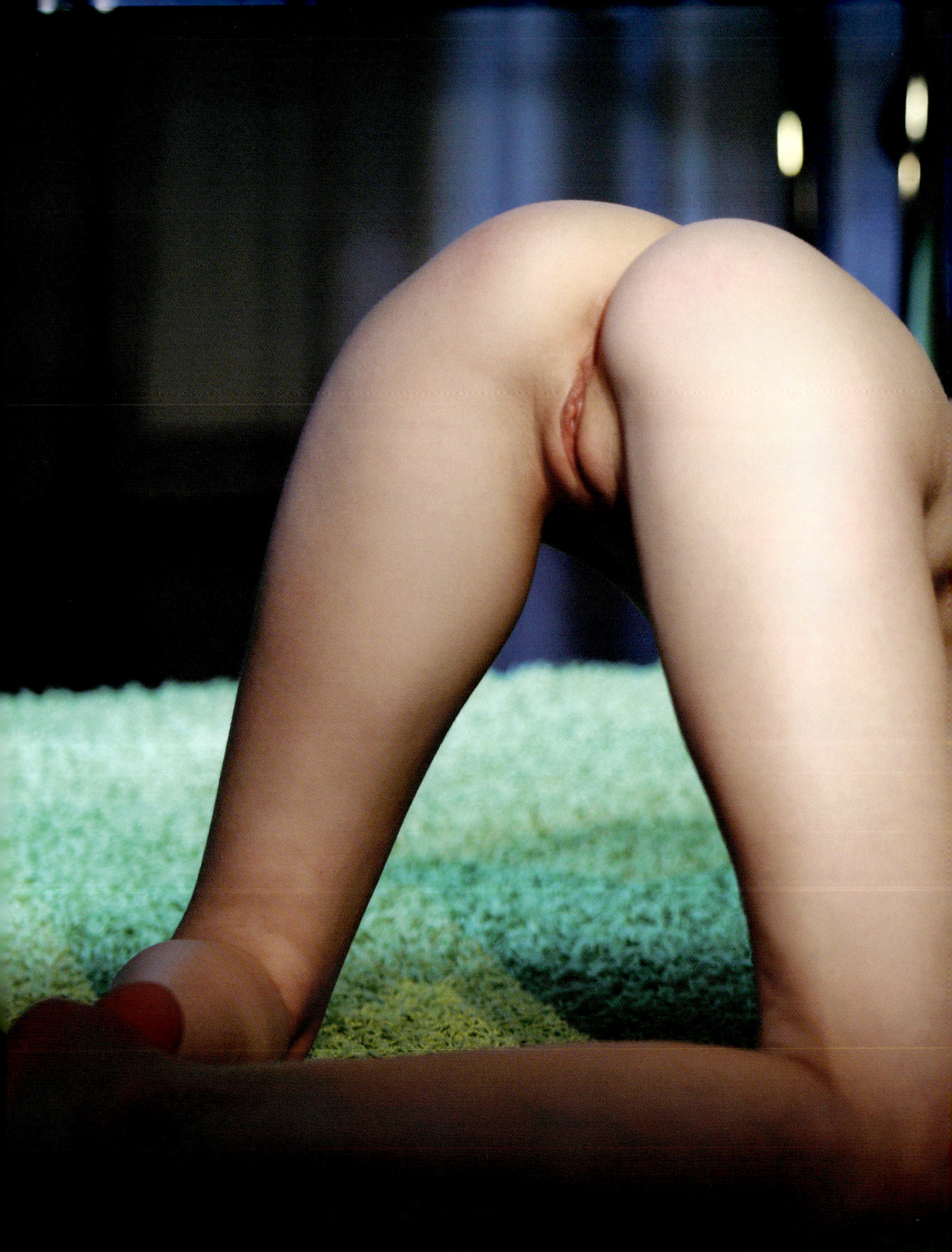

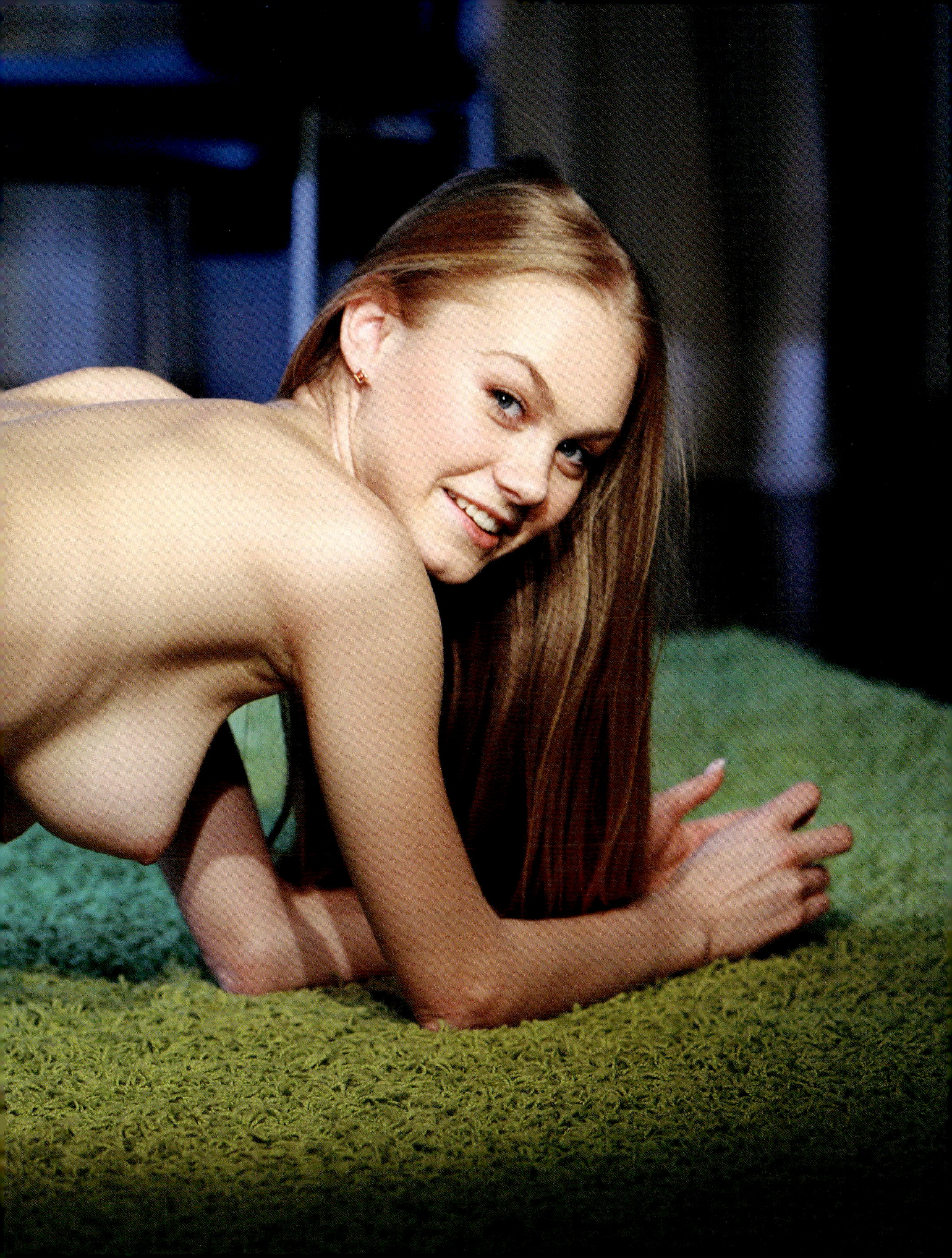

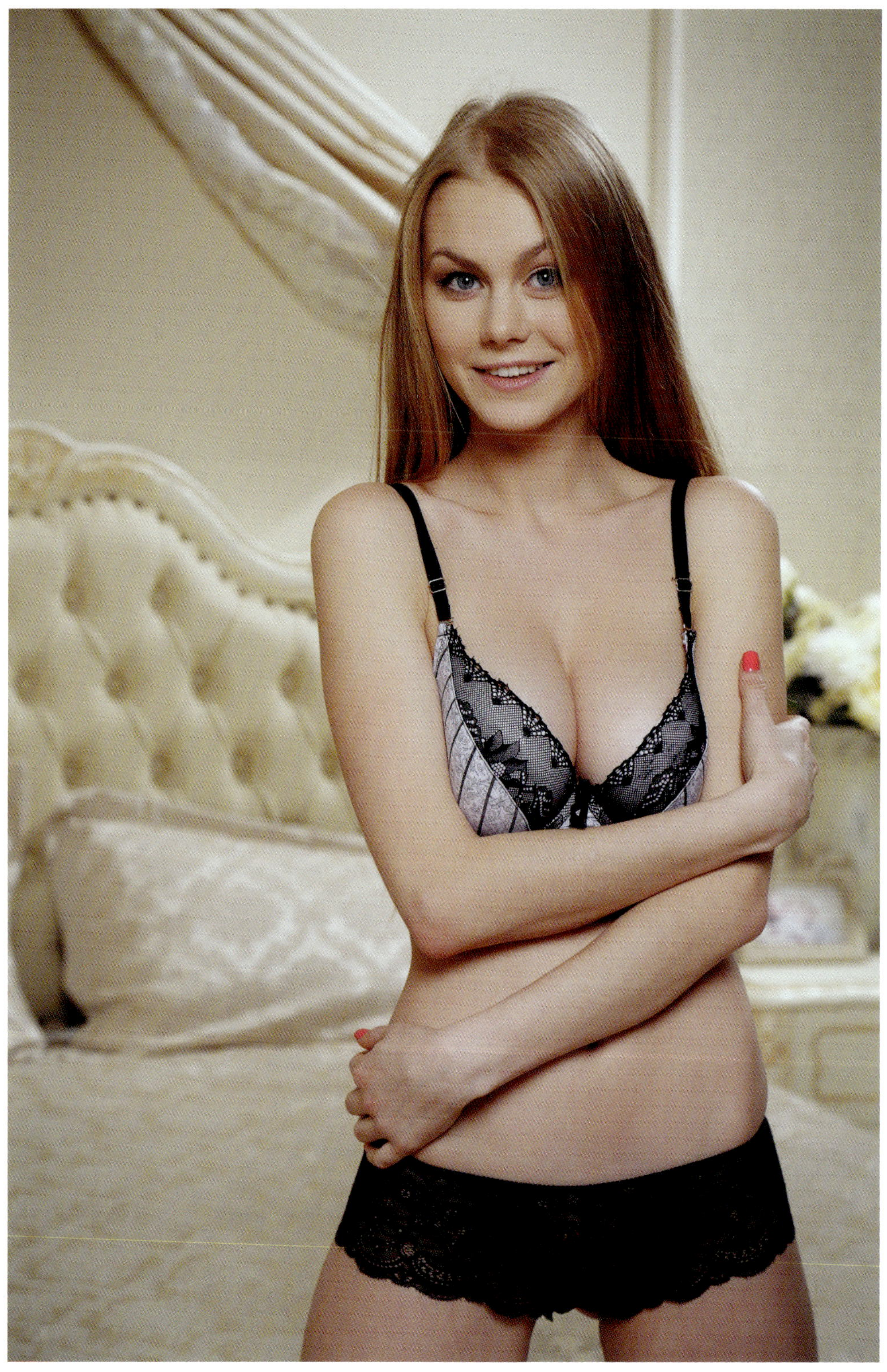

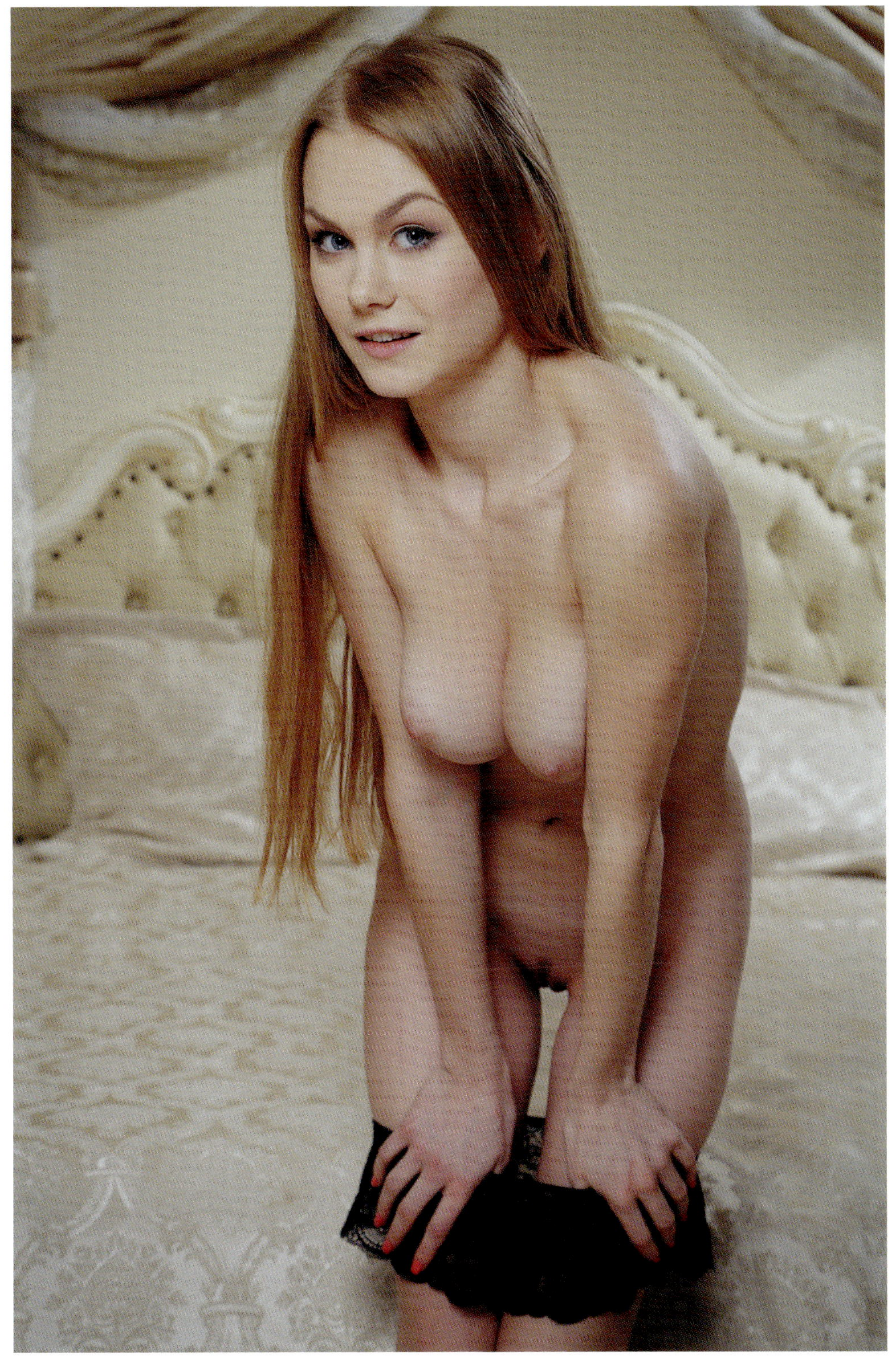

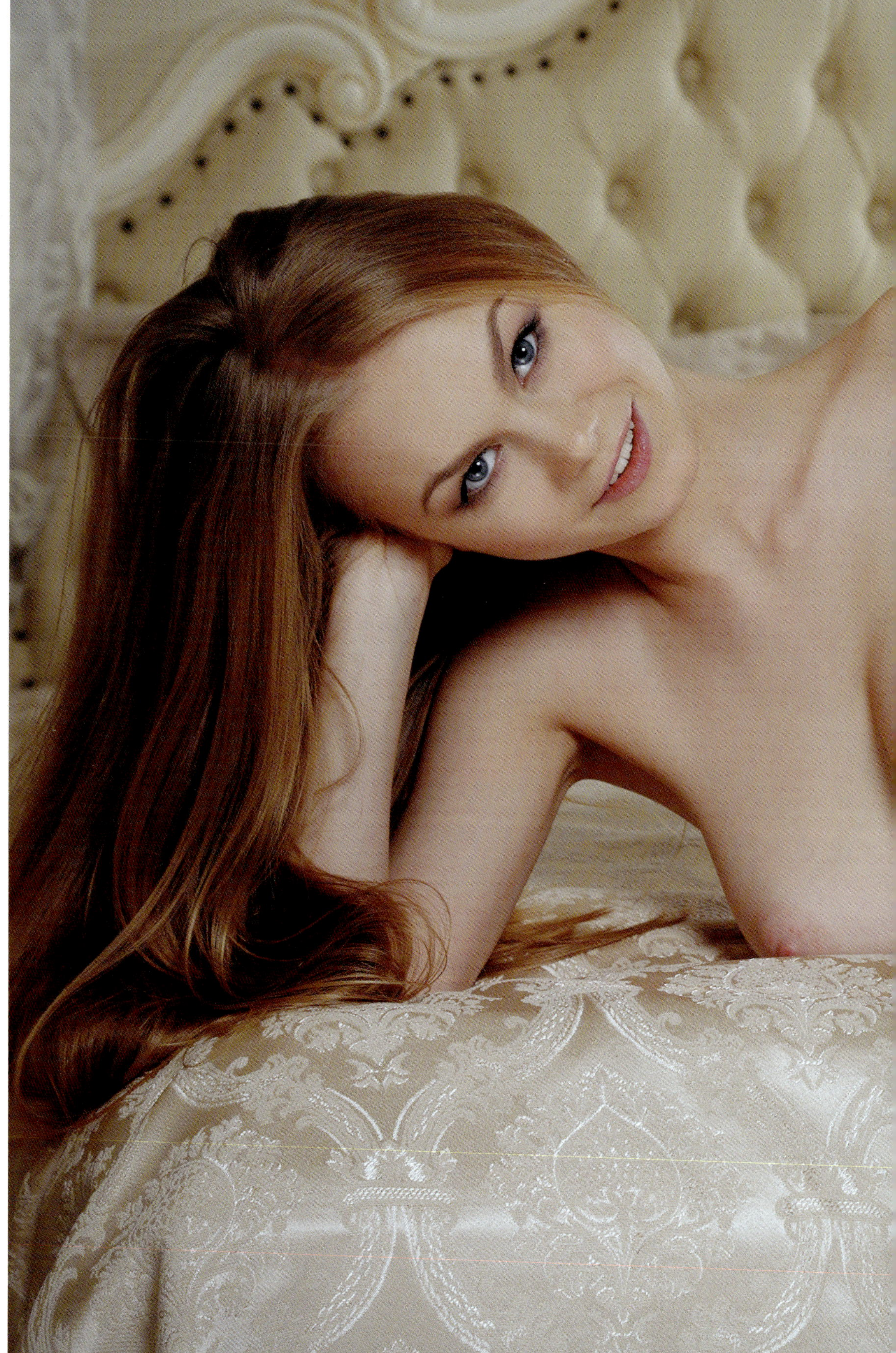

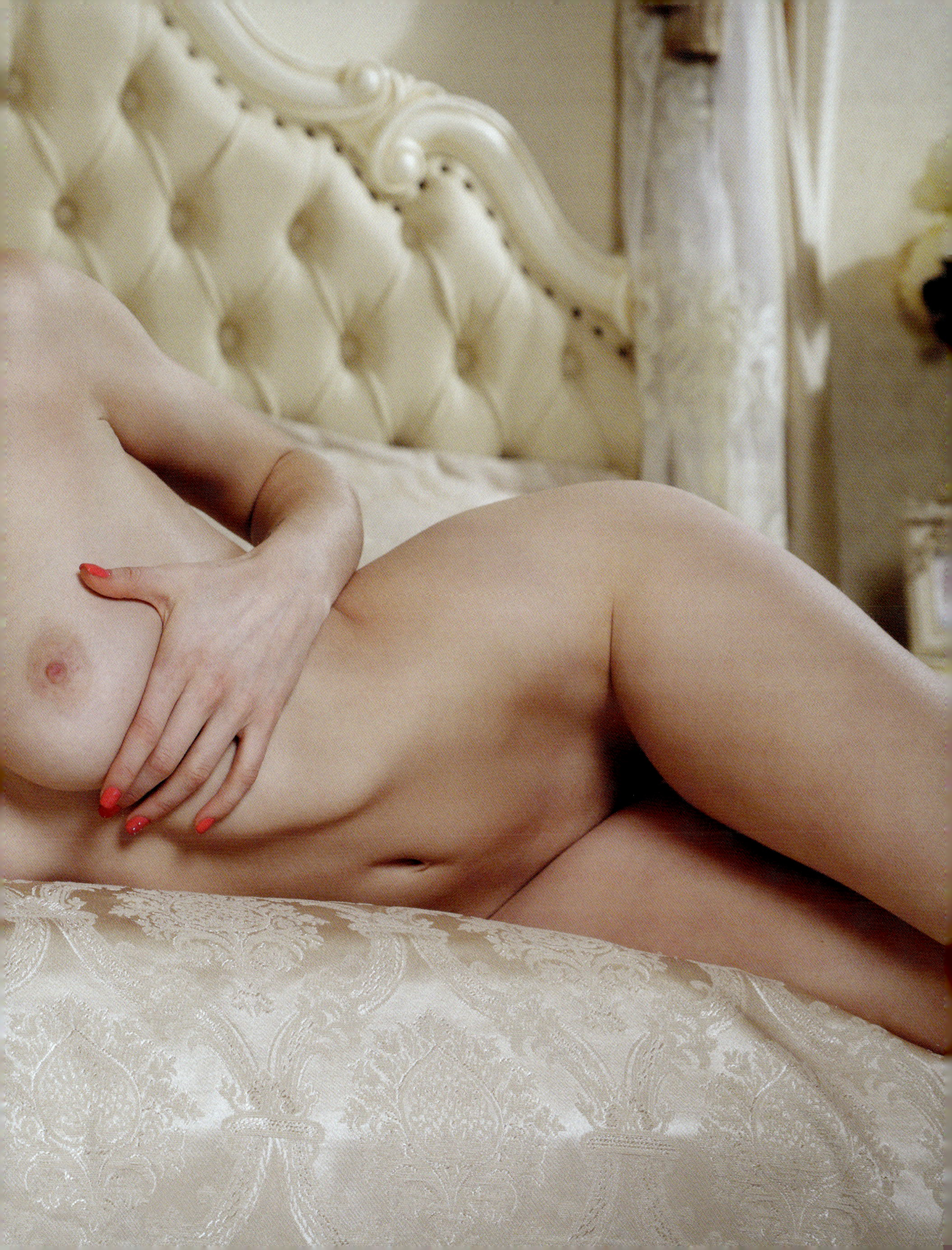

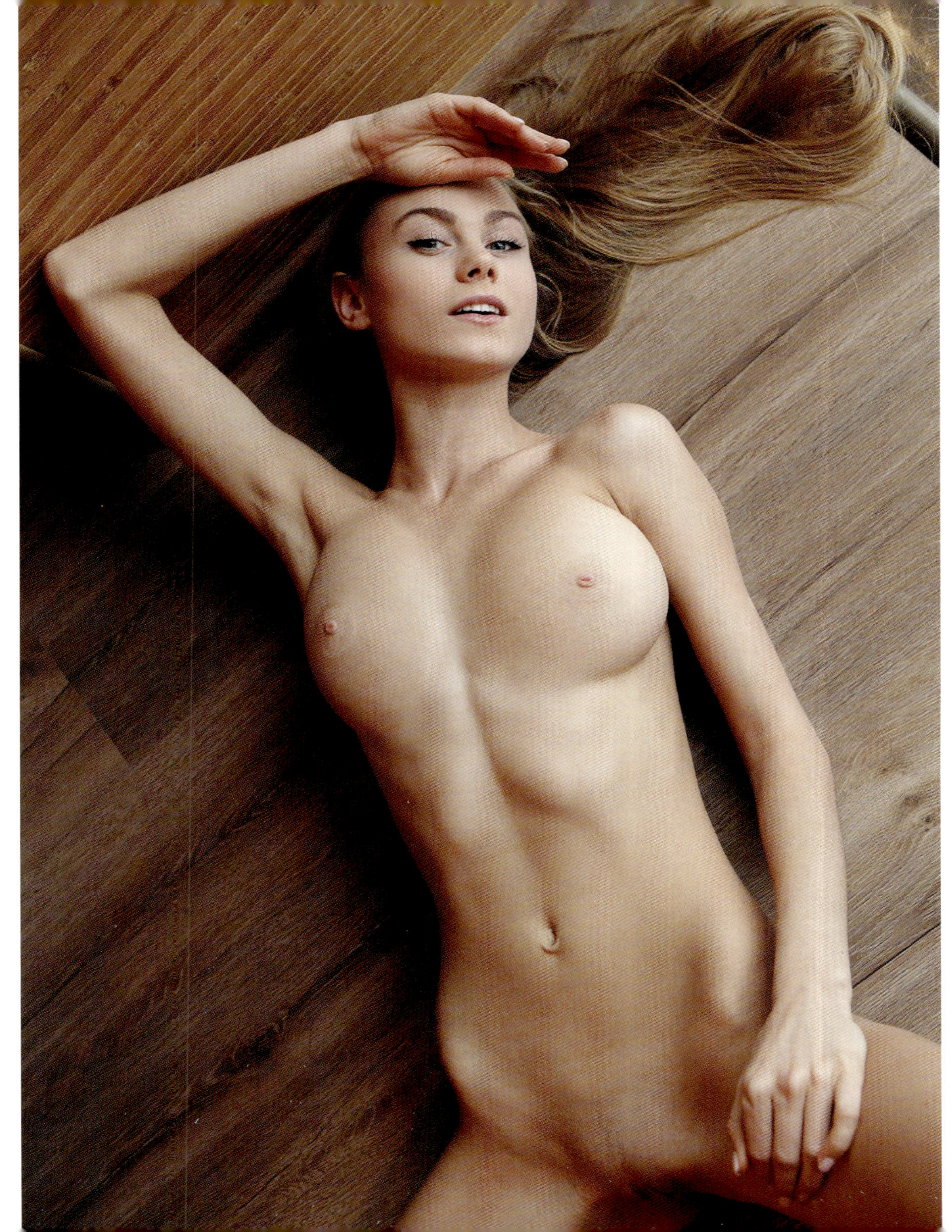

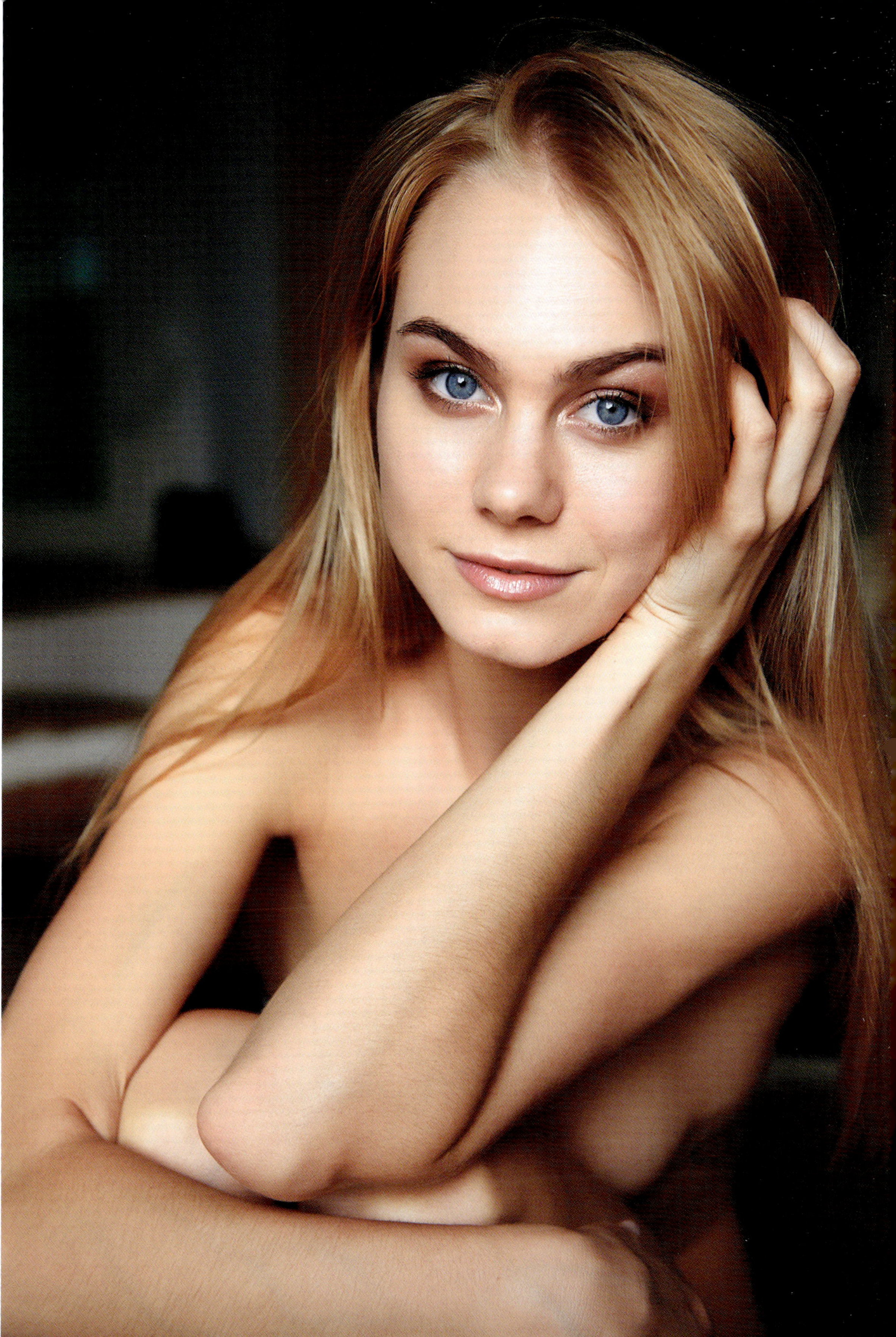

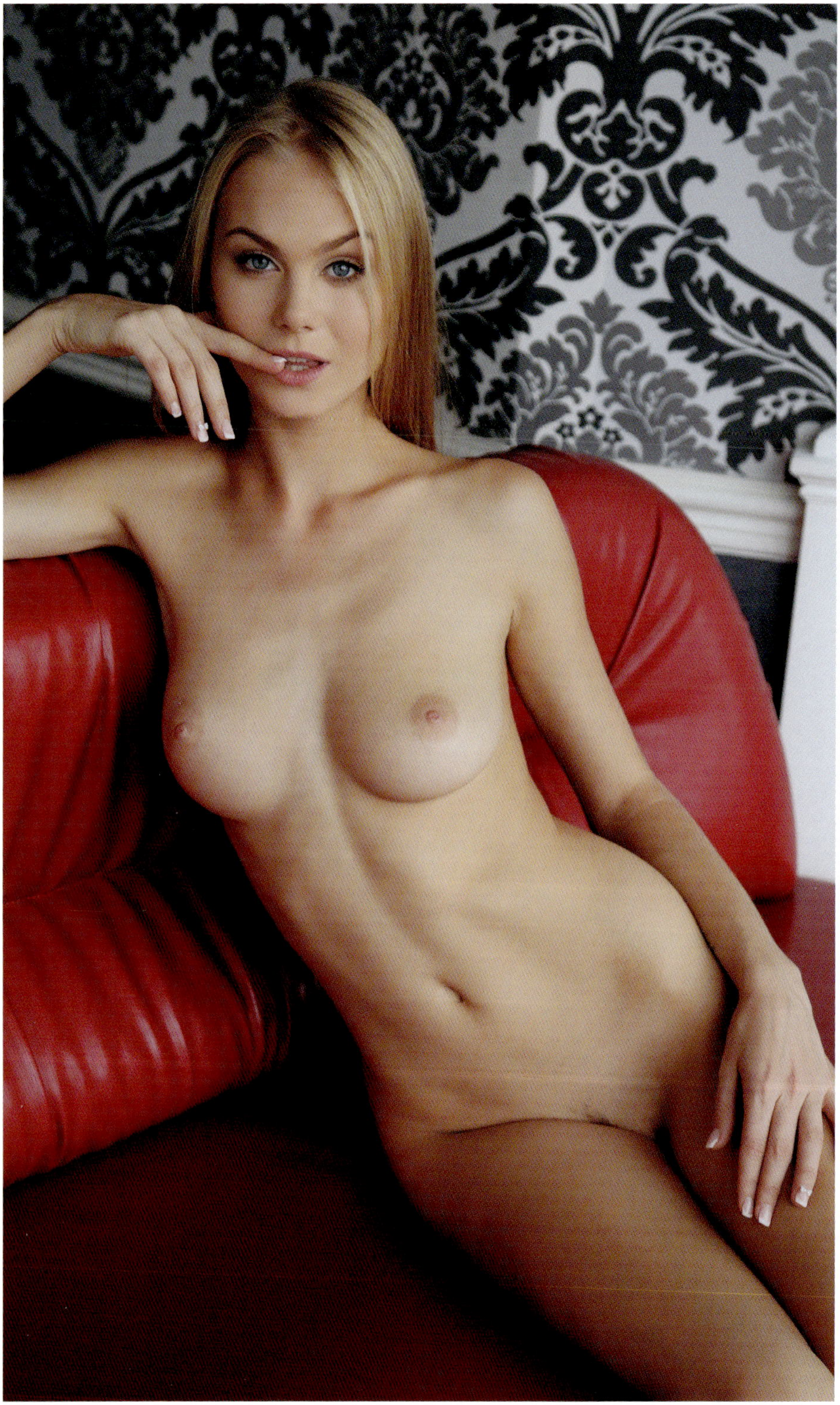

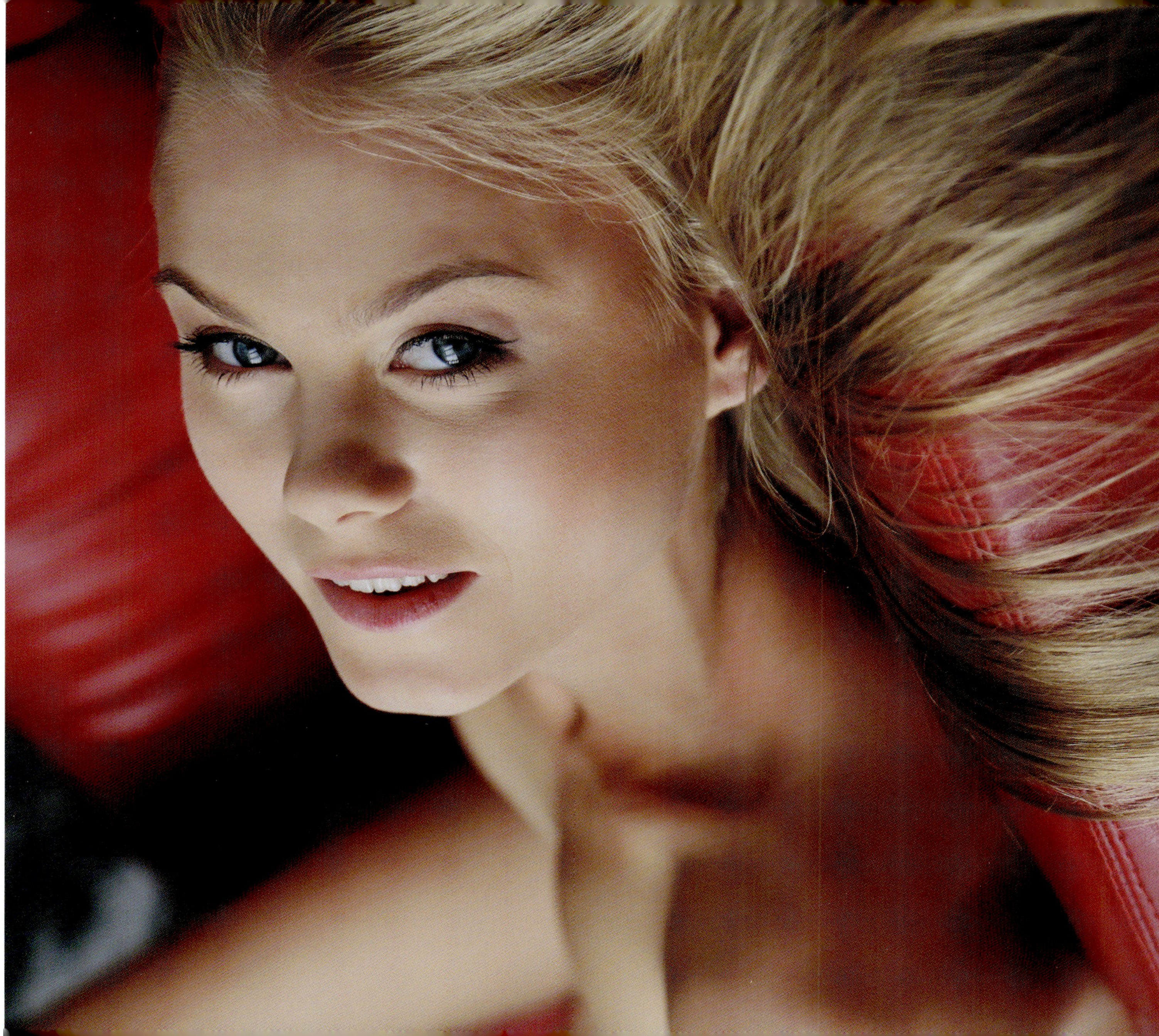

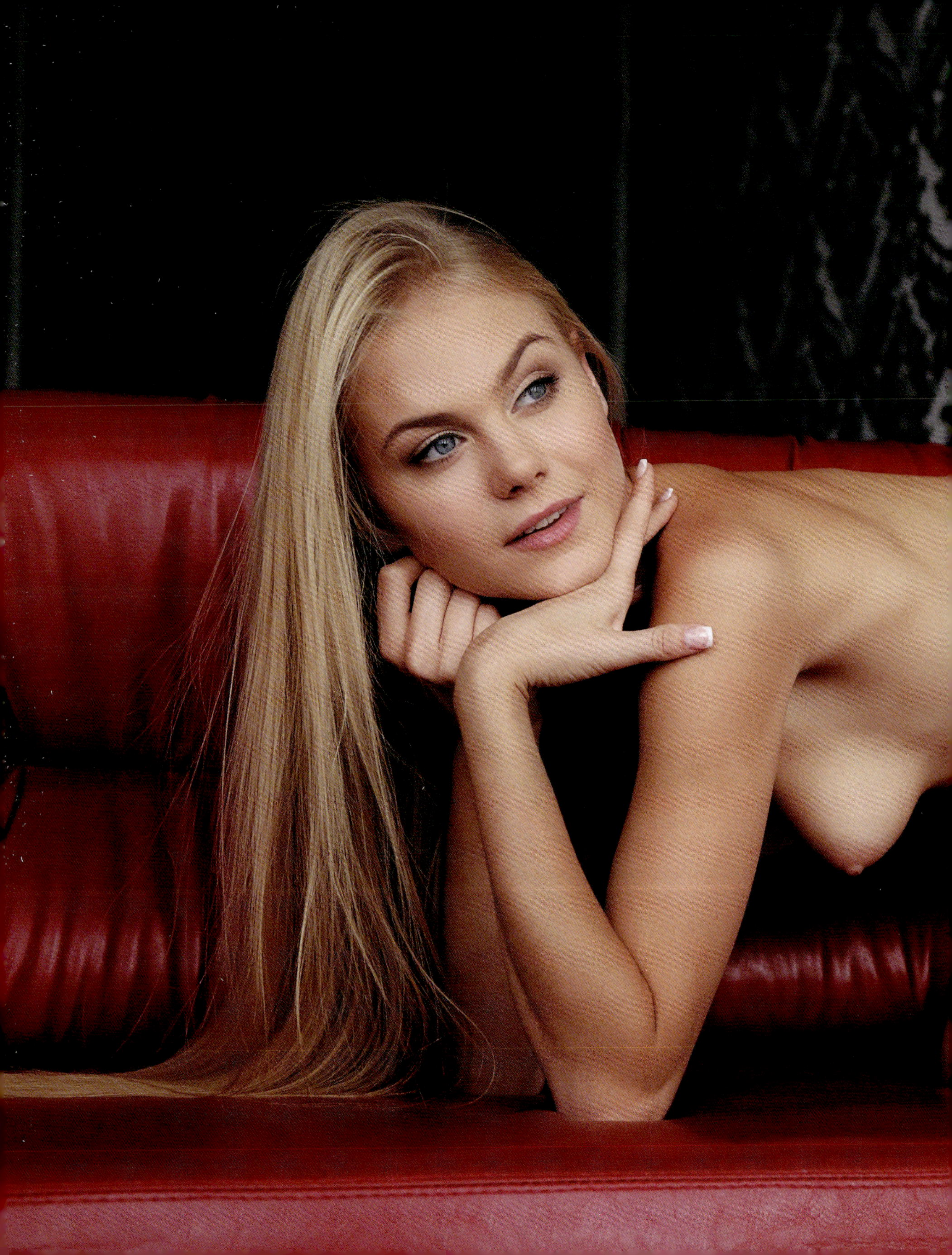

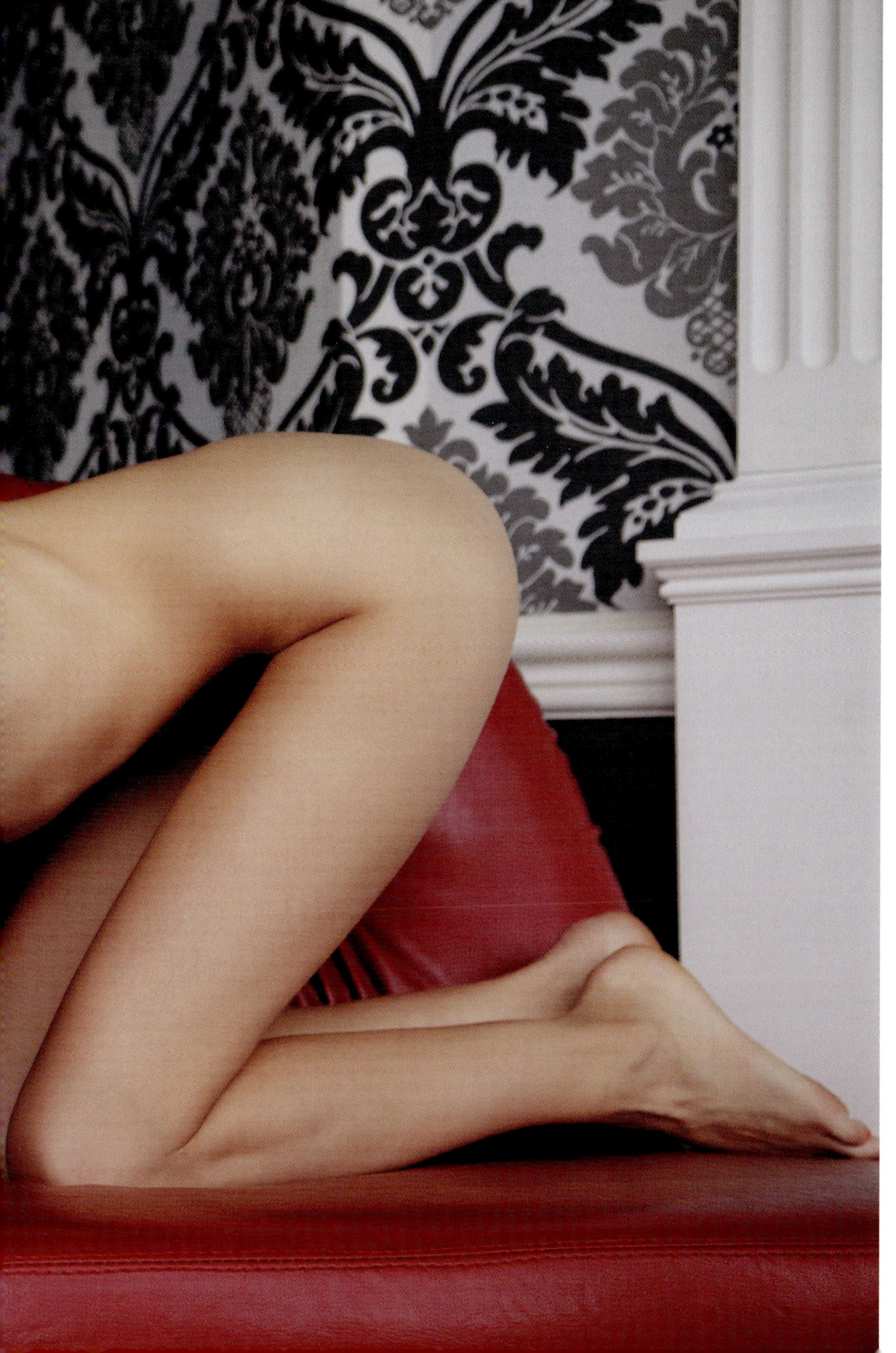

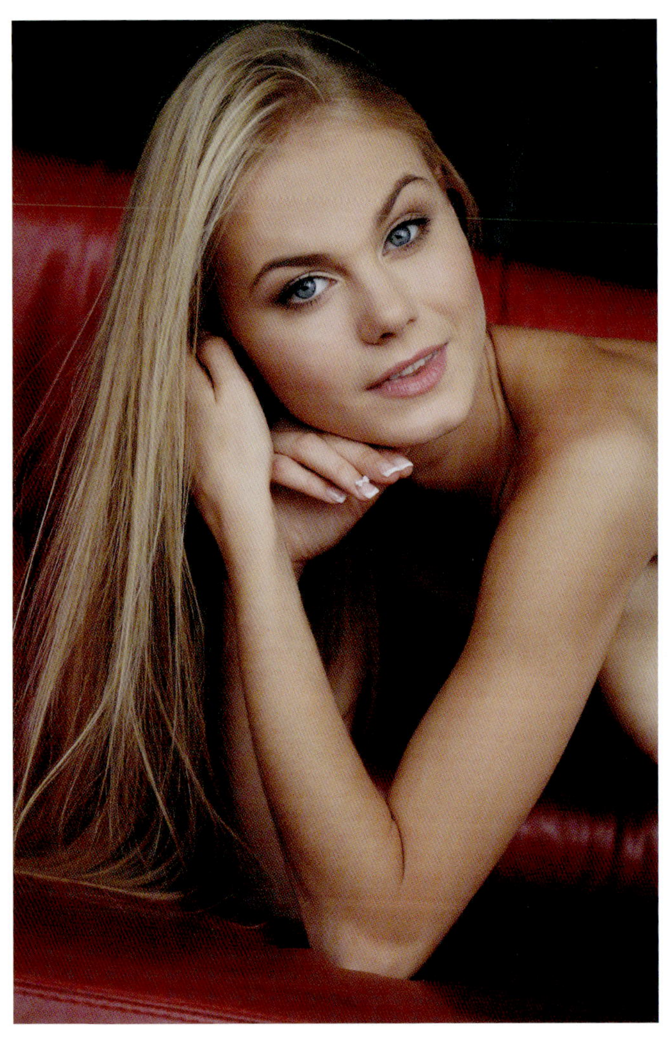

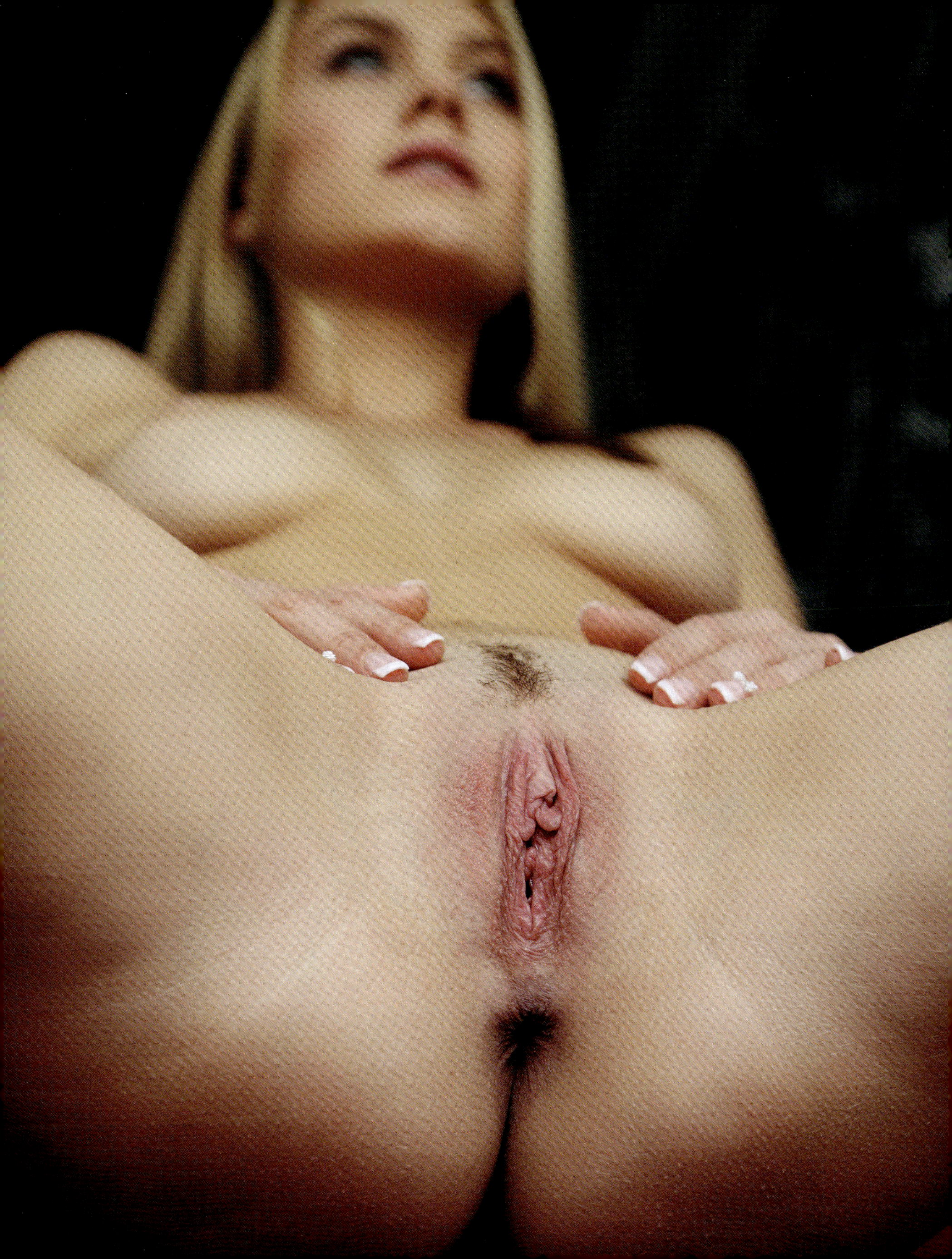

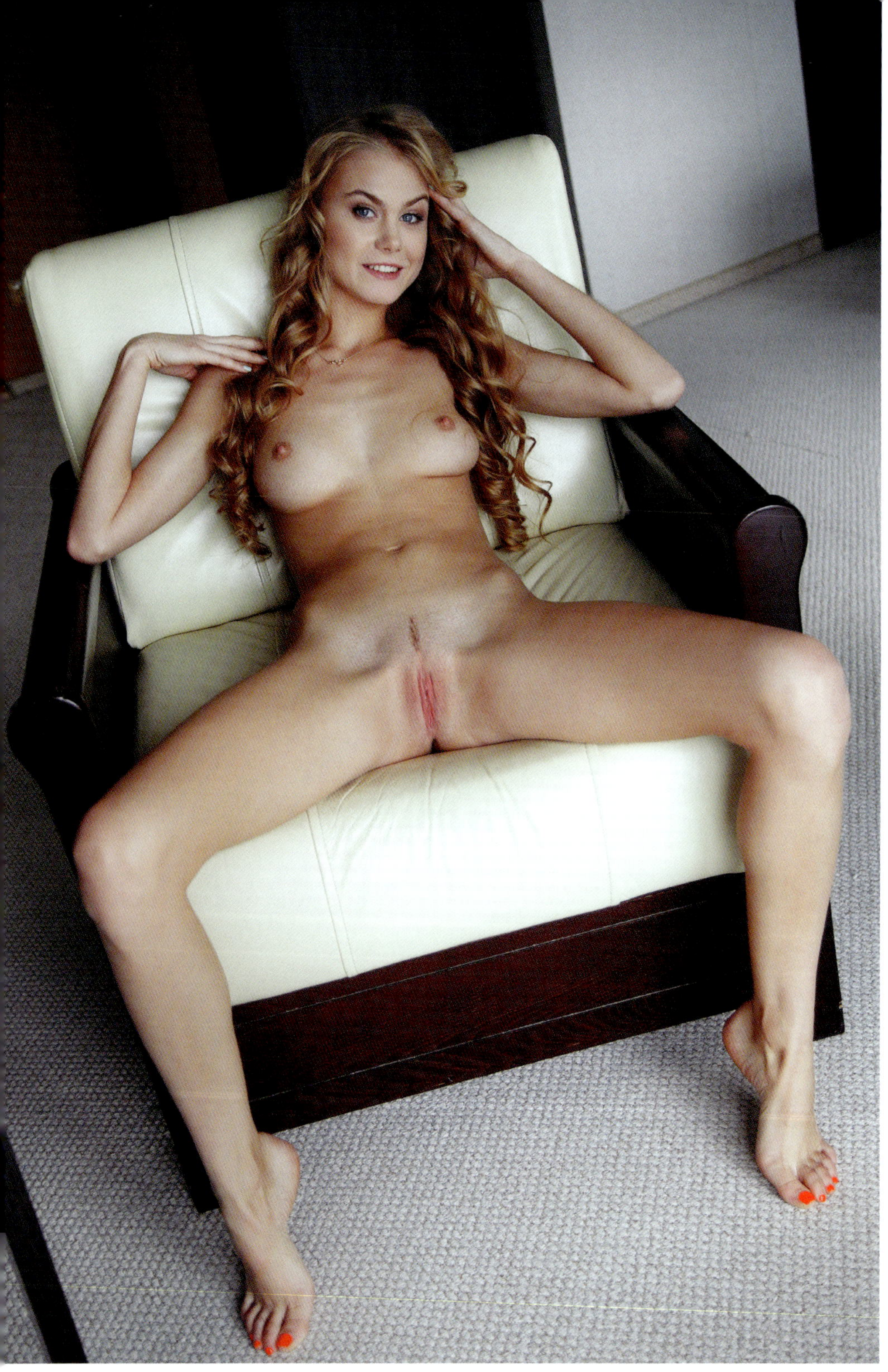

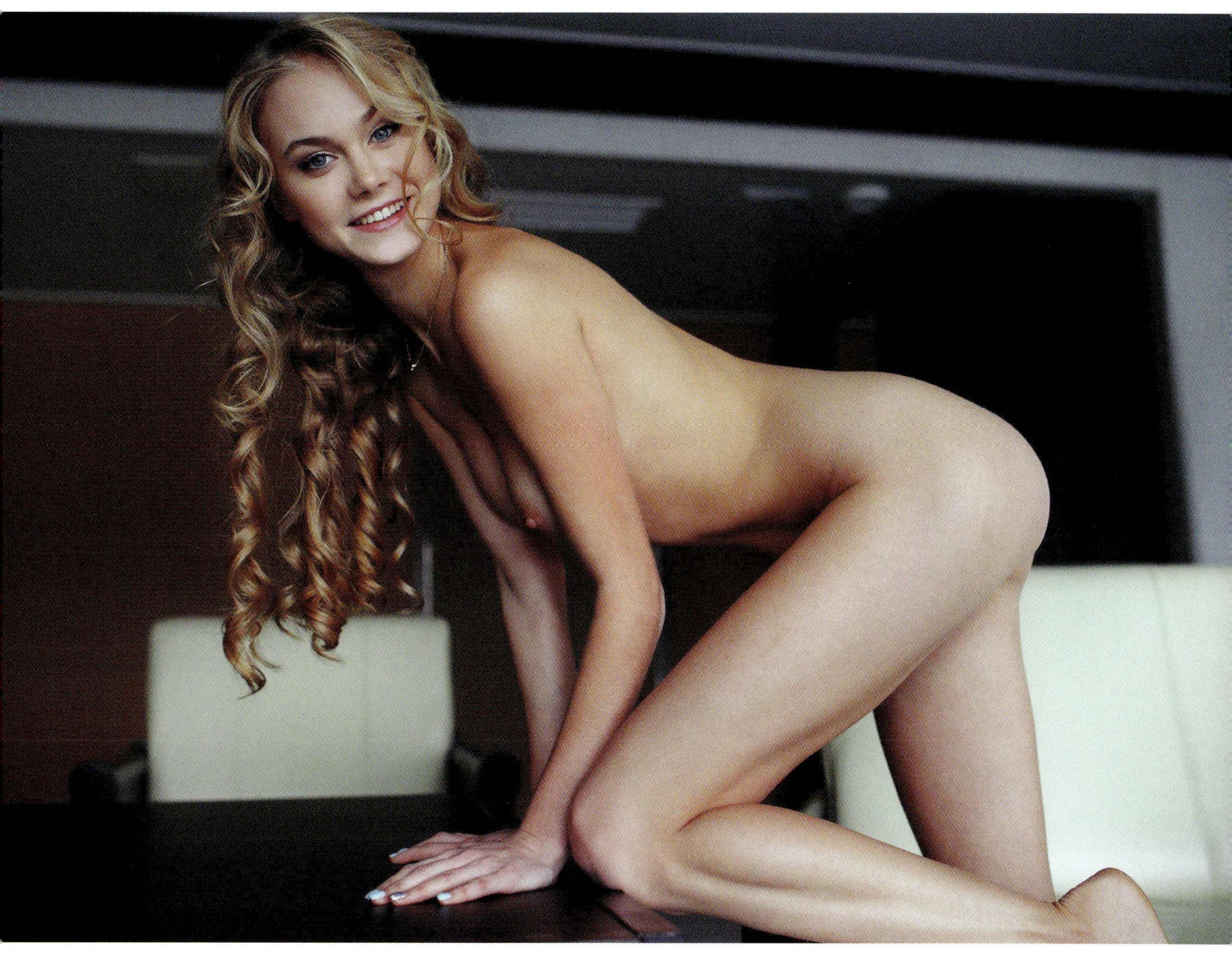

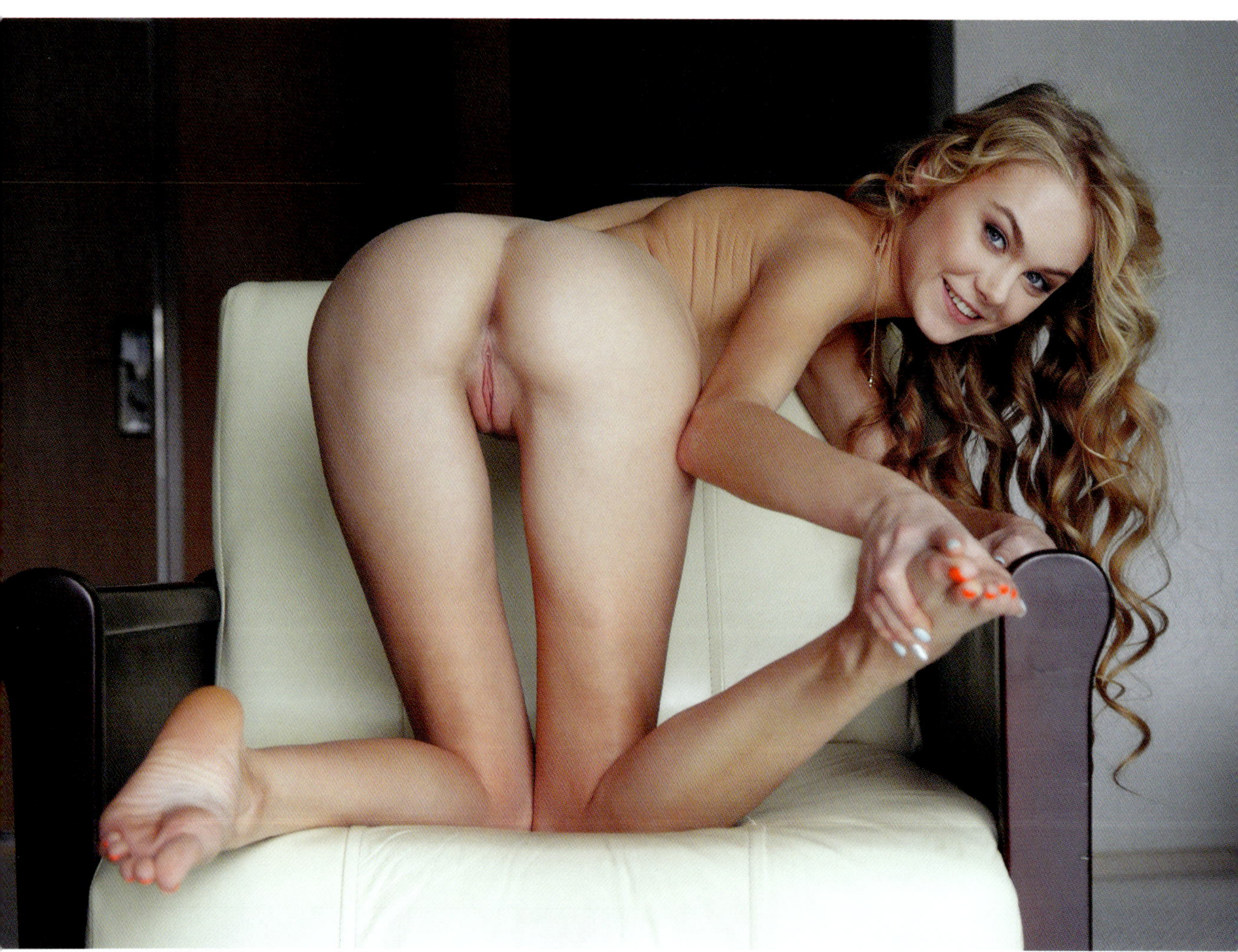

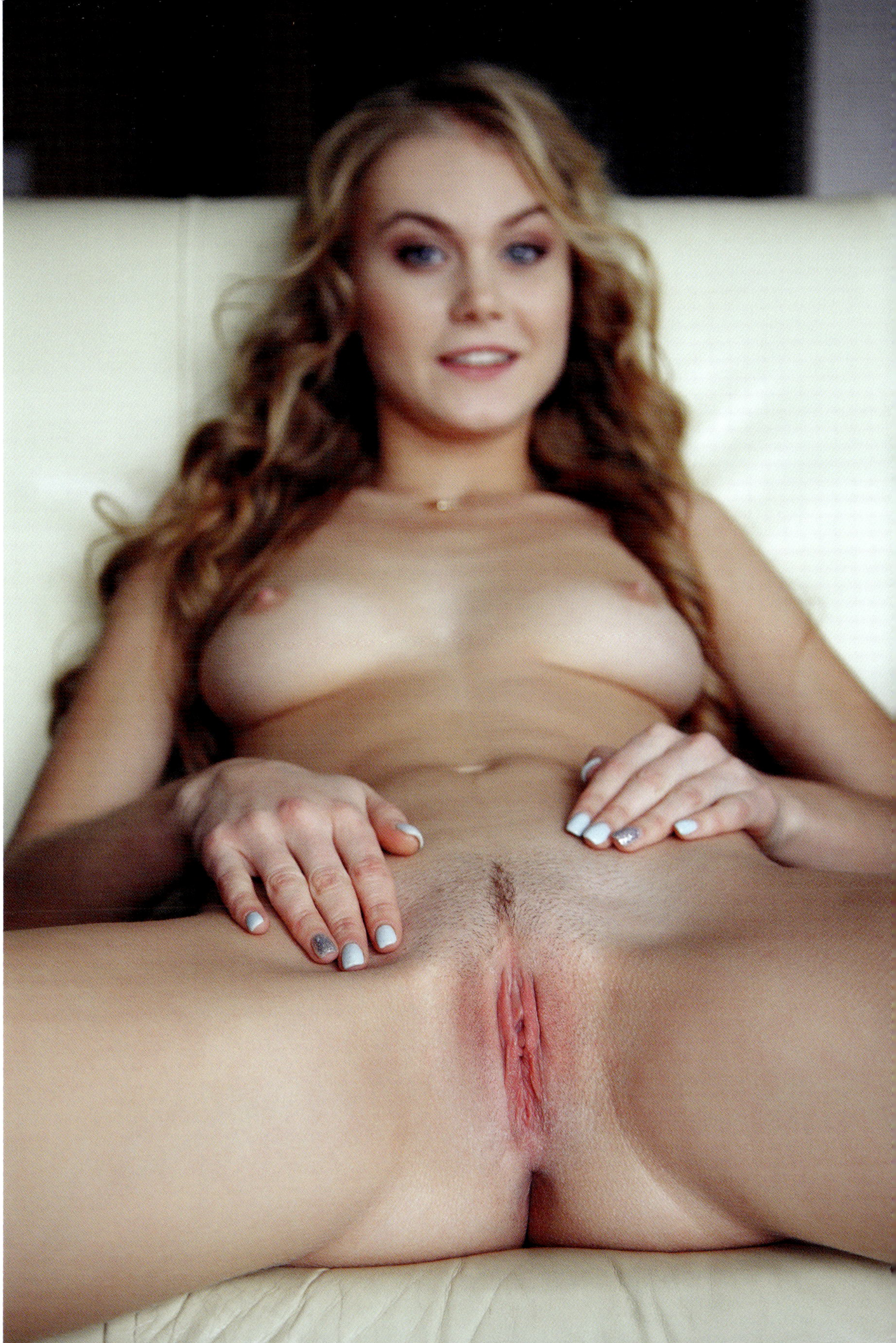

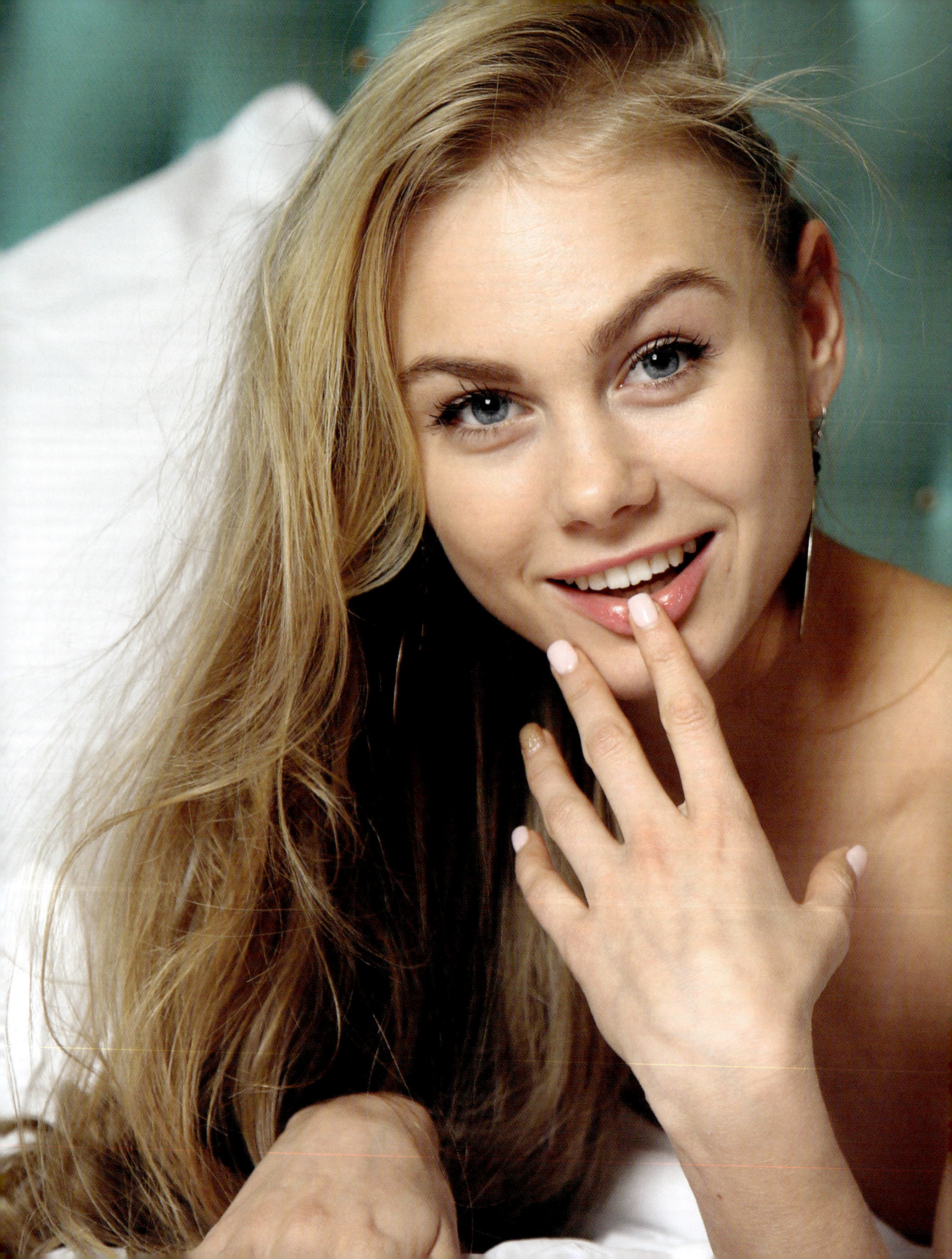

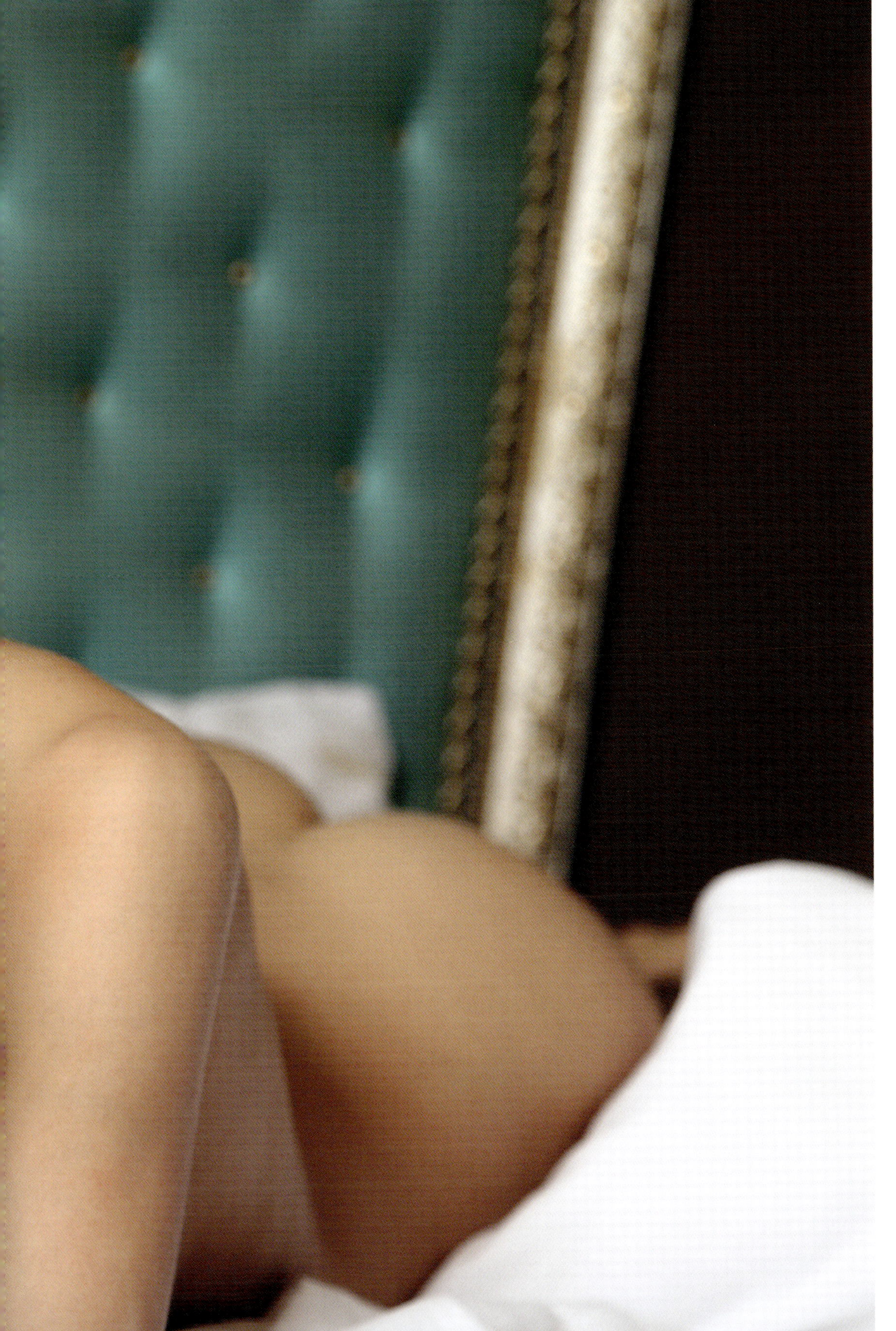

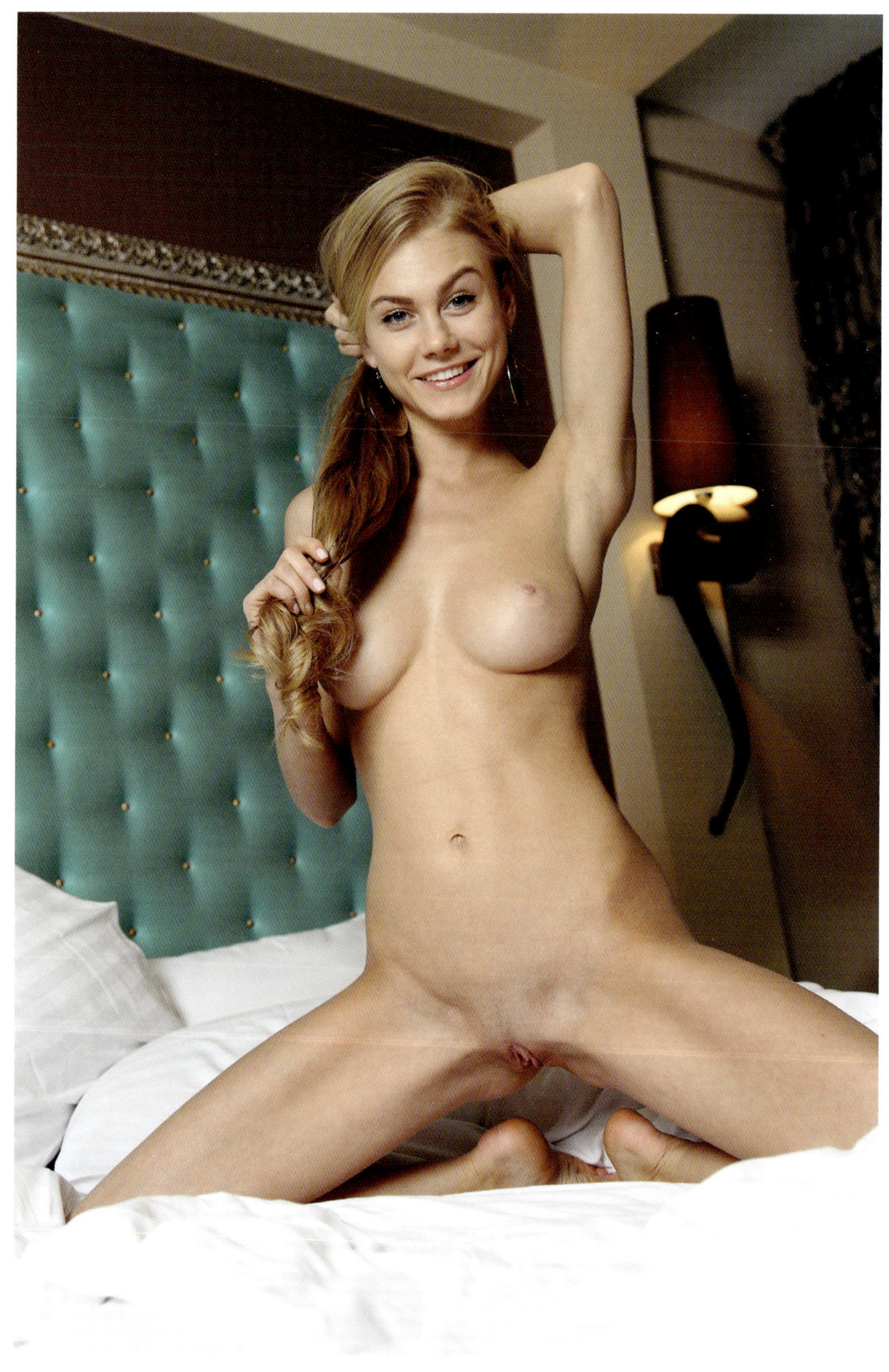

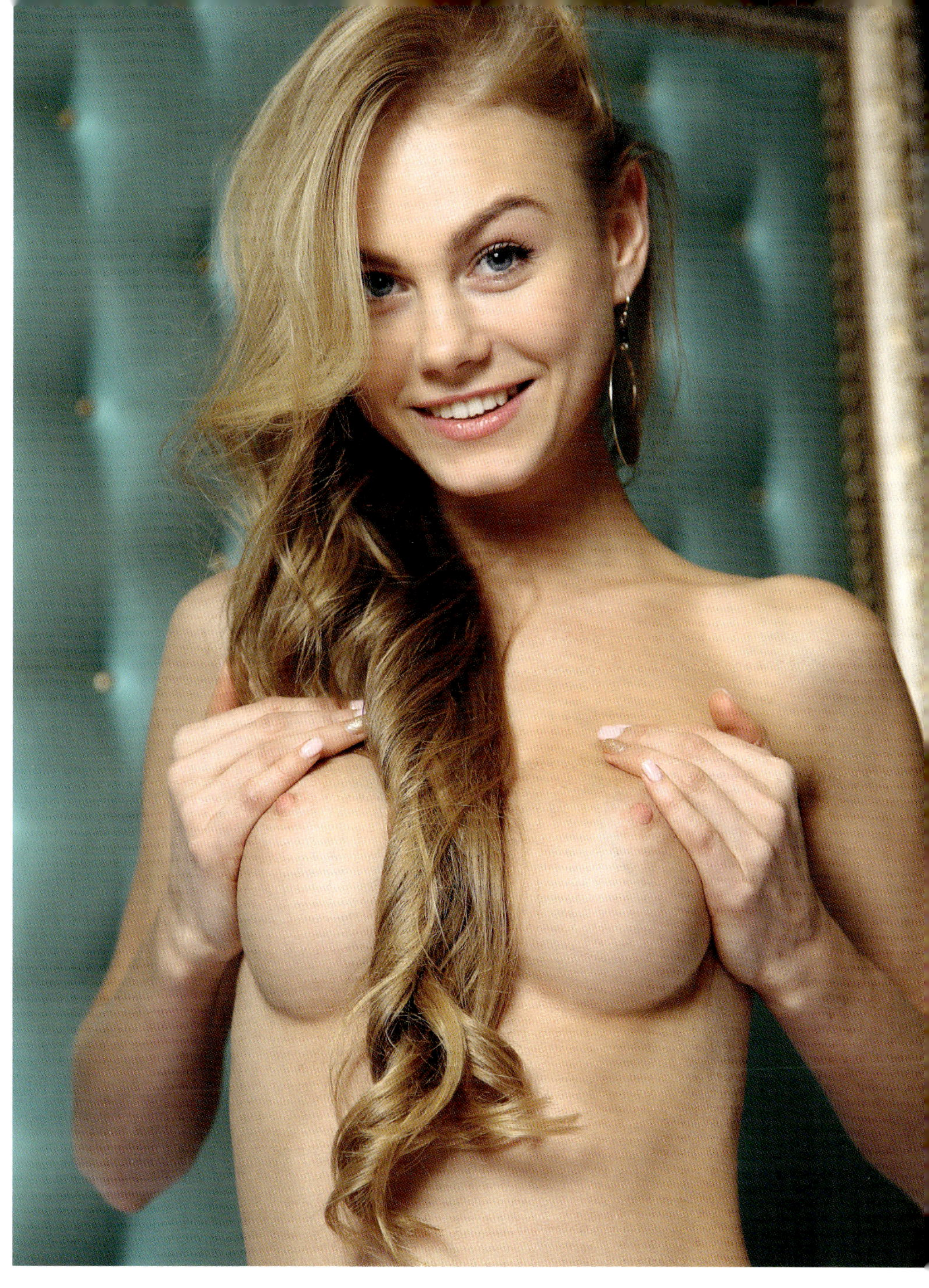

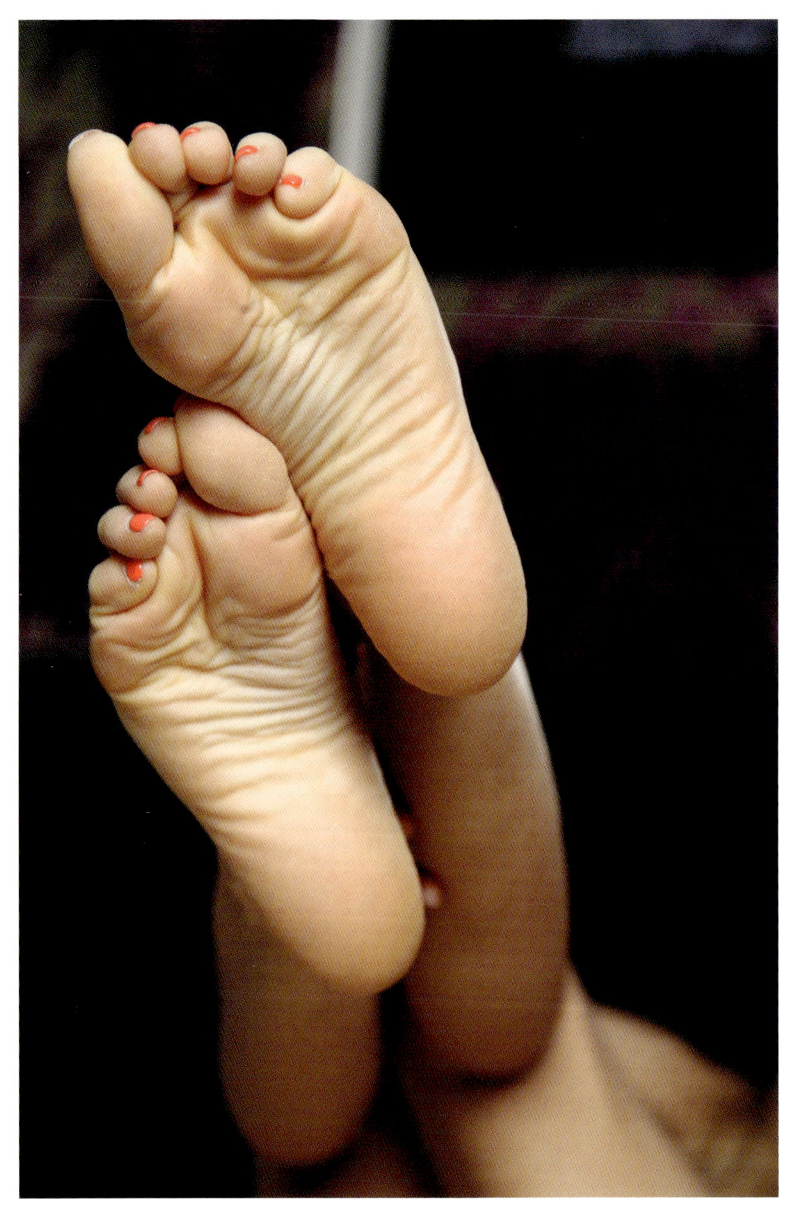

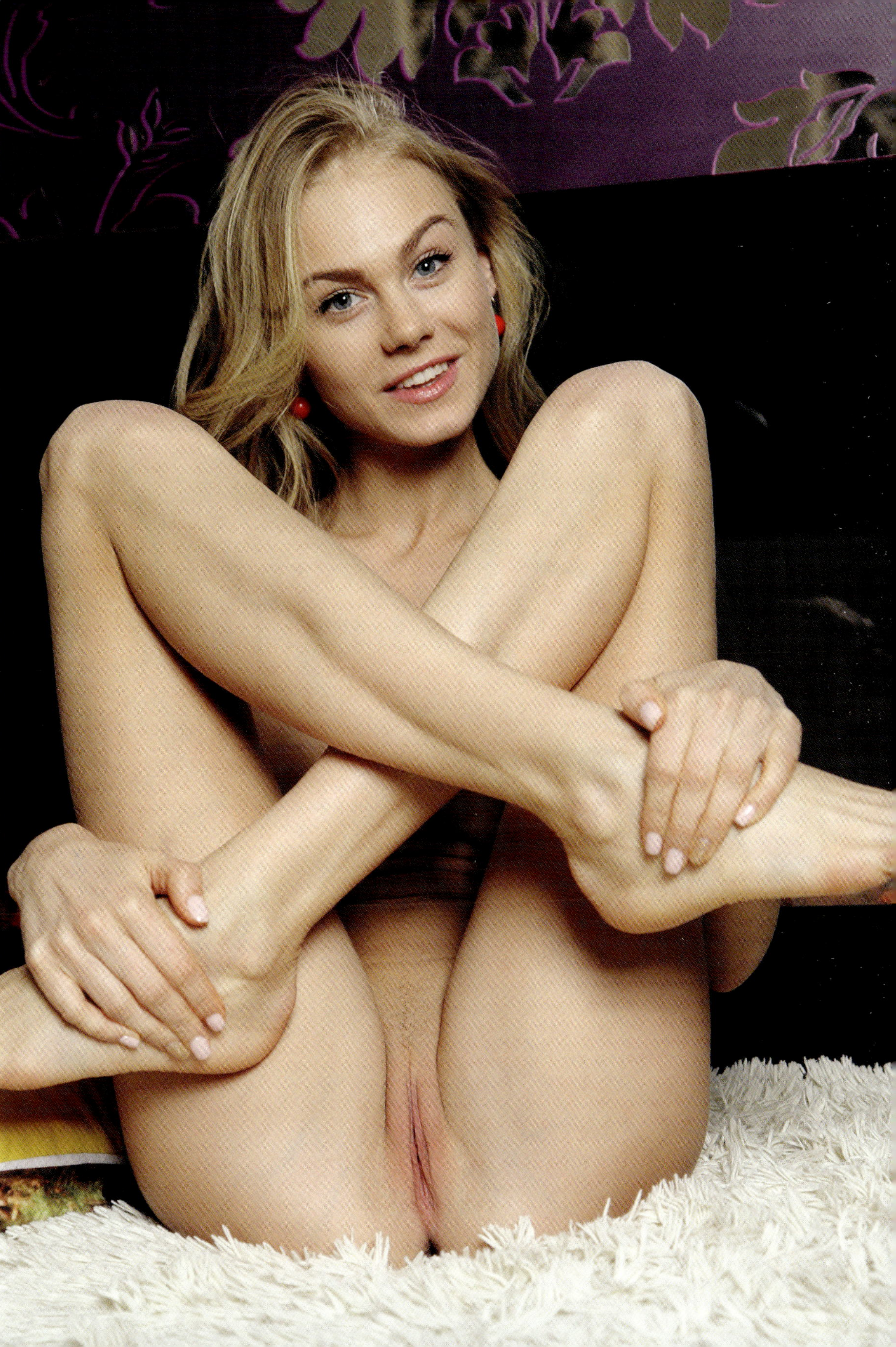

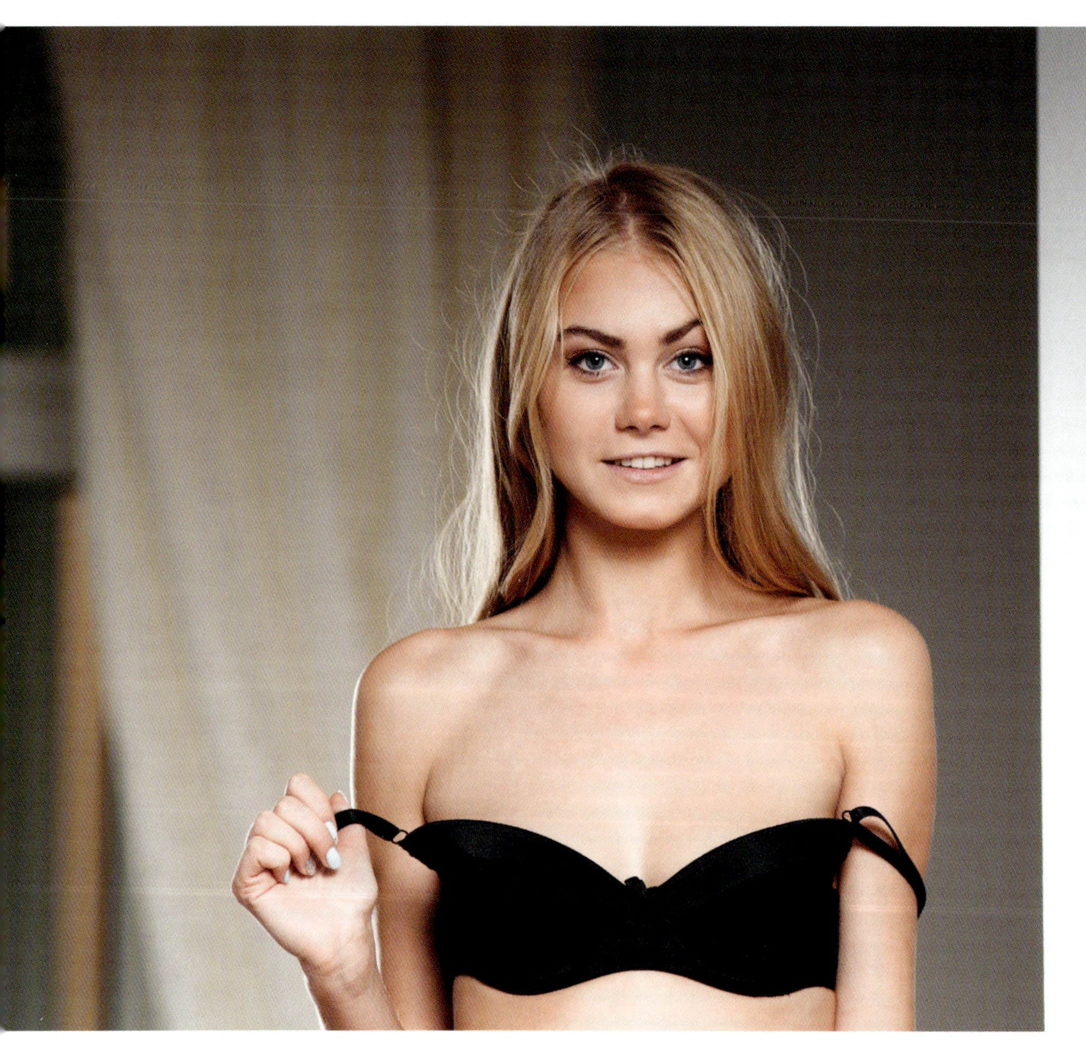

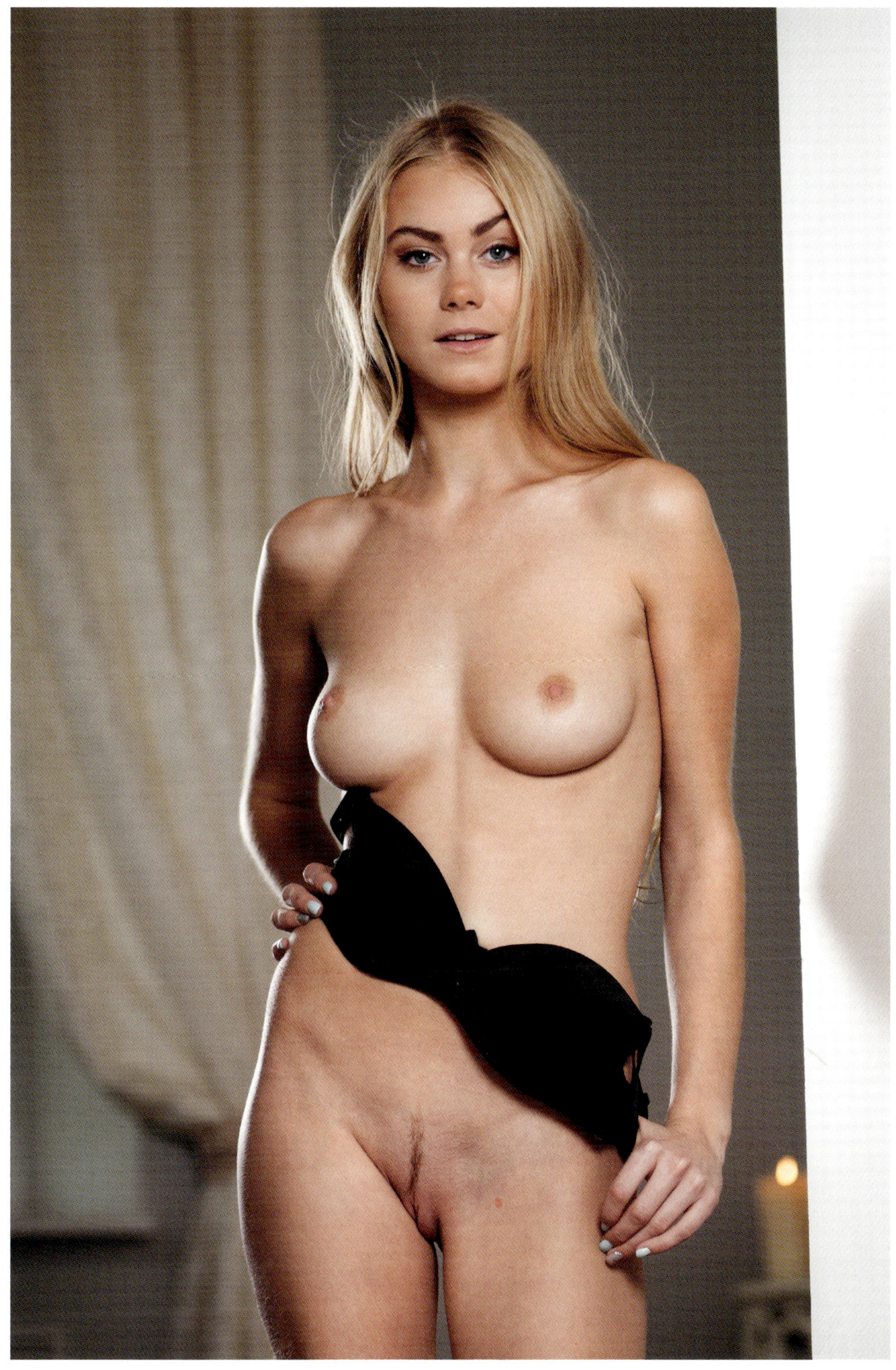

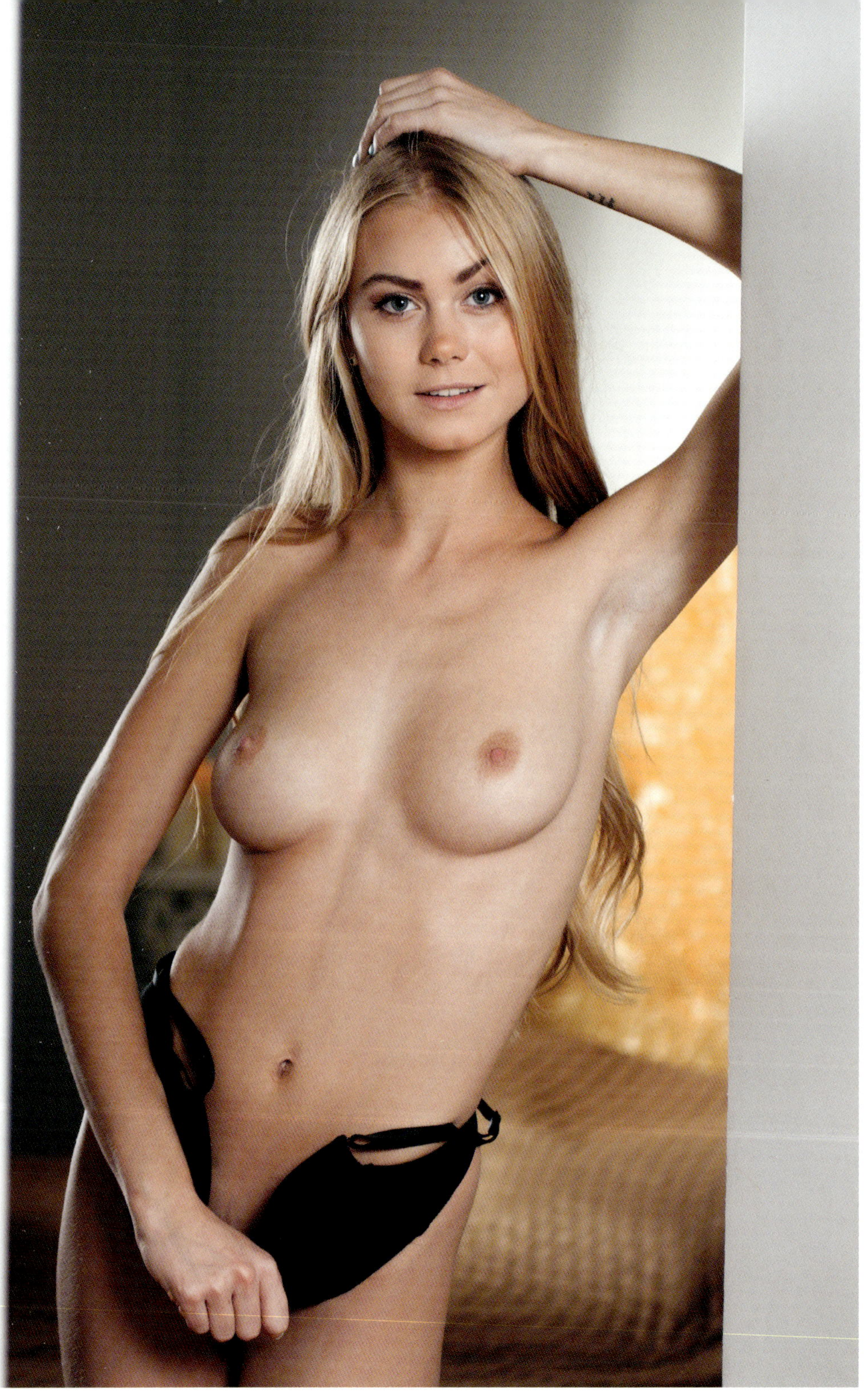

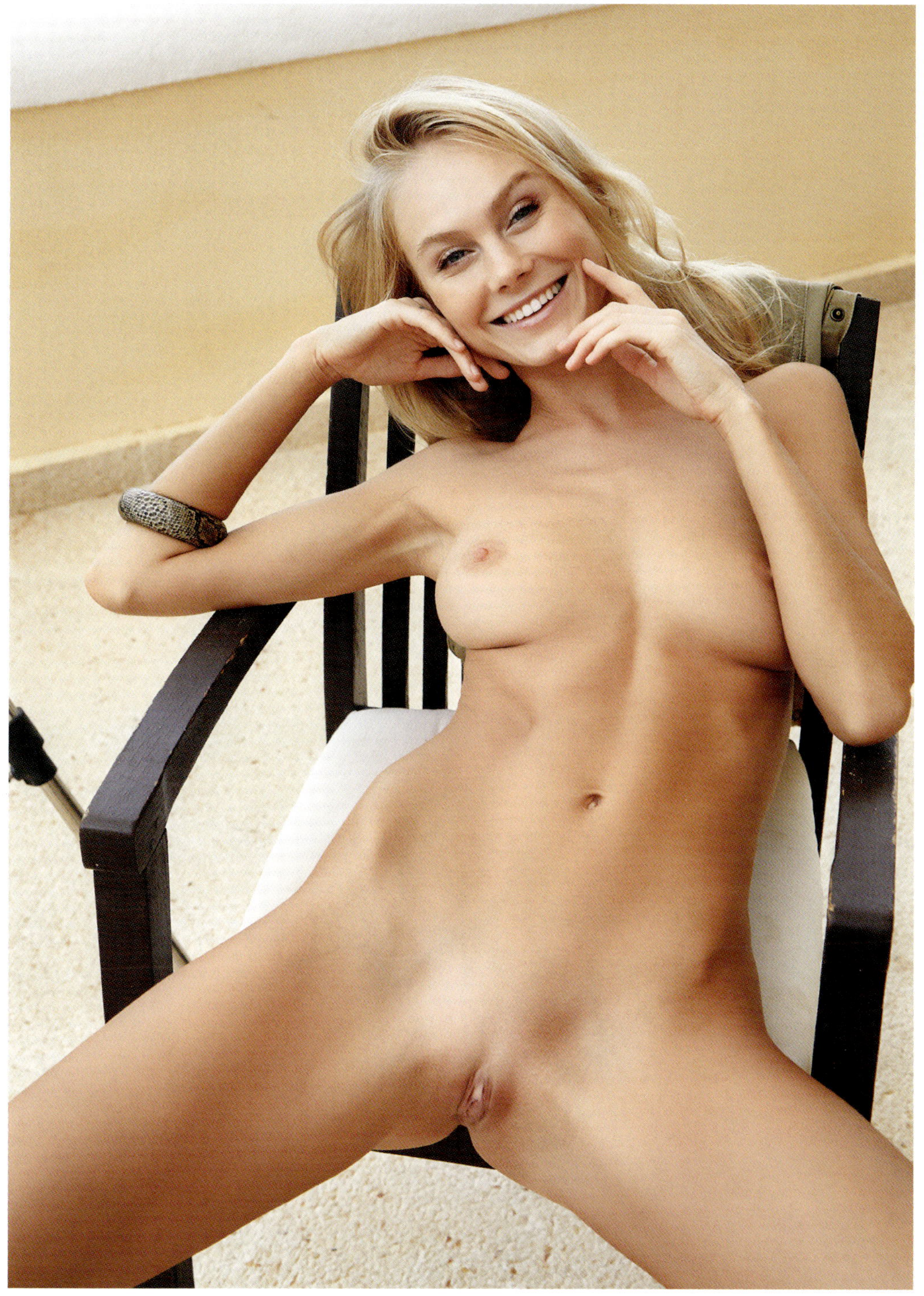

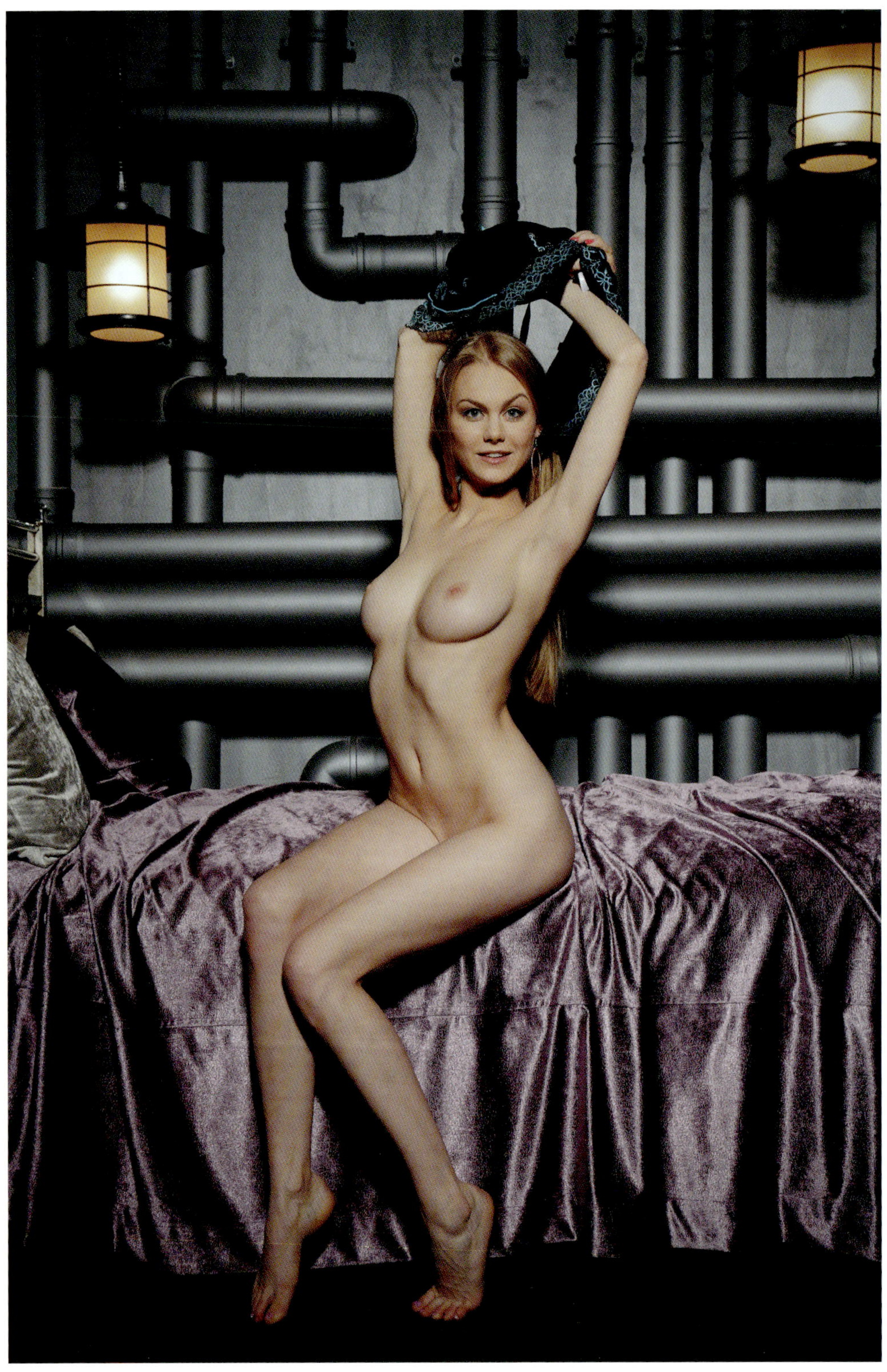

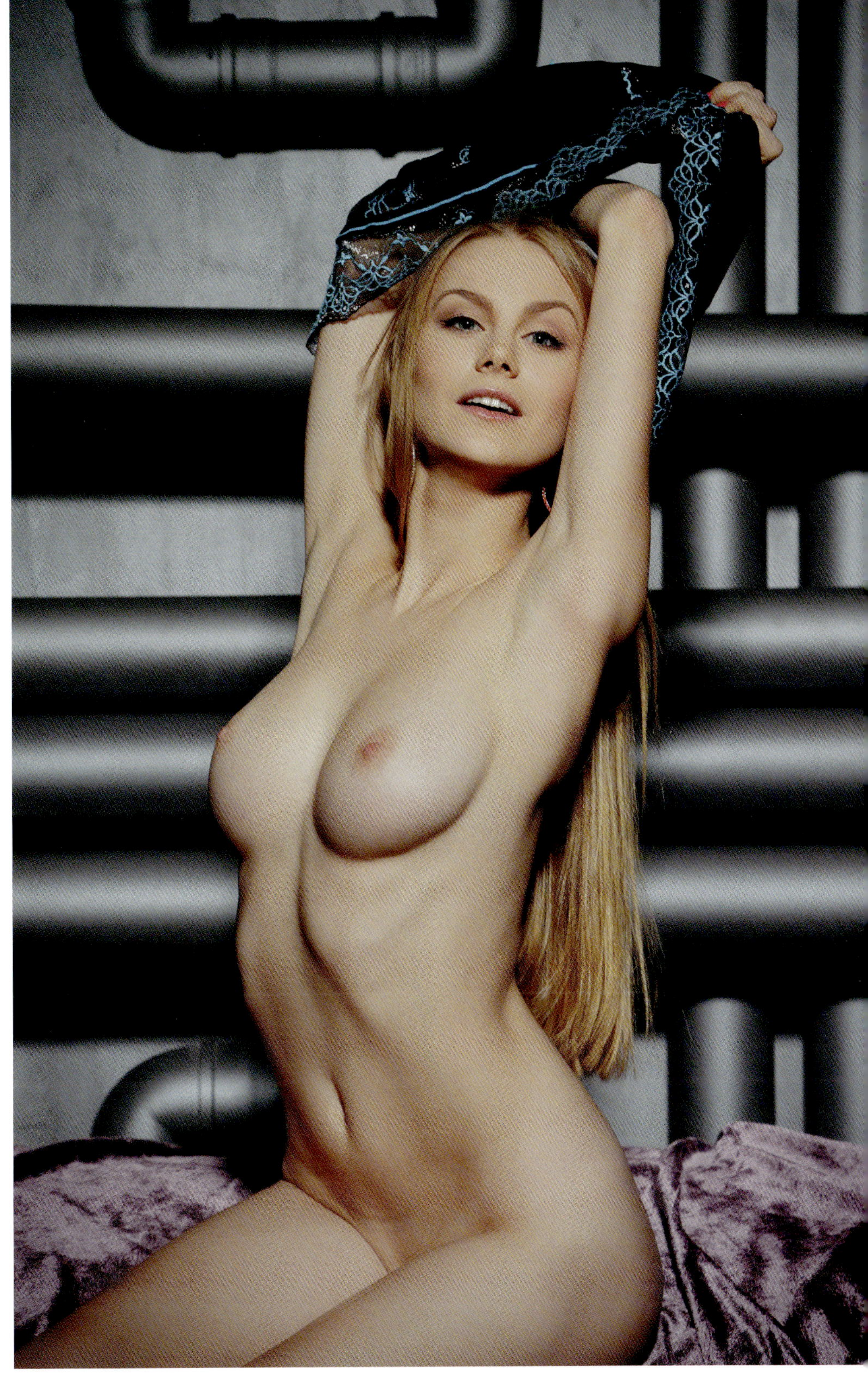

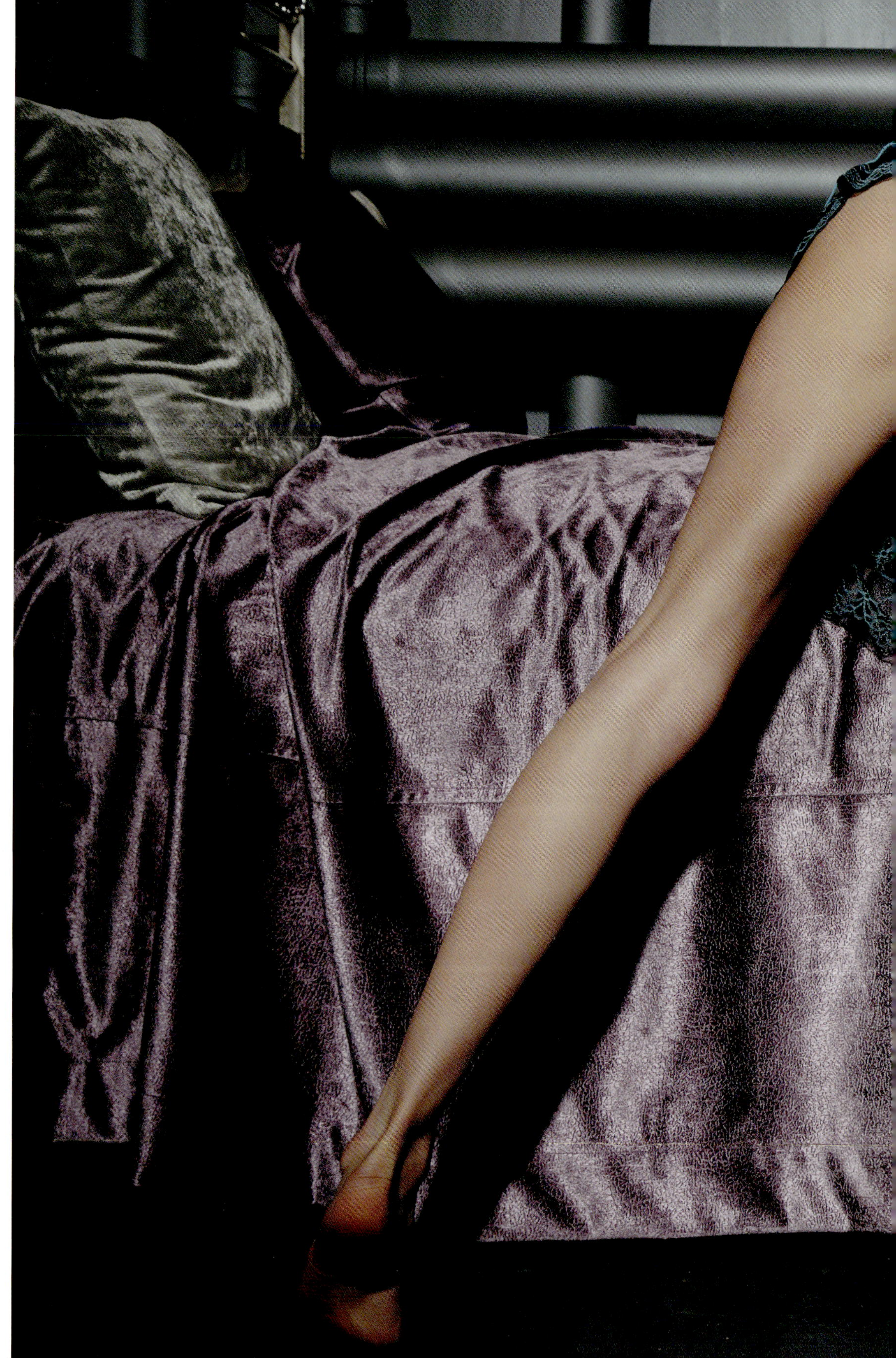

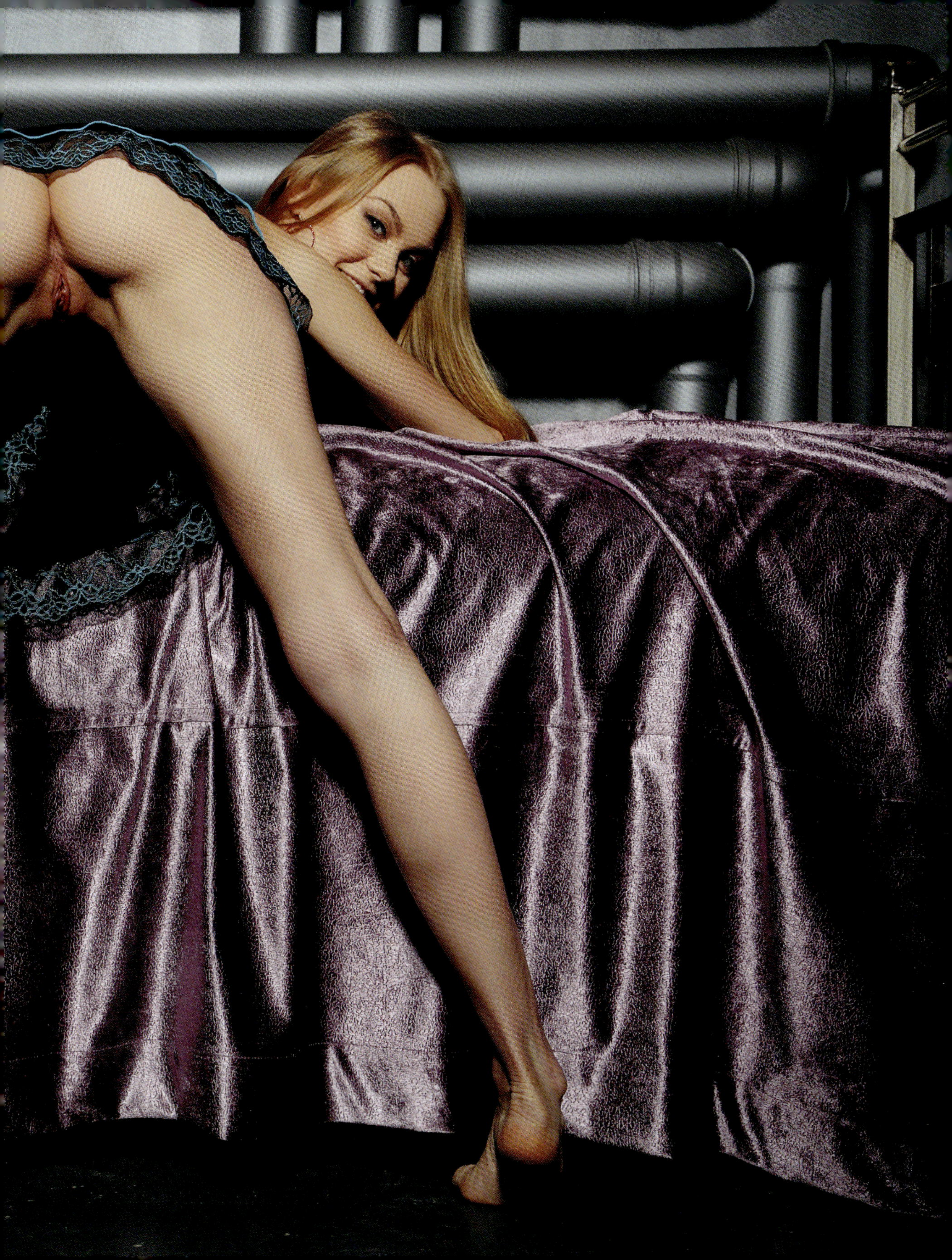

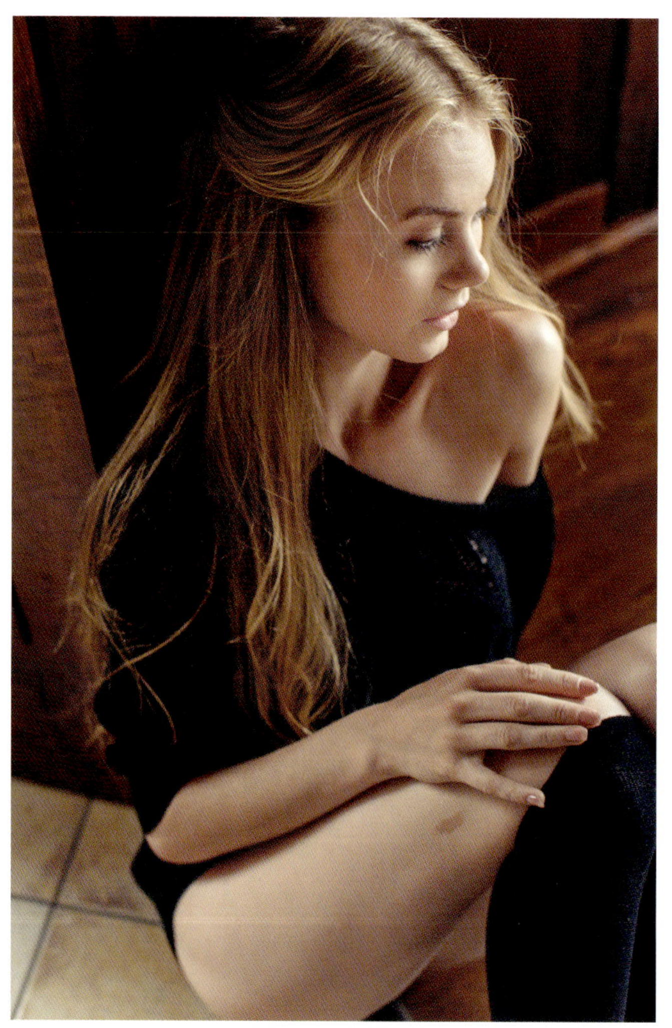

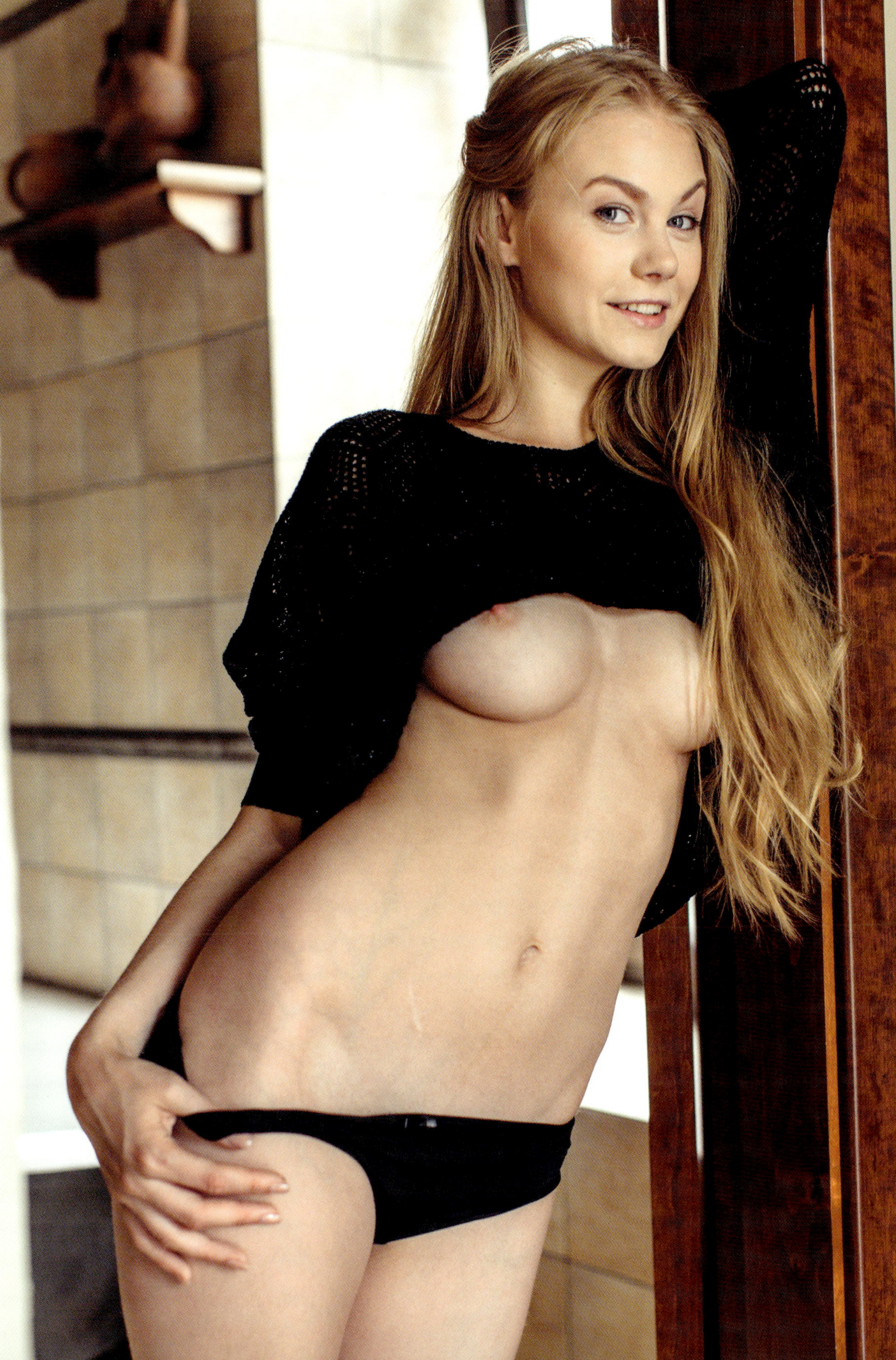

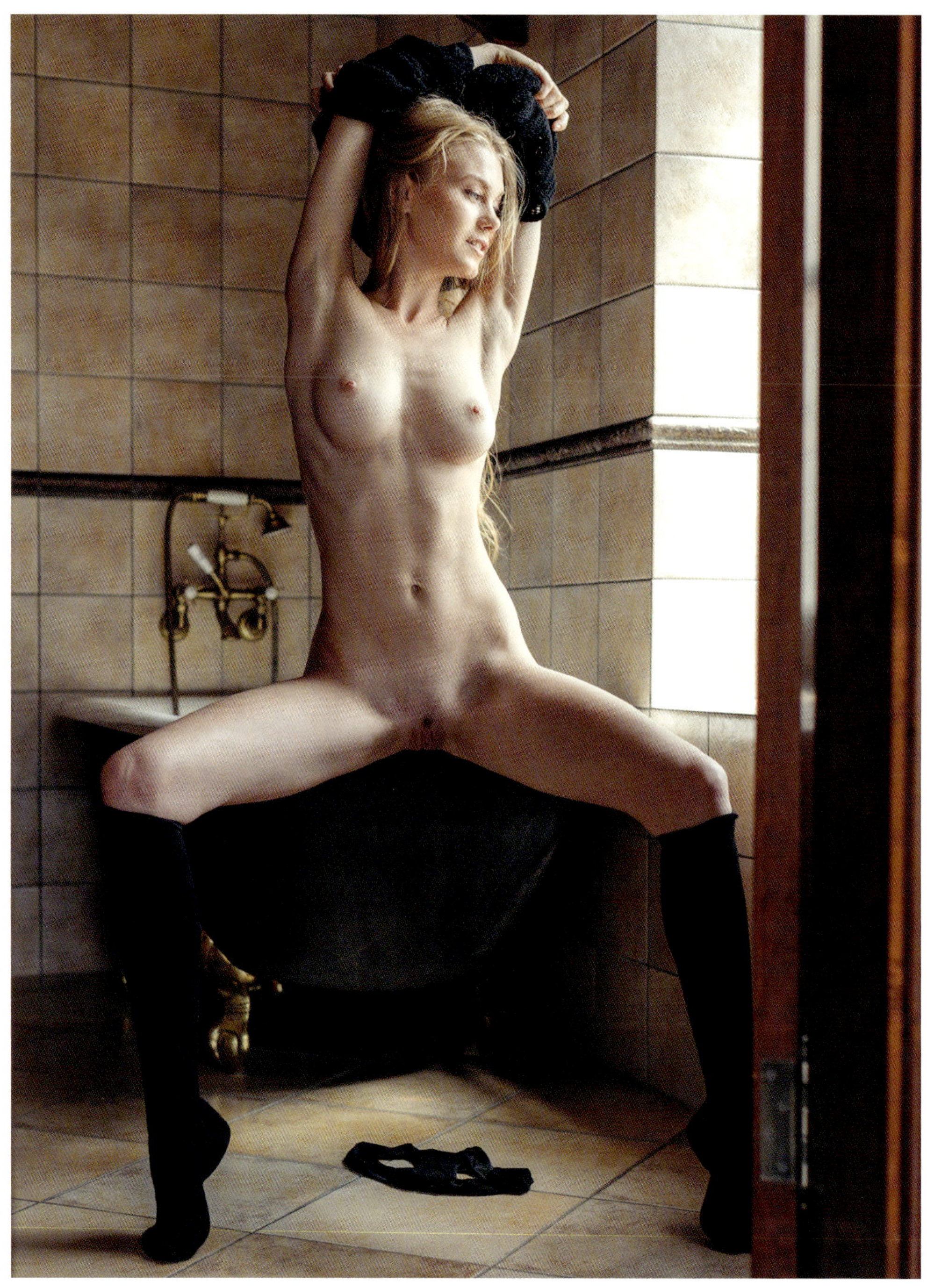

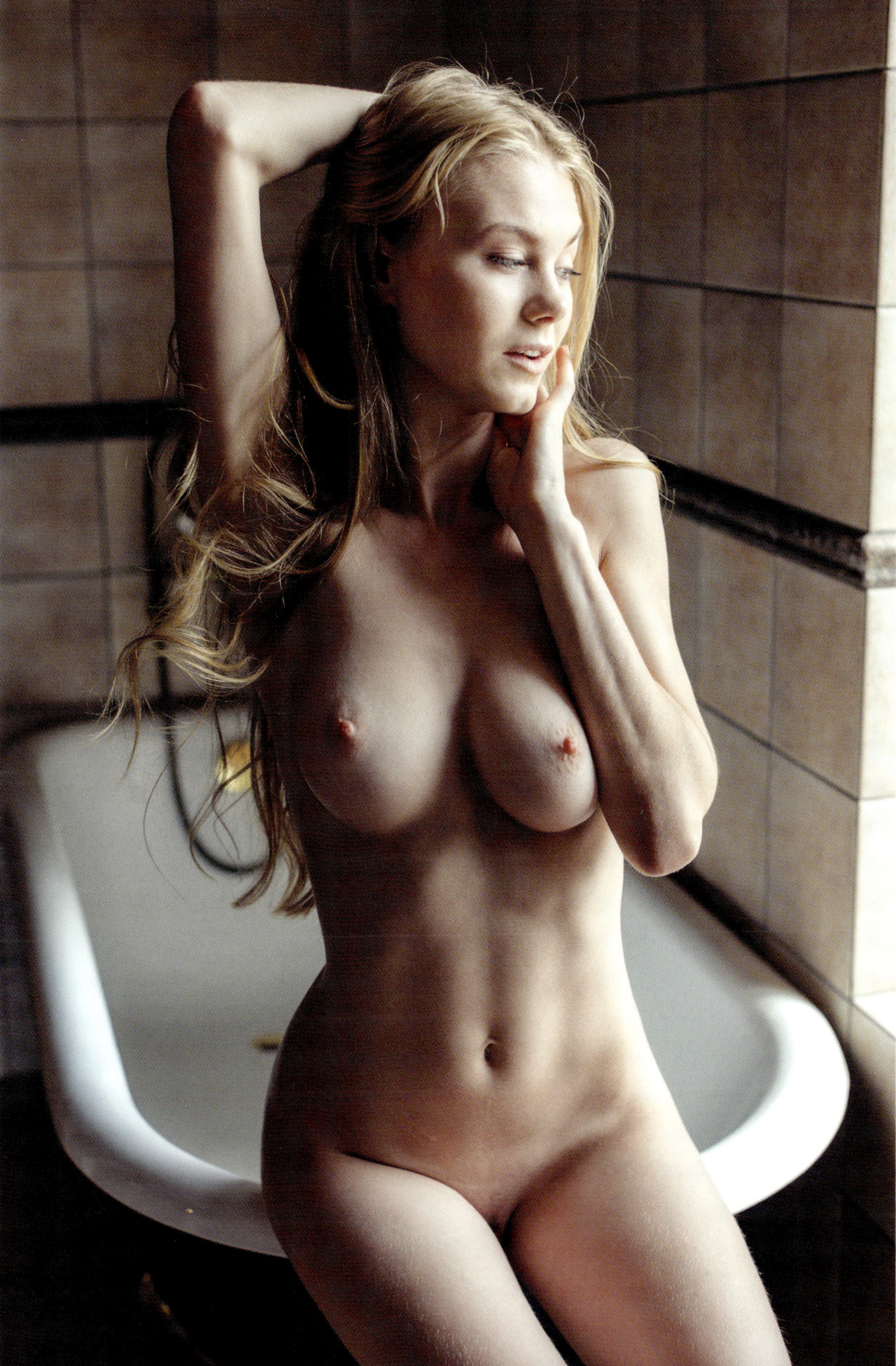

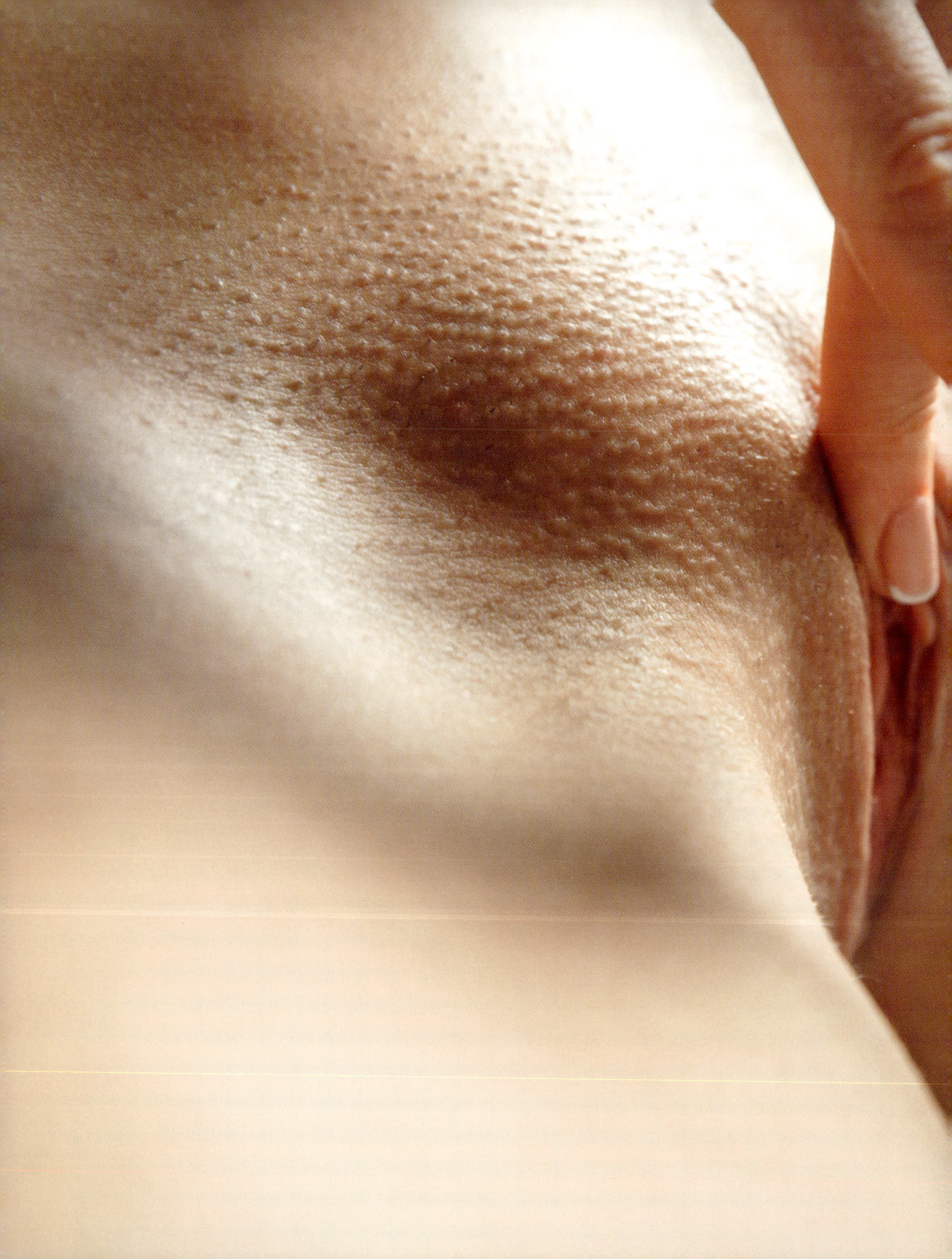

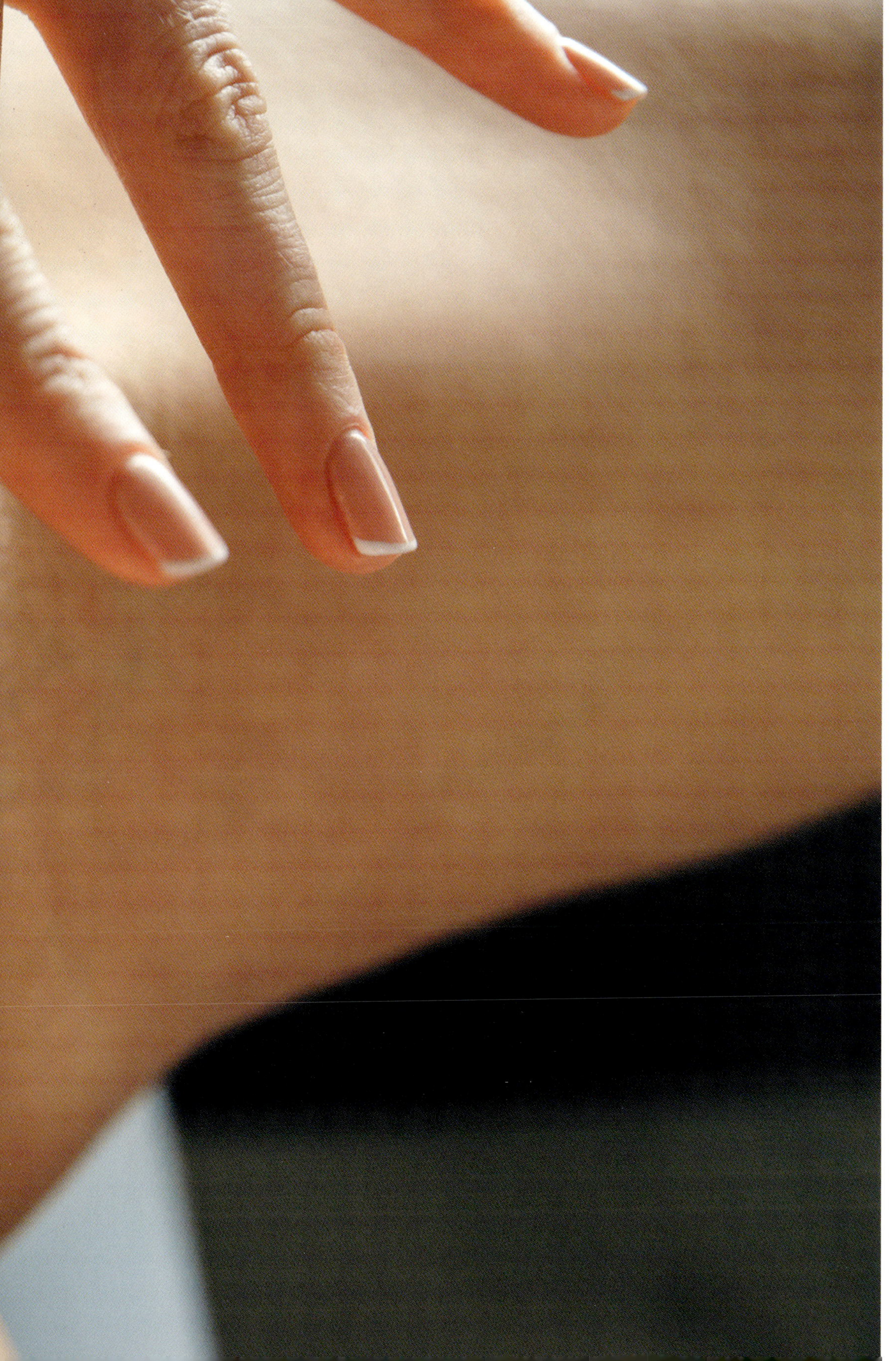

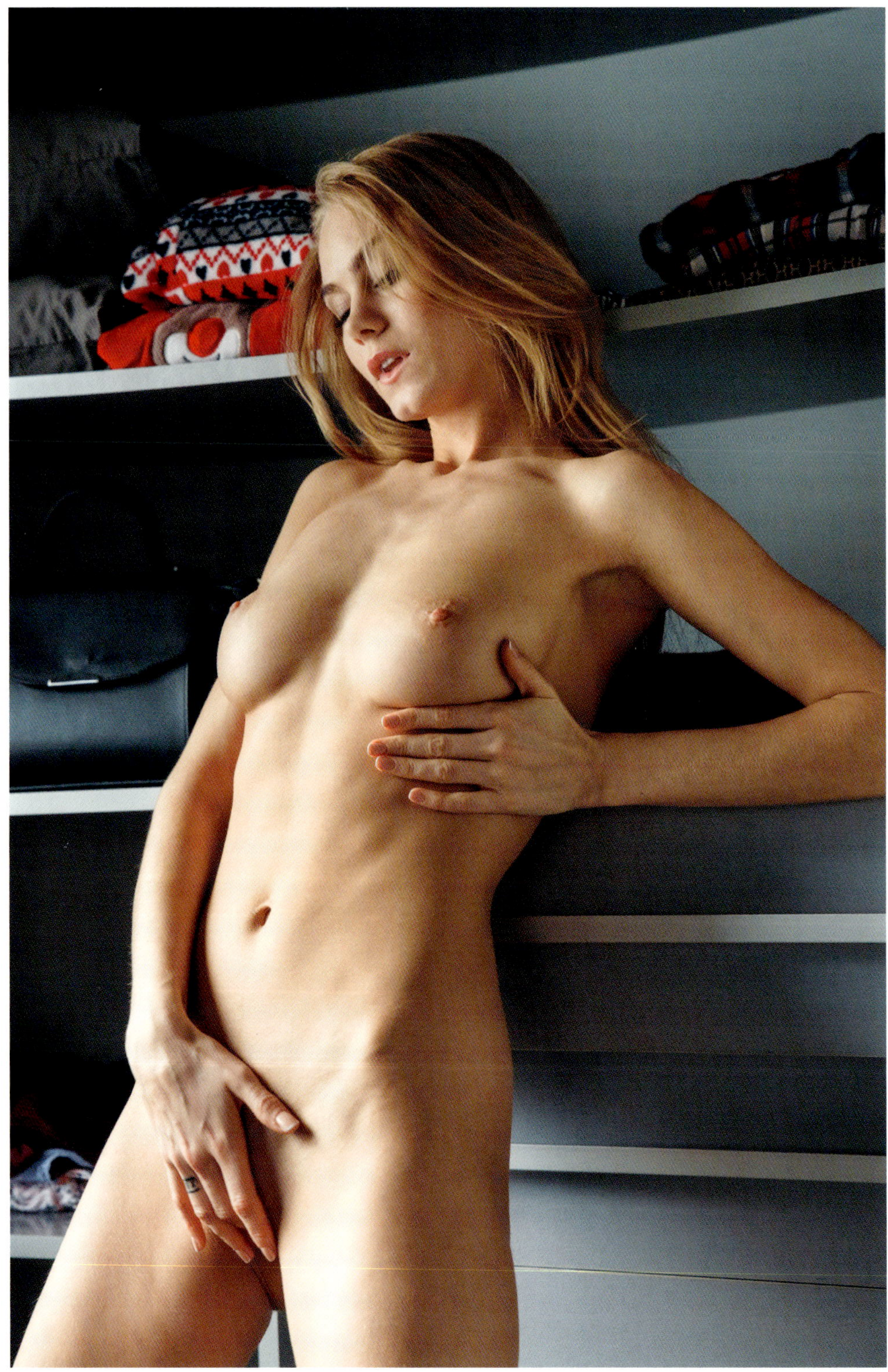

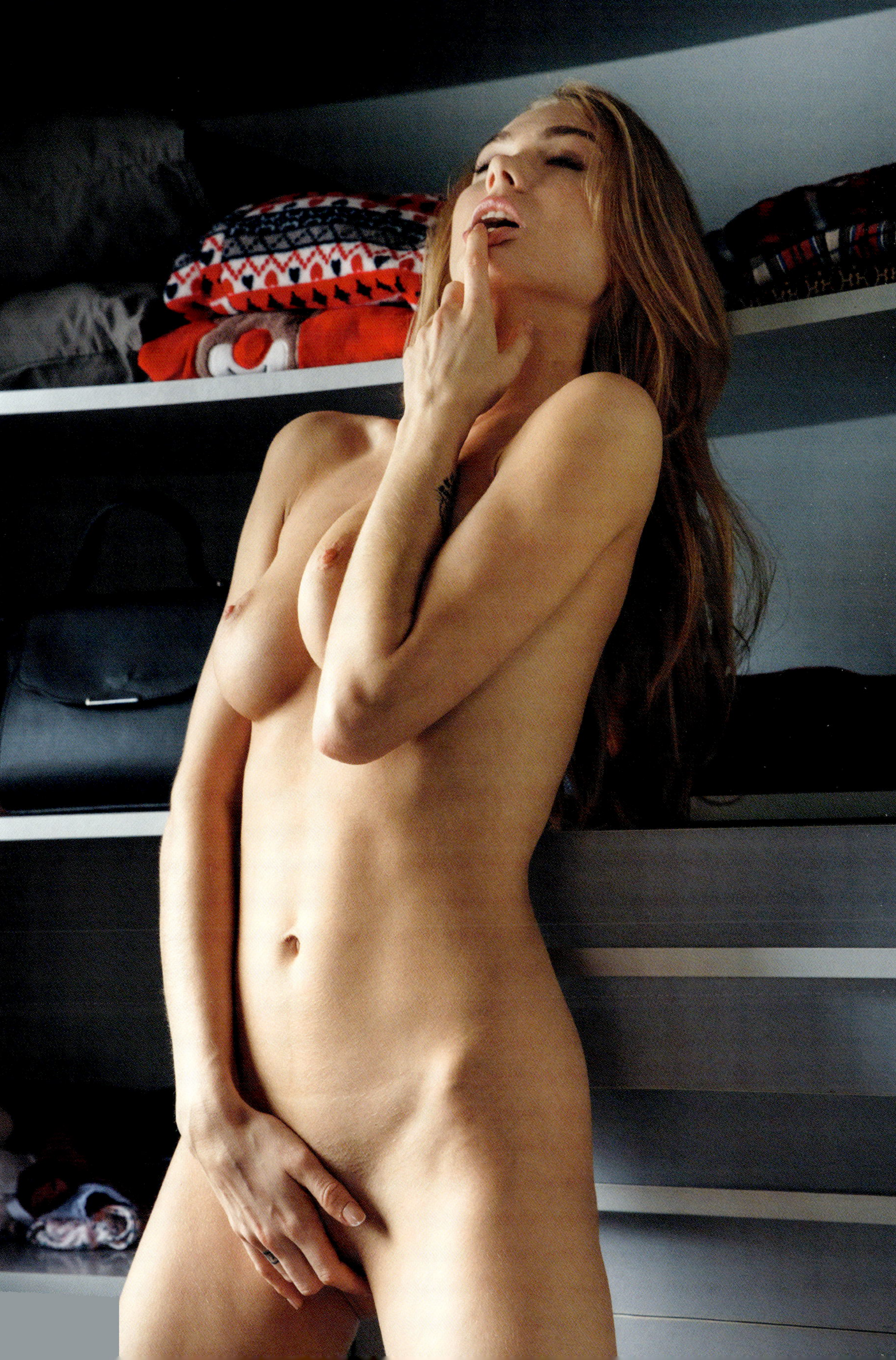

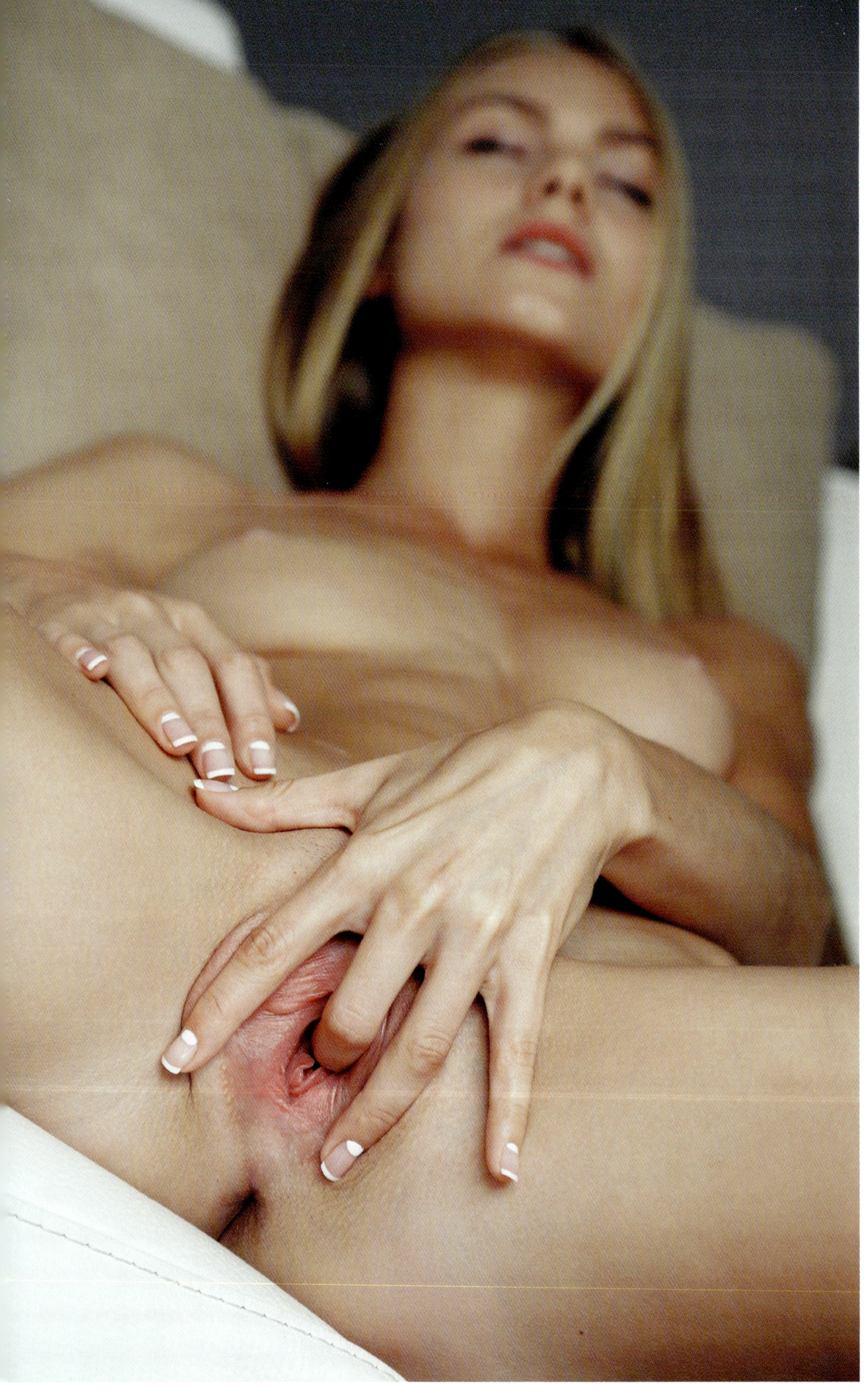

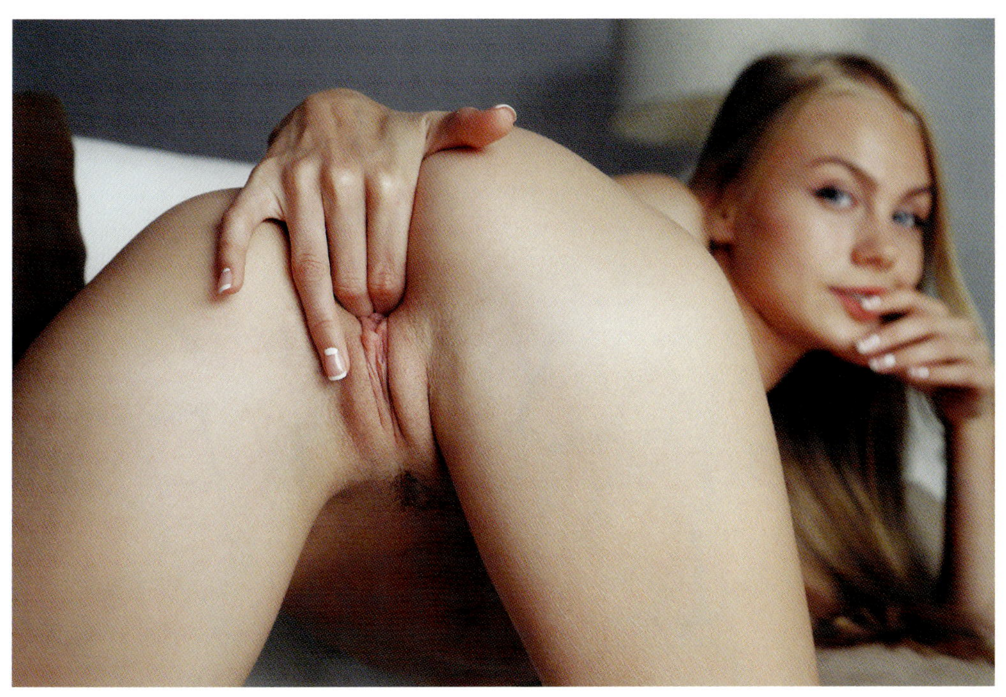

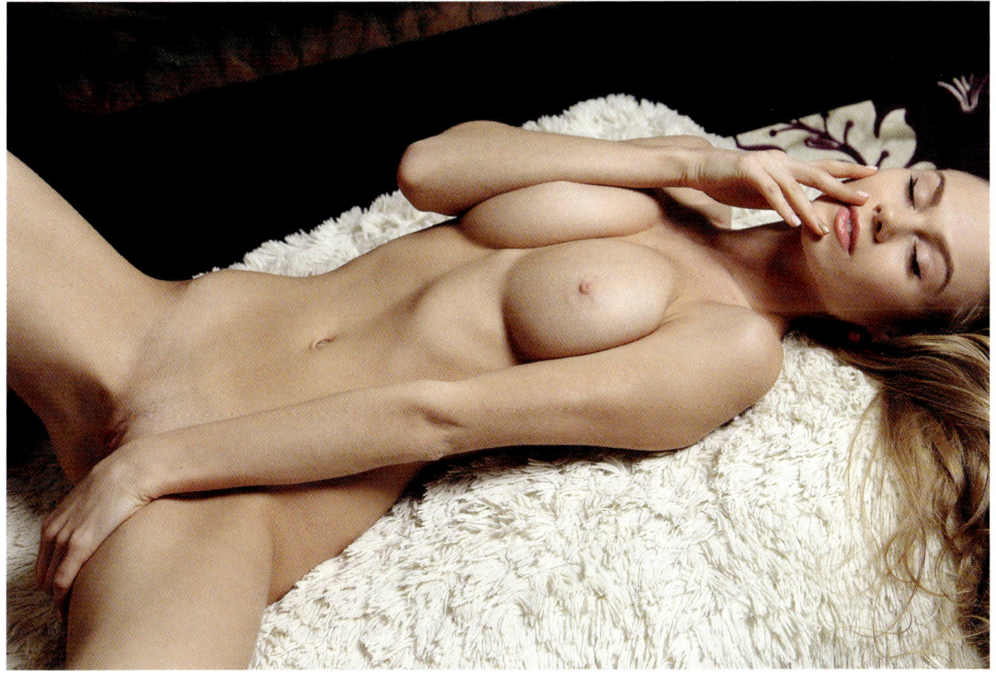

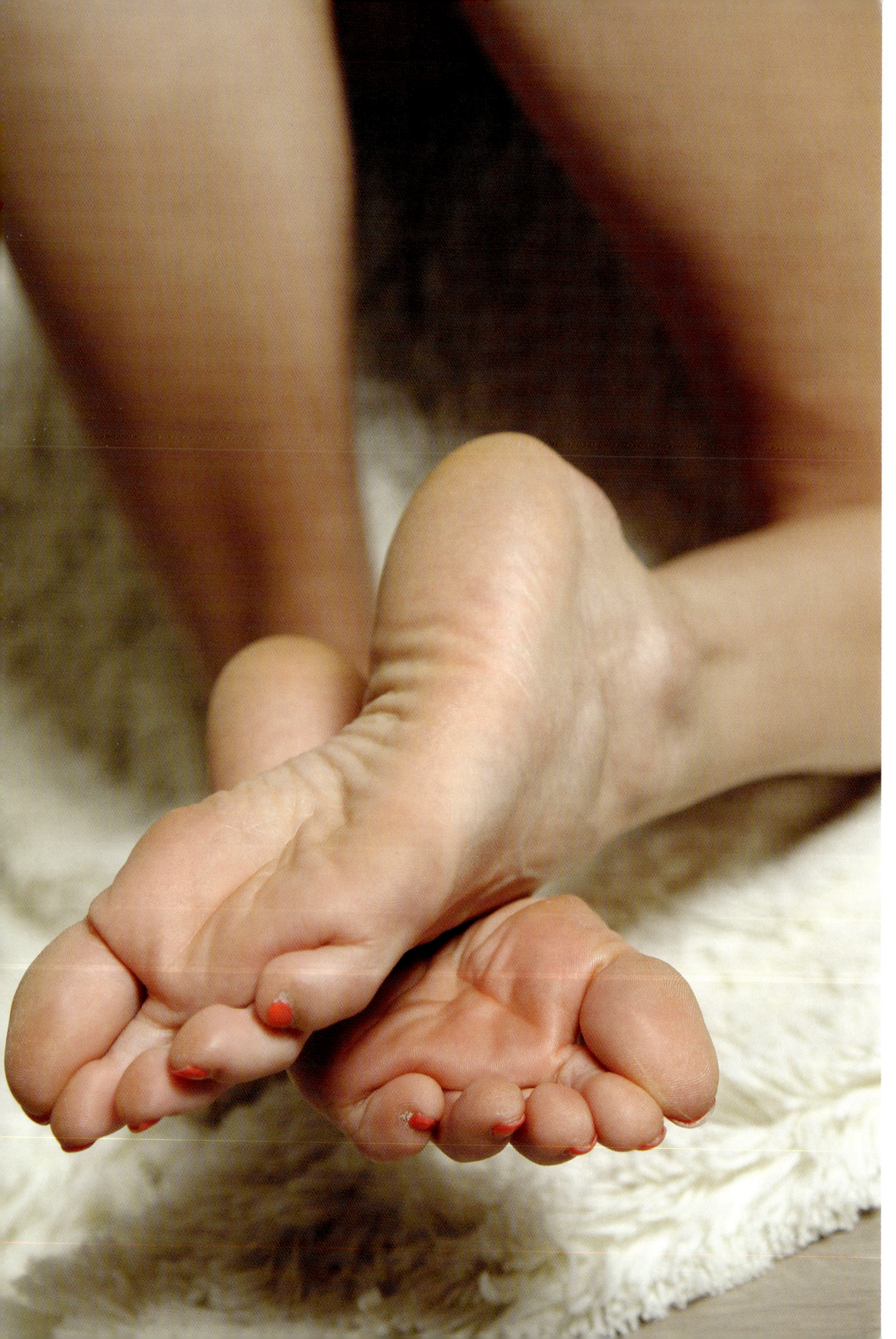

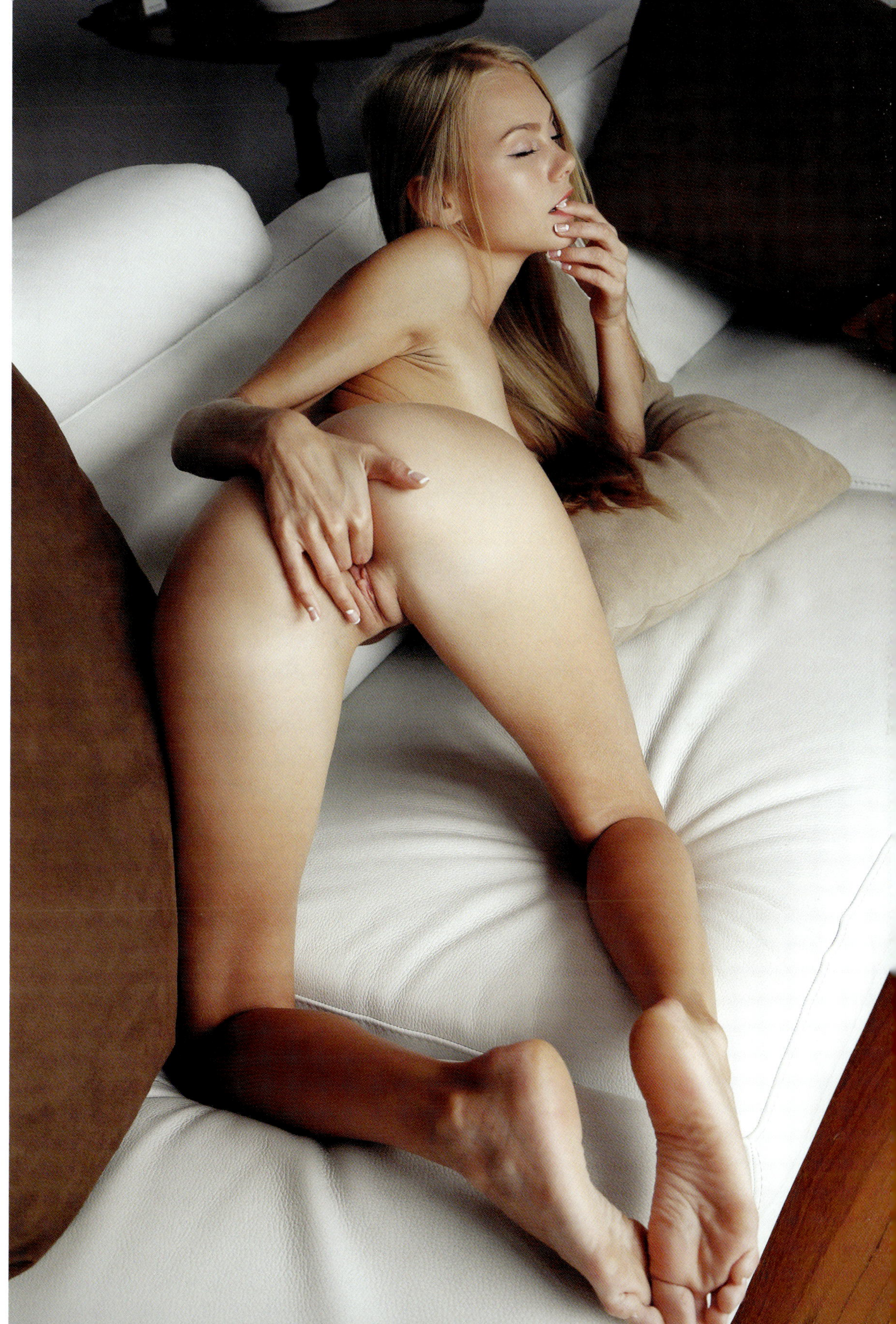

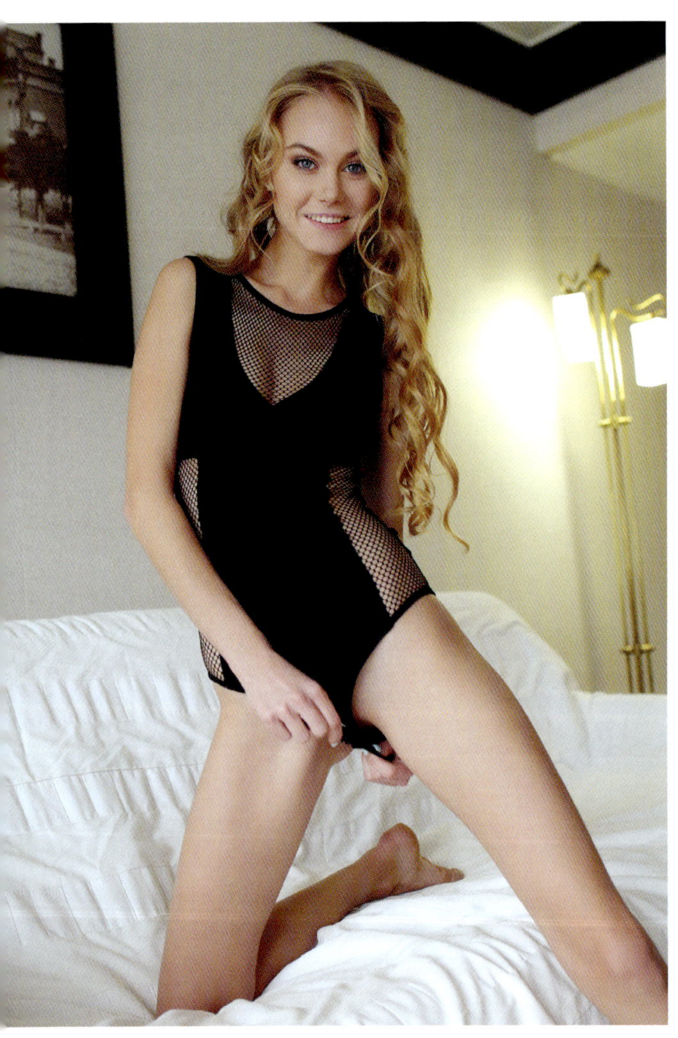
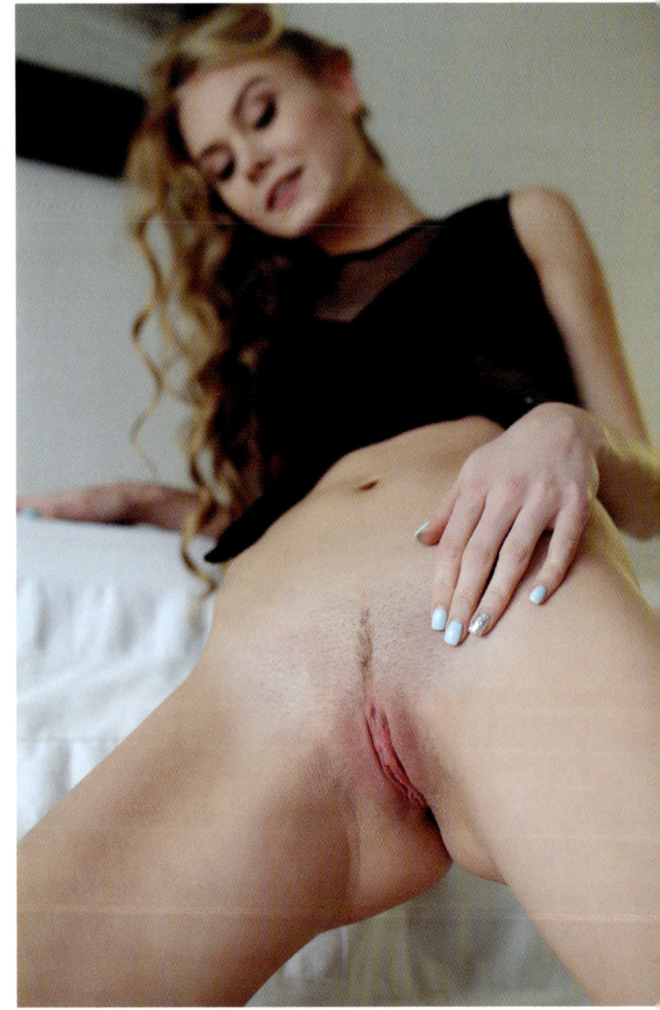

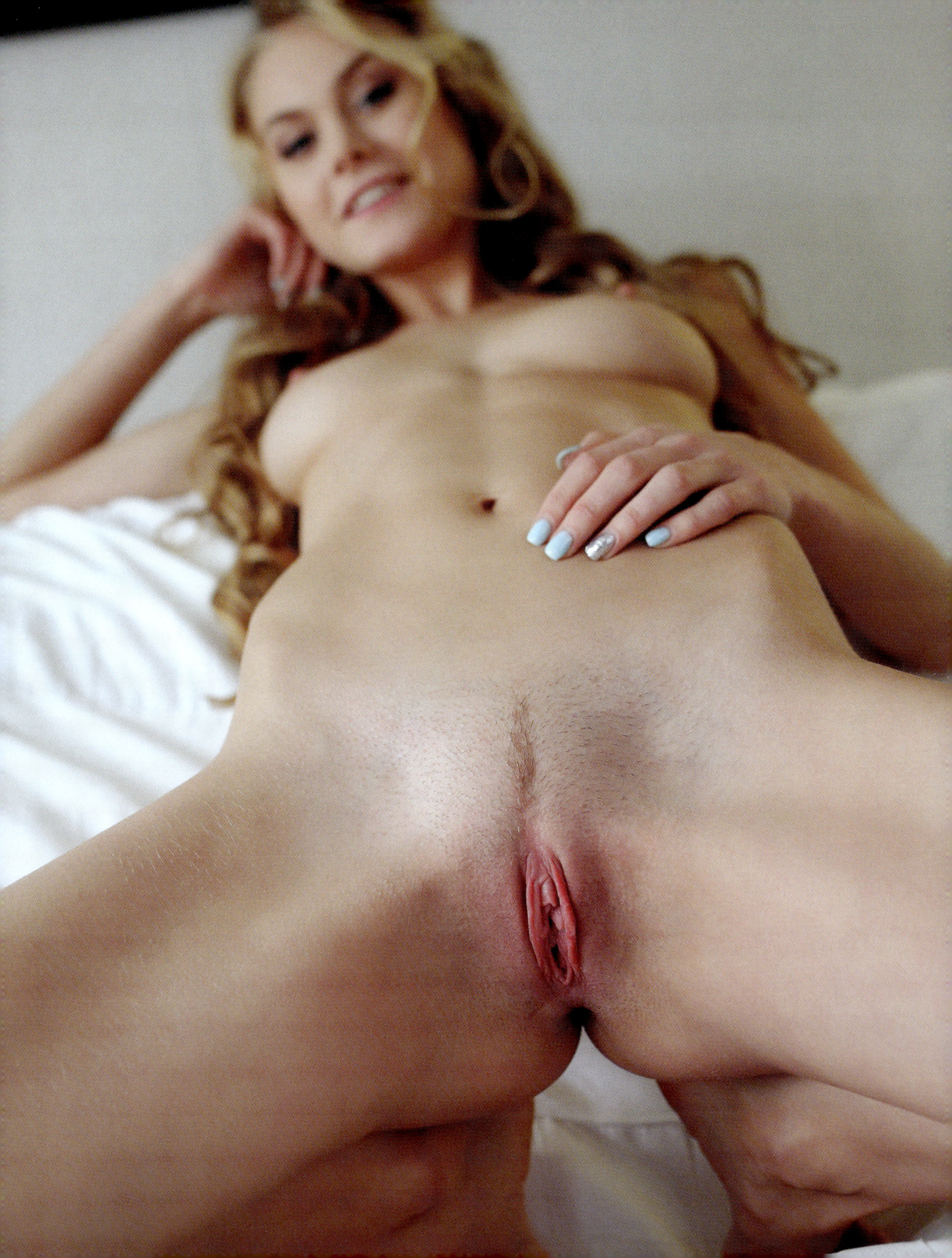

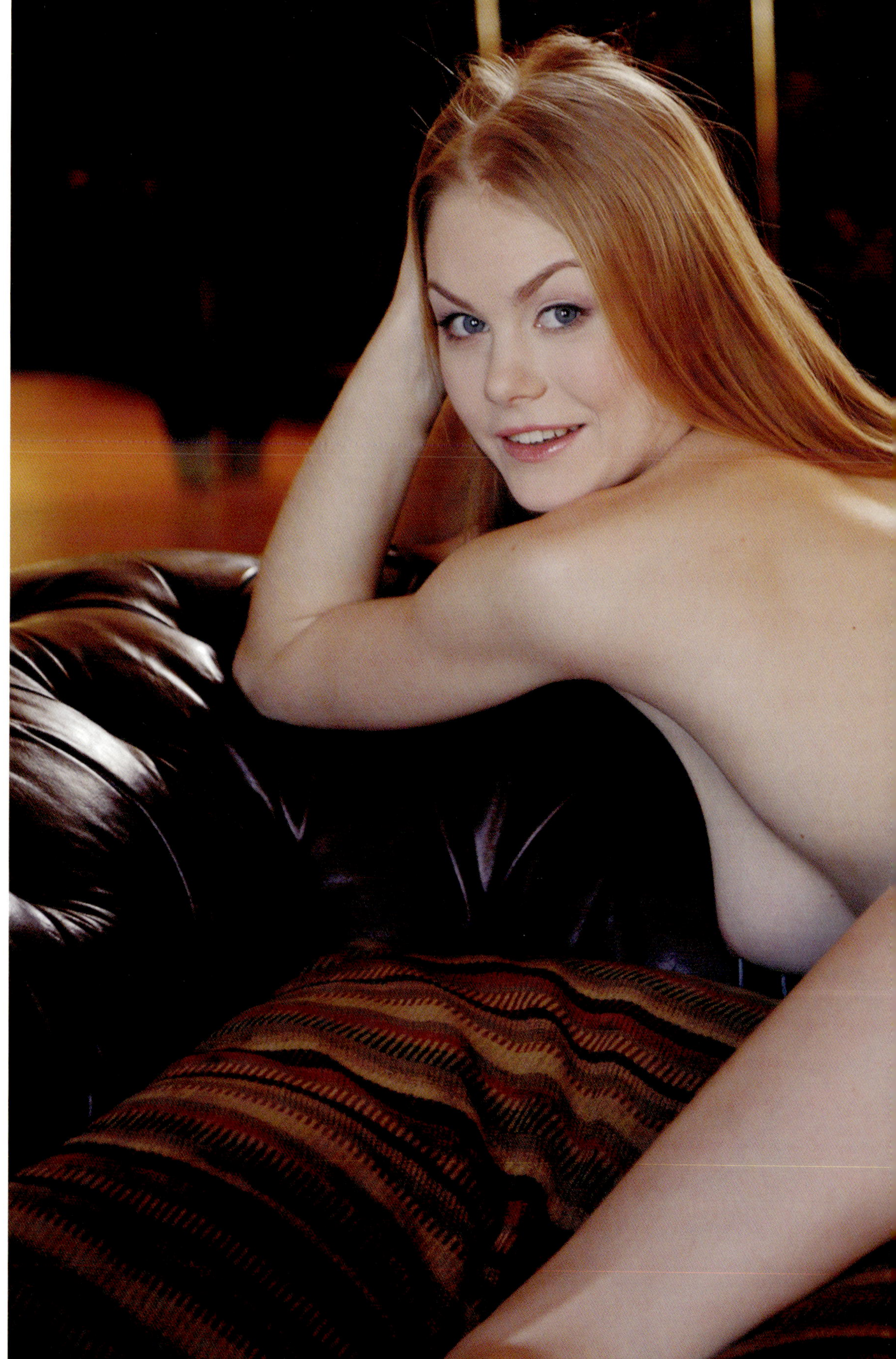

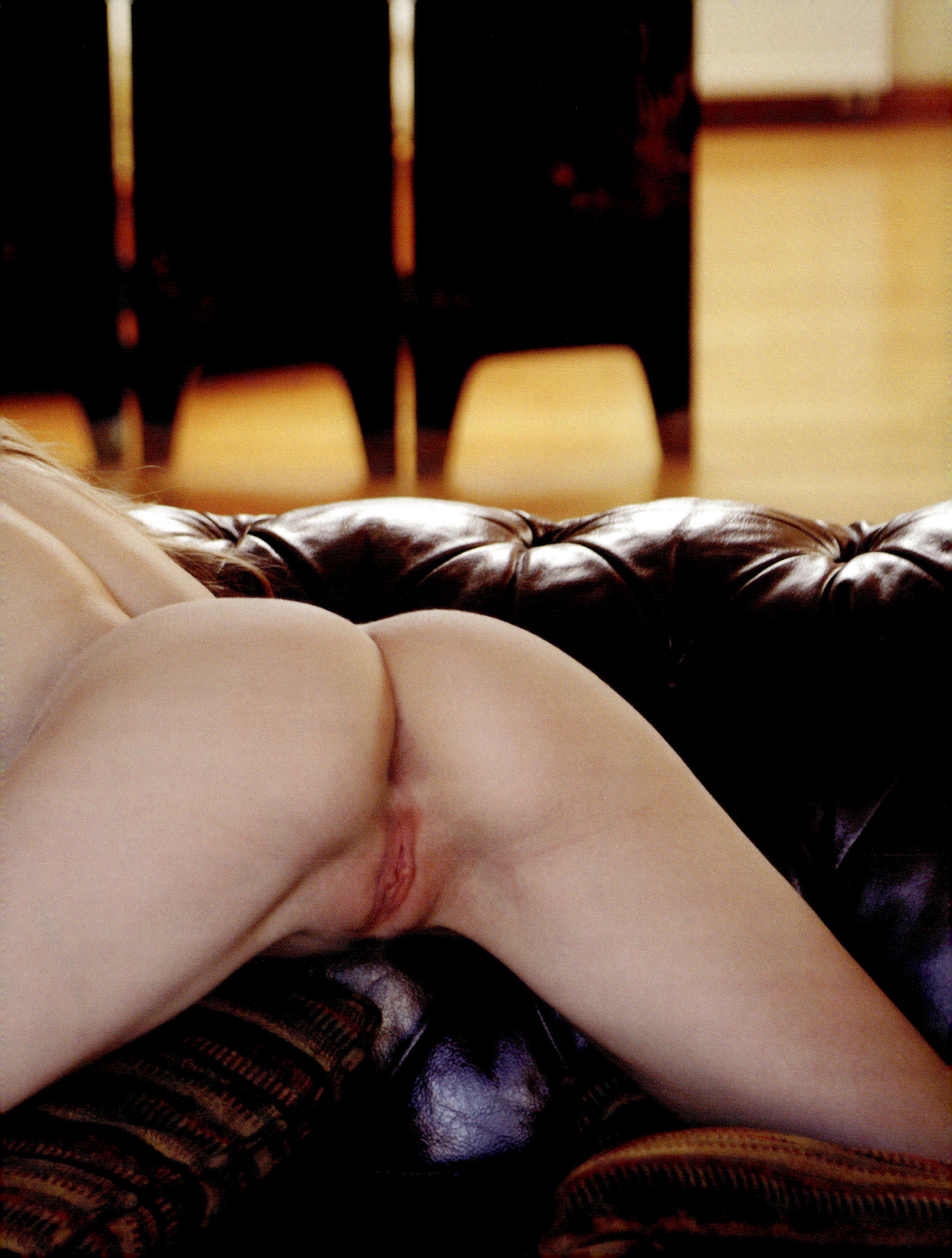

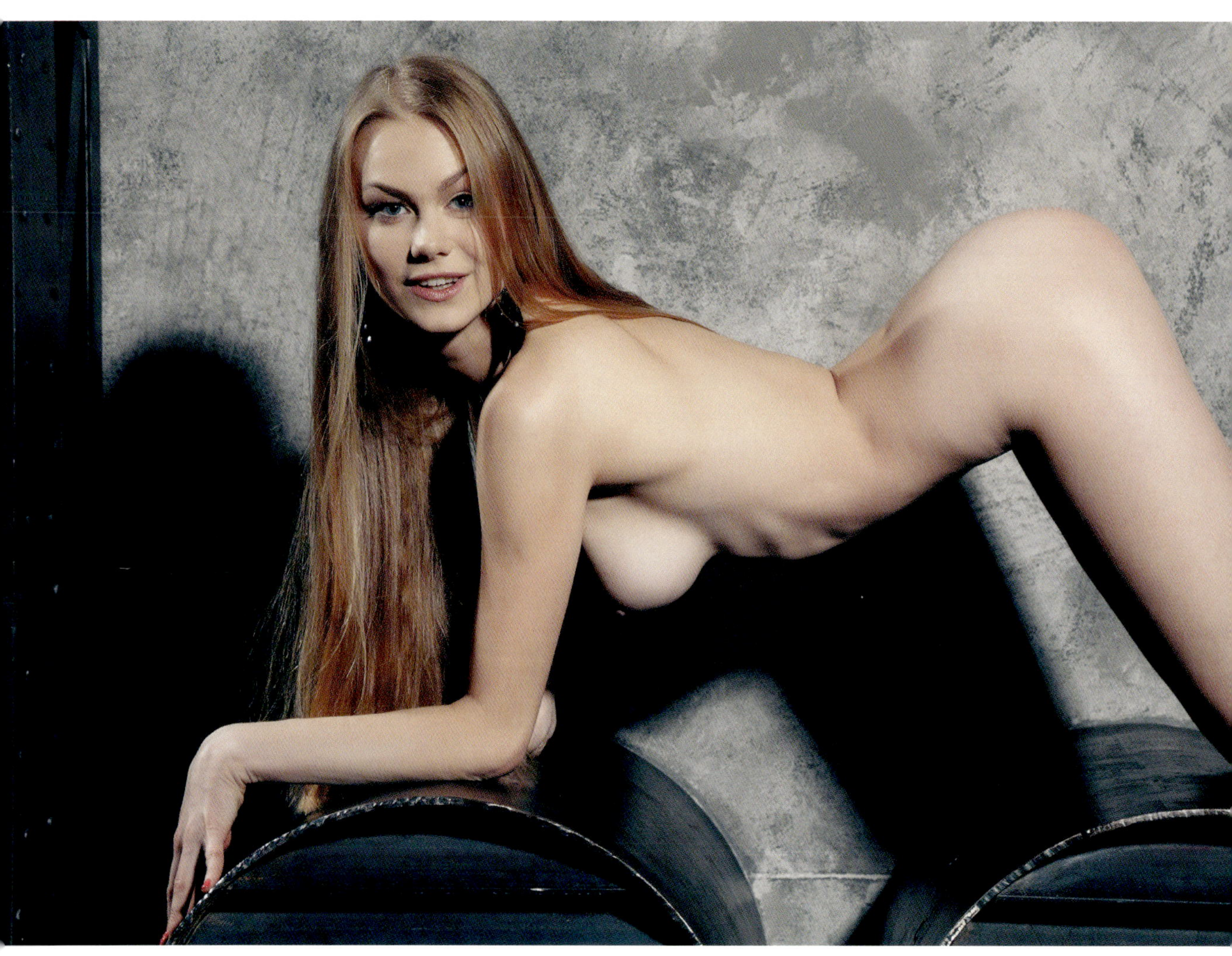

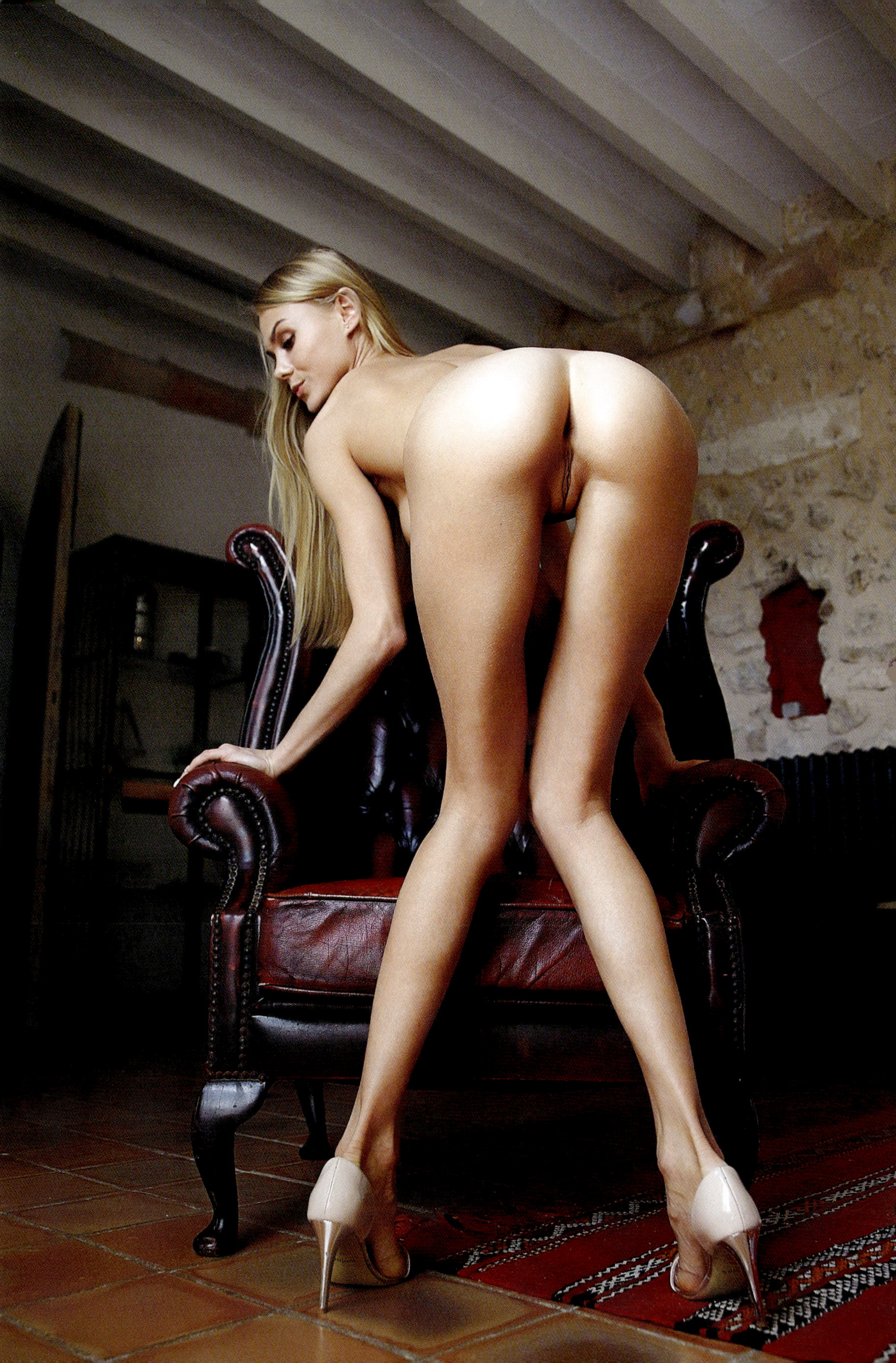

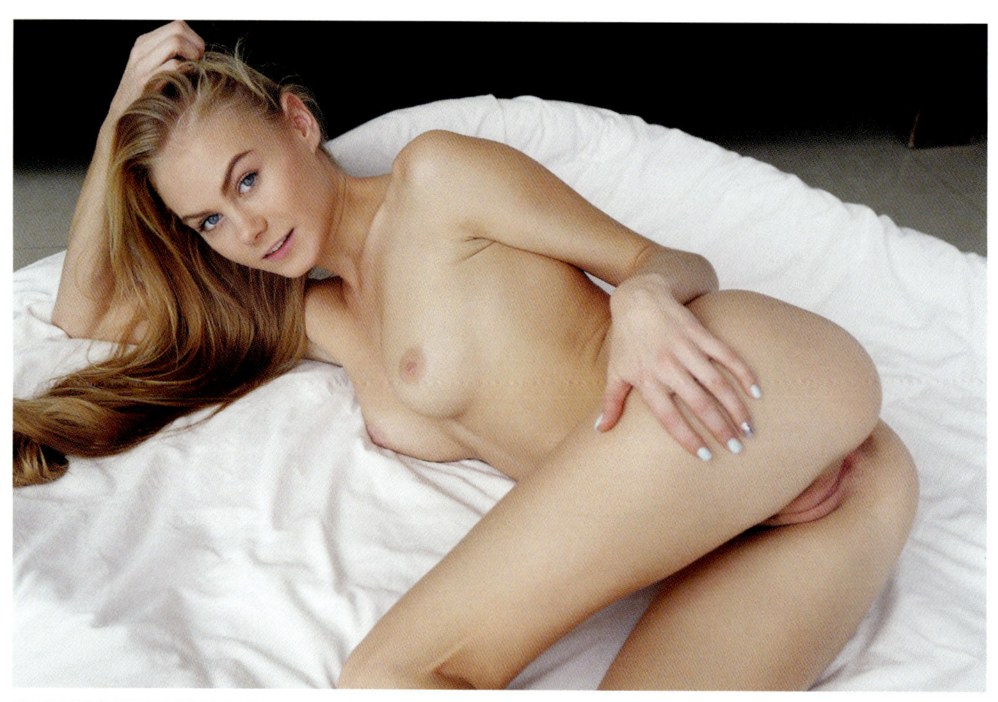

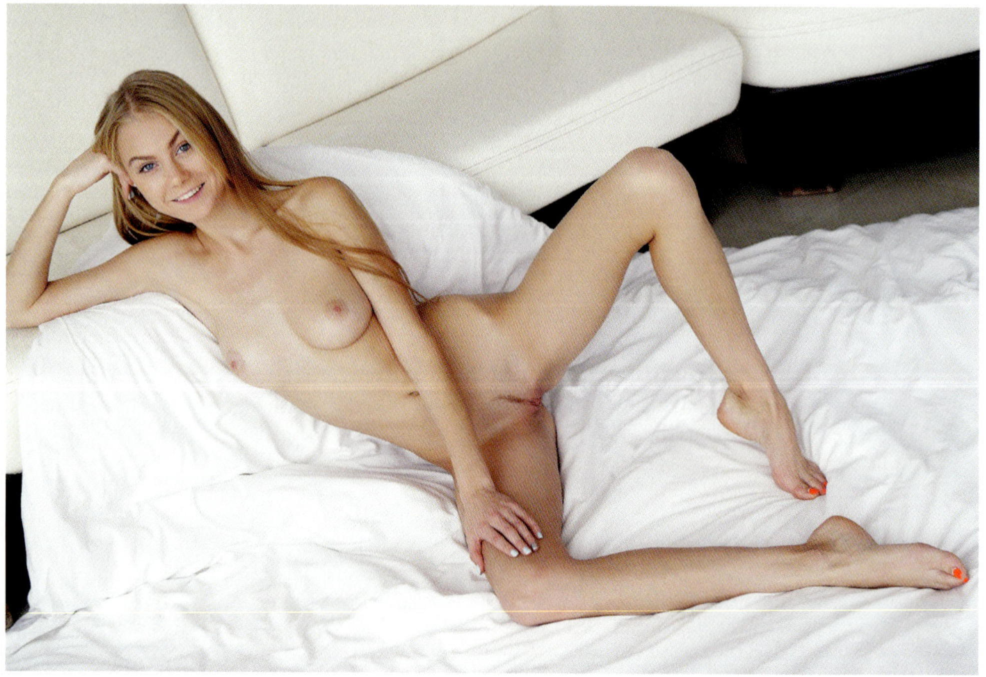

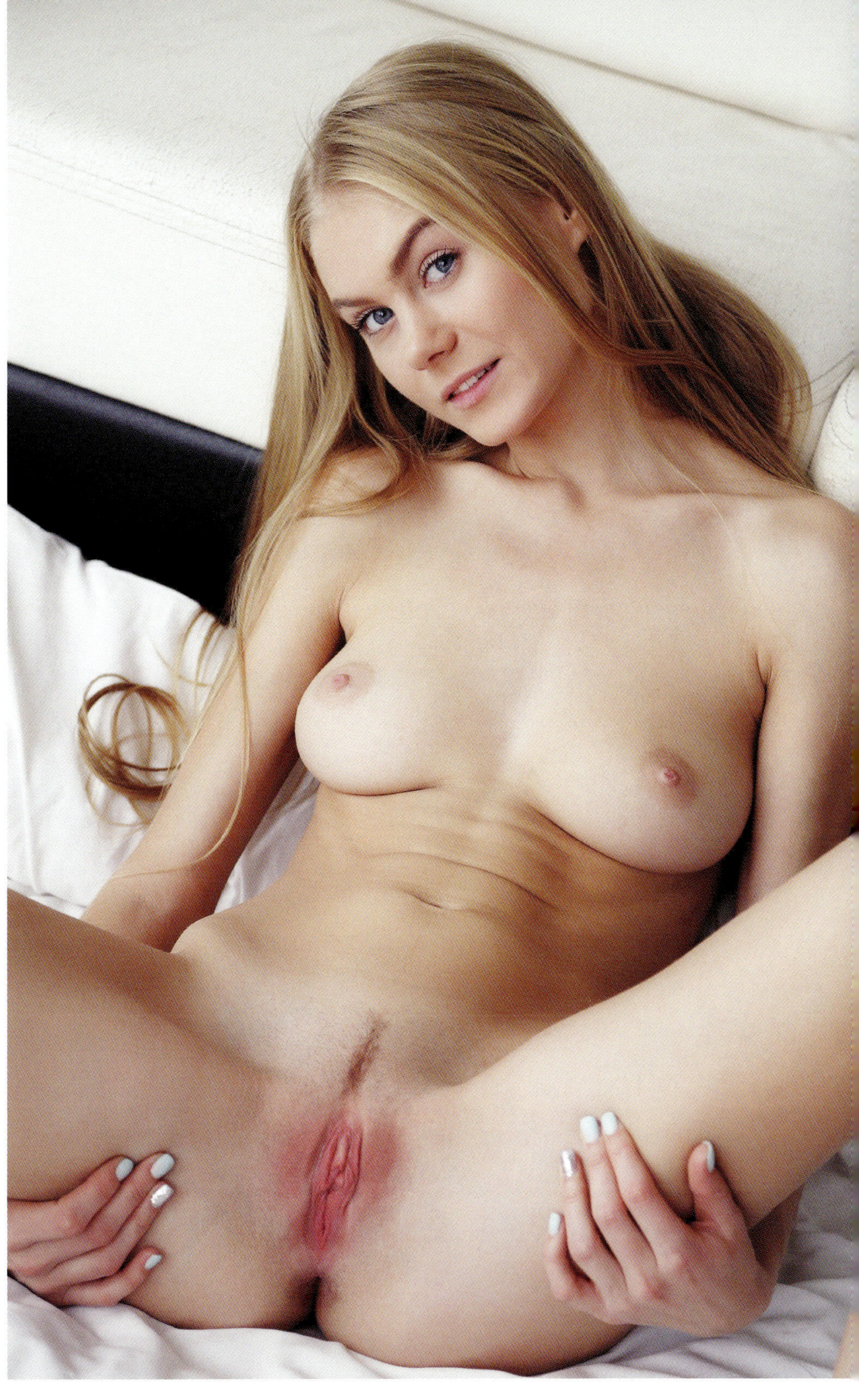

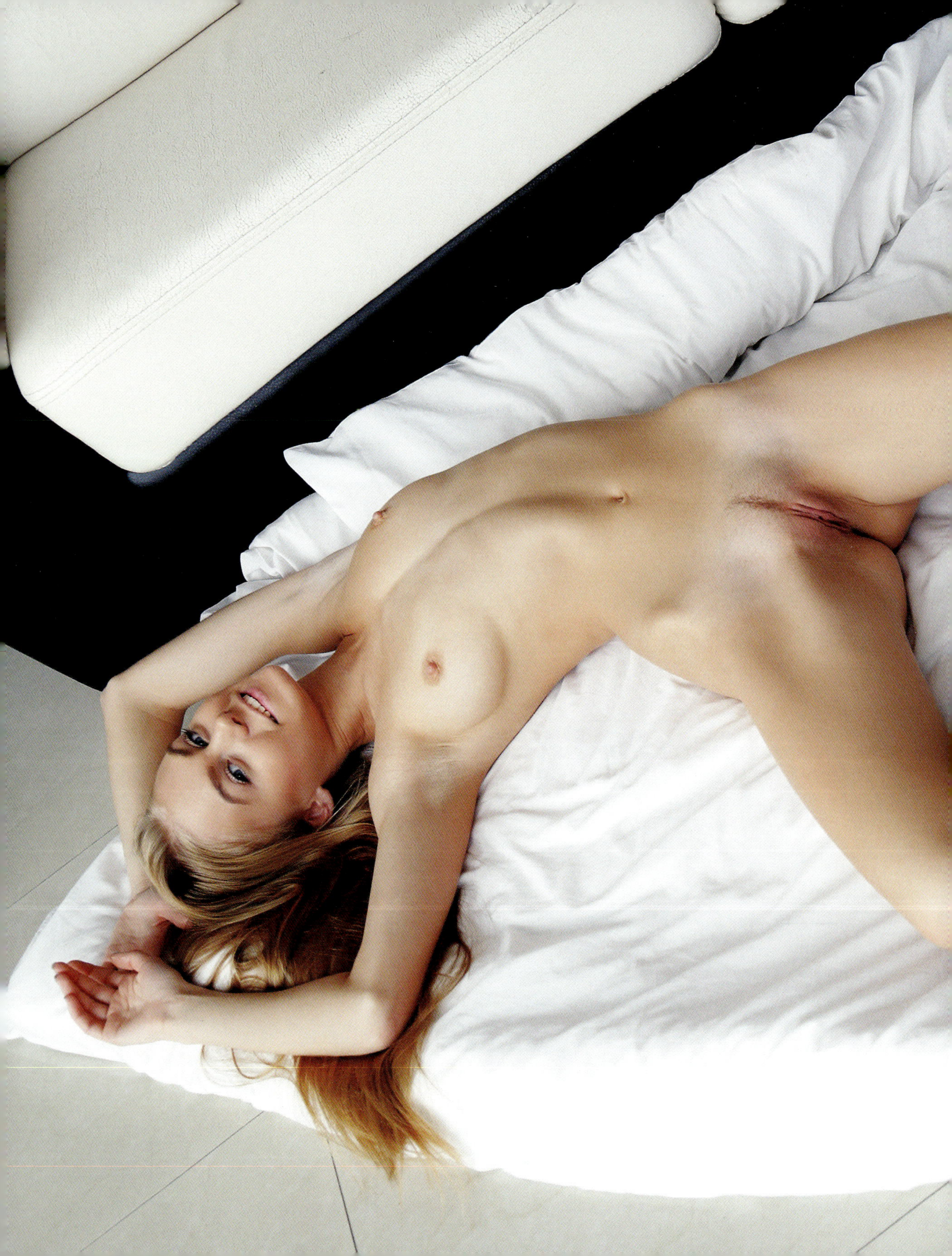

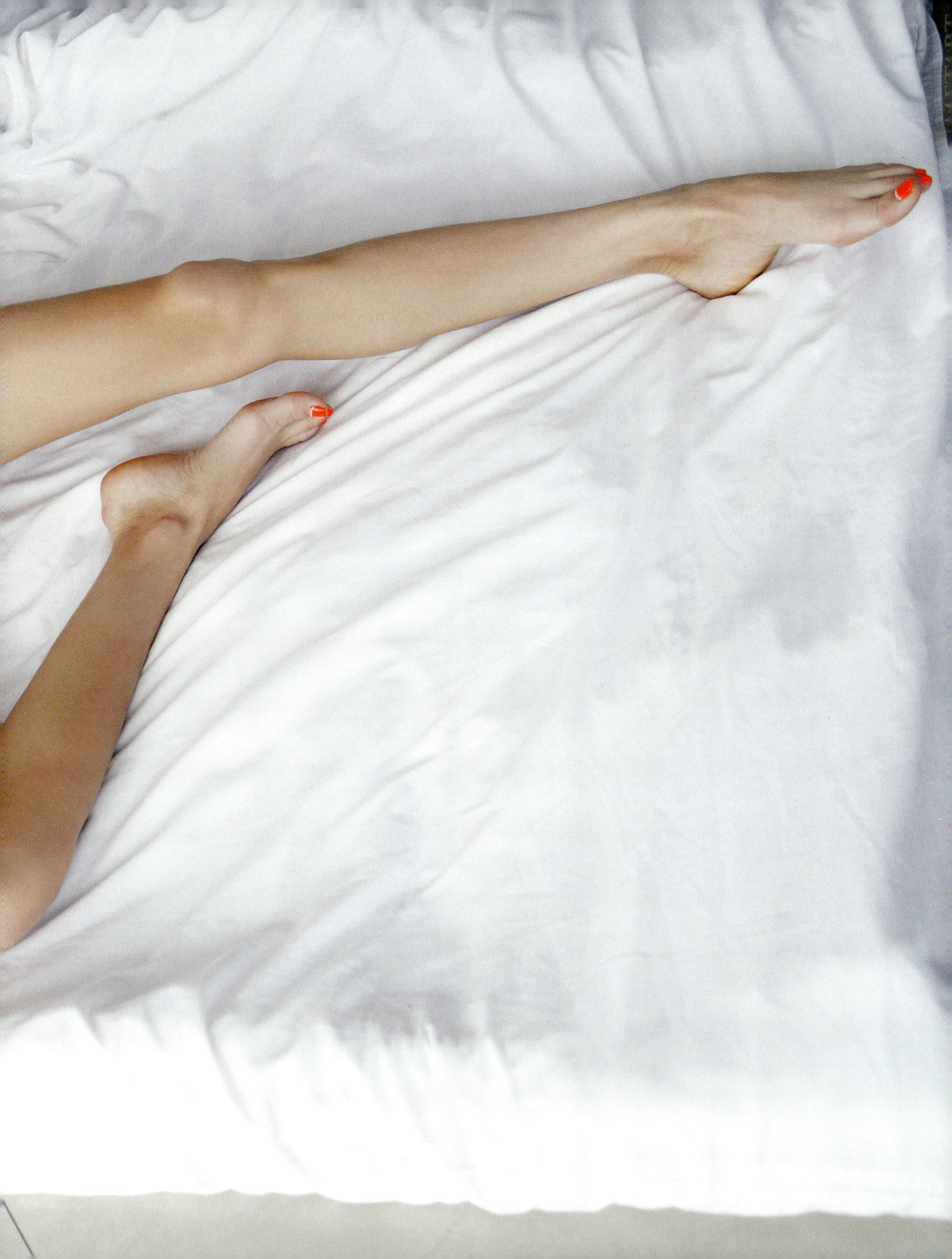

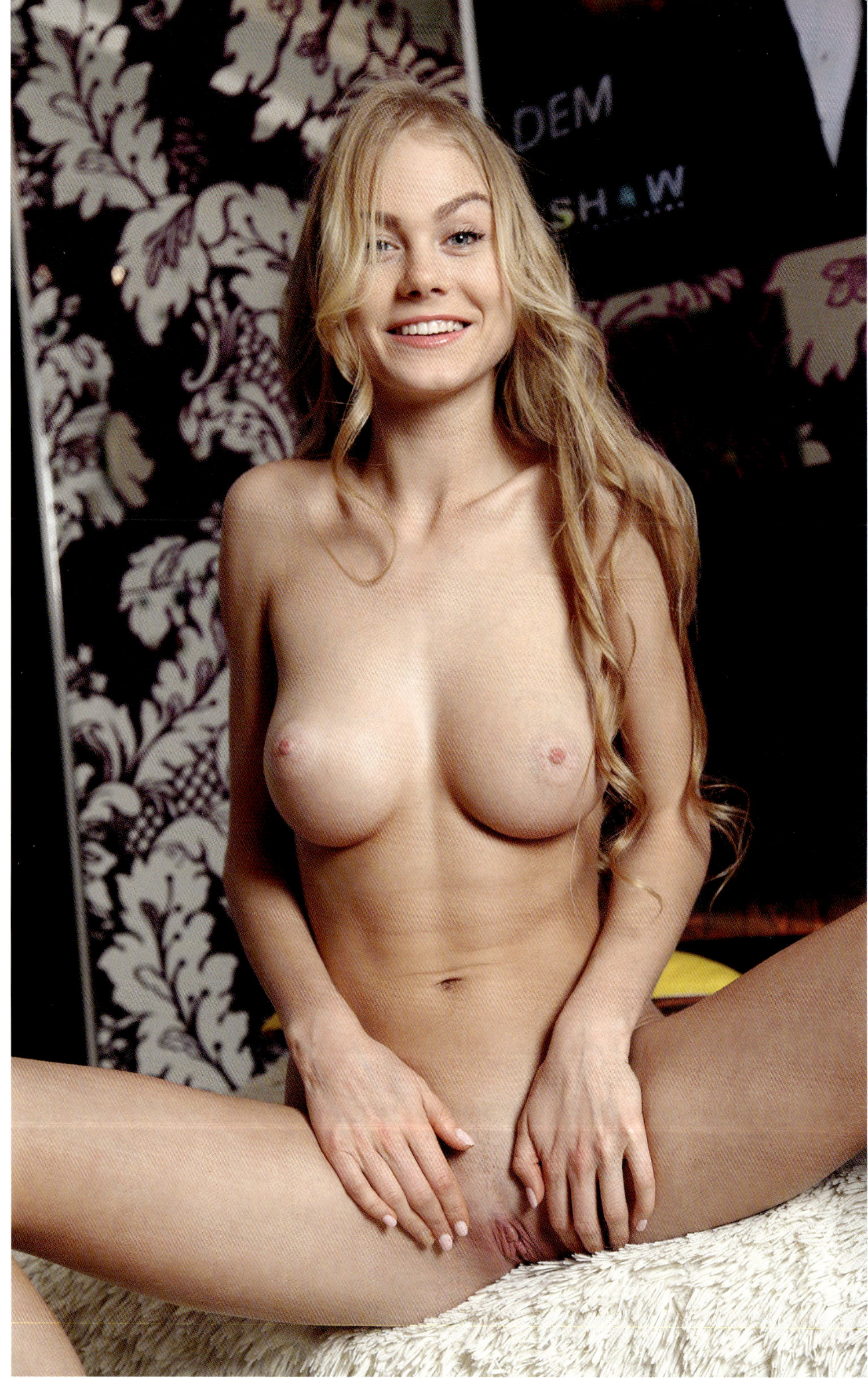

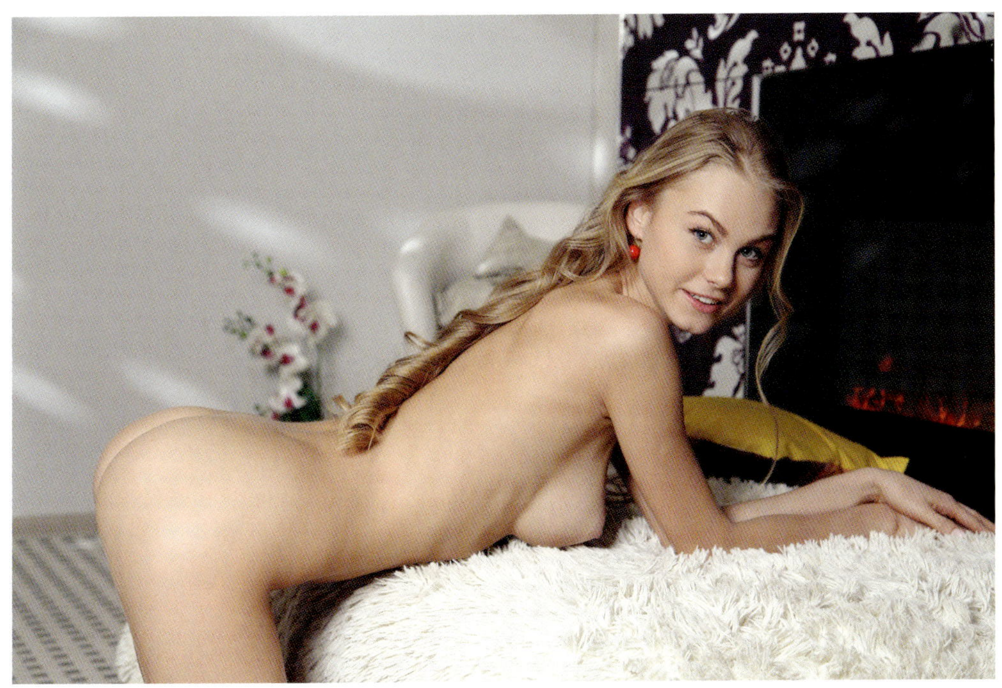

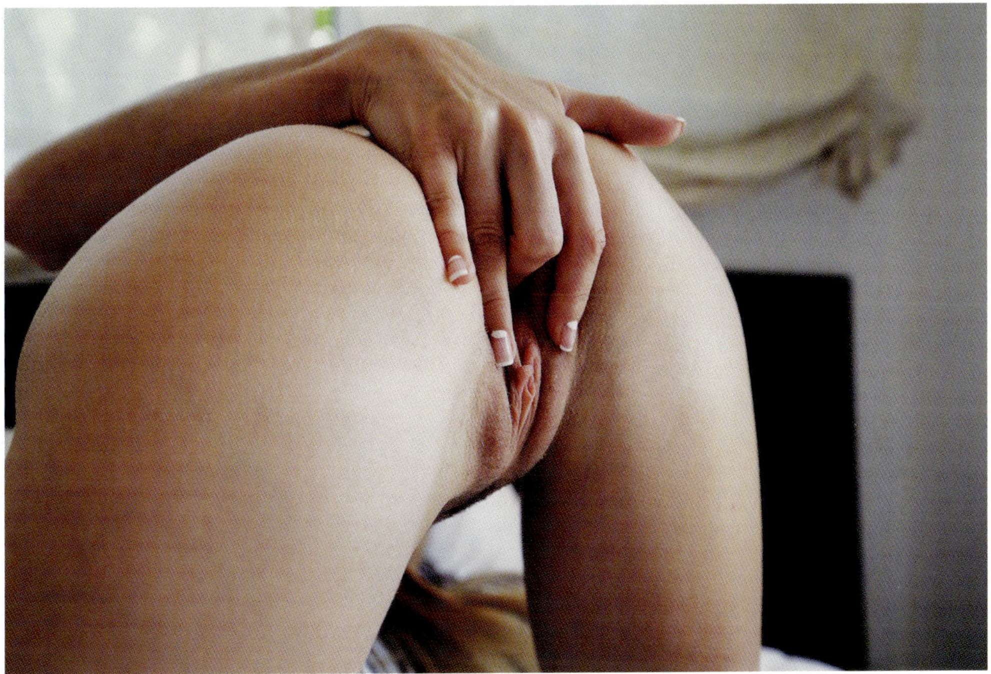

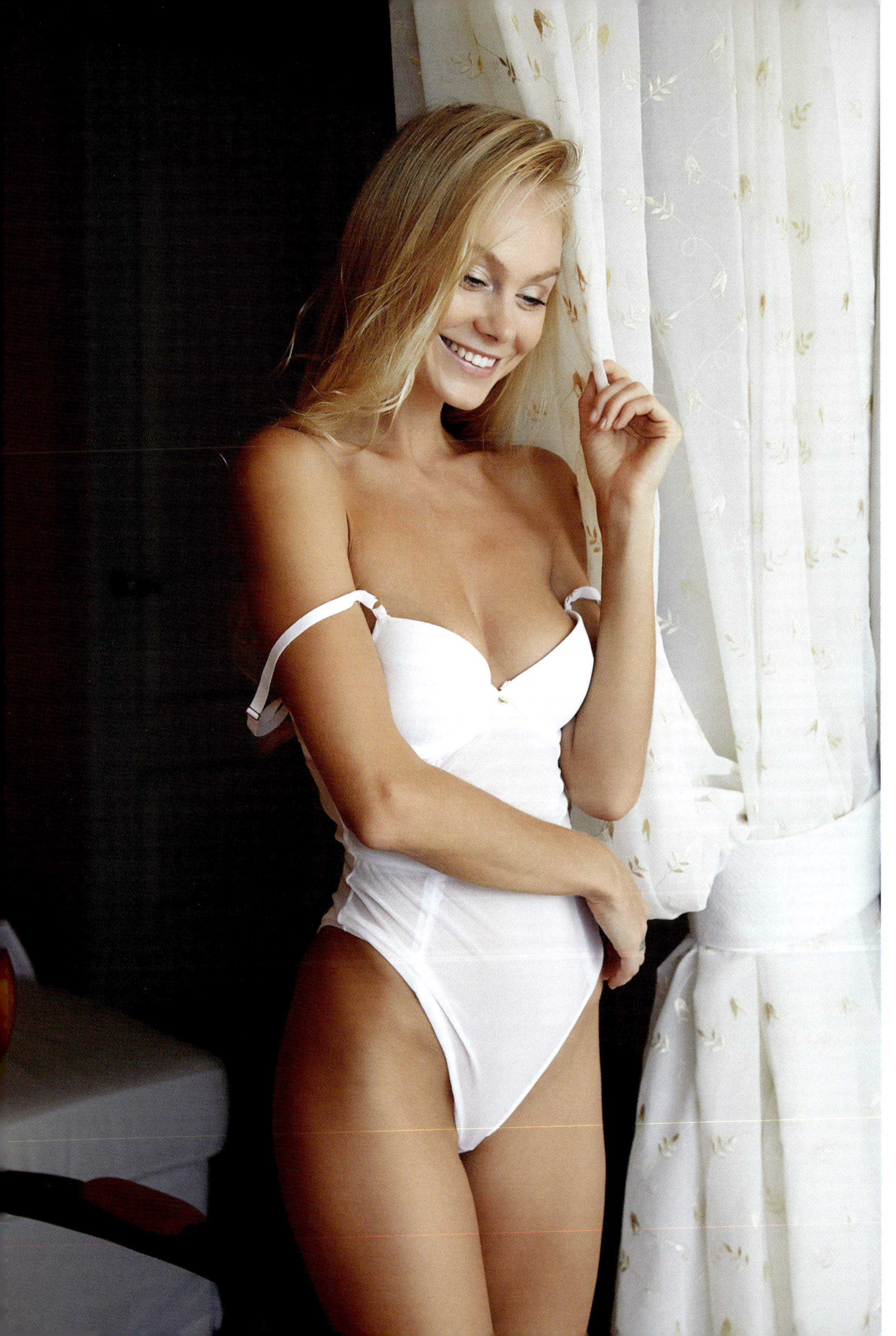

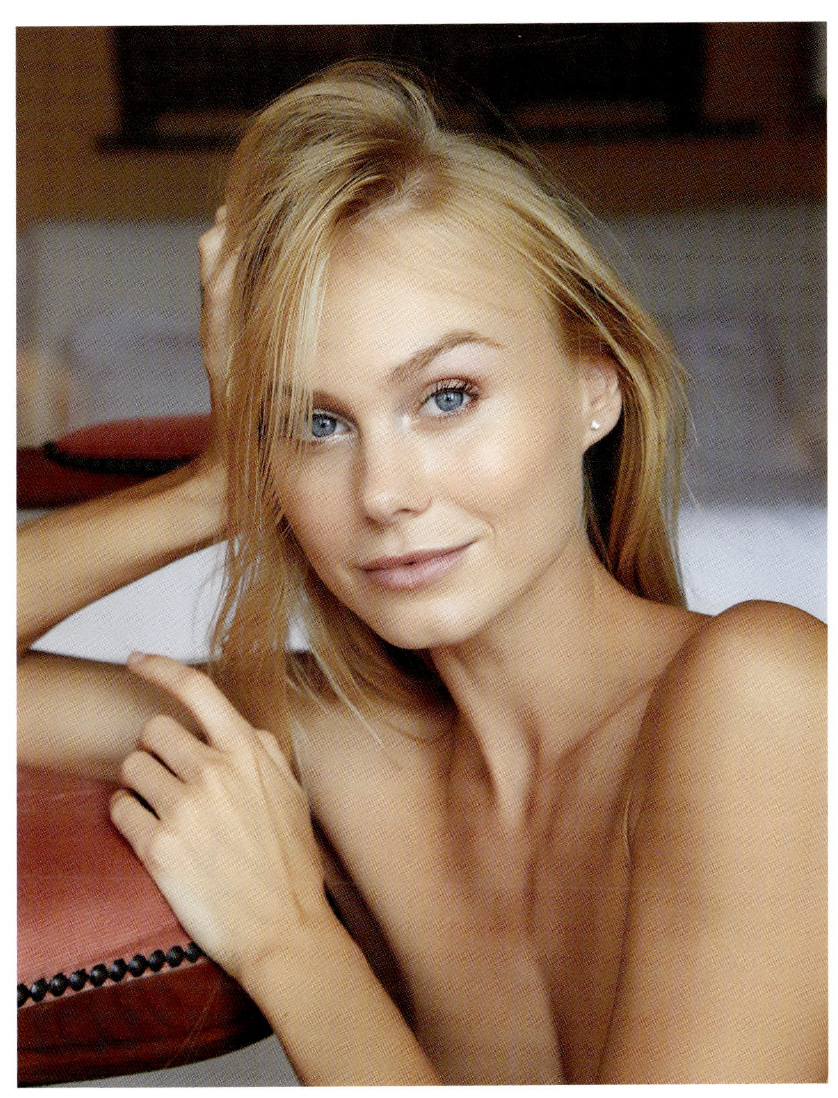

COLLECT THEM ALL: OUR MOST BEAUTIFUL

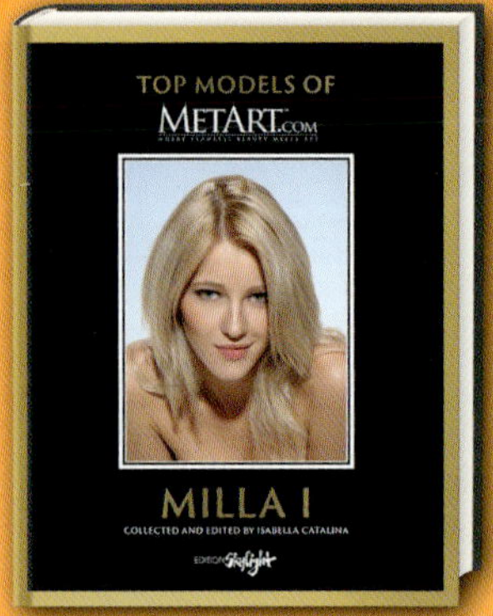

MILLA I

ISBN 978-3-03766-703-3

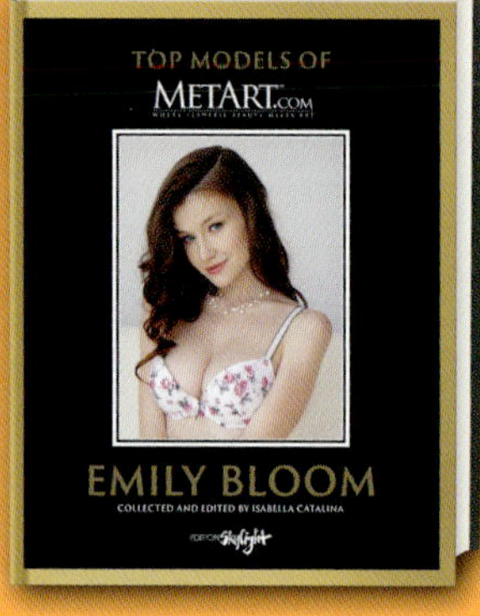

EMILY BLOOM

ISBN 978-3-03766-704-0

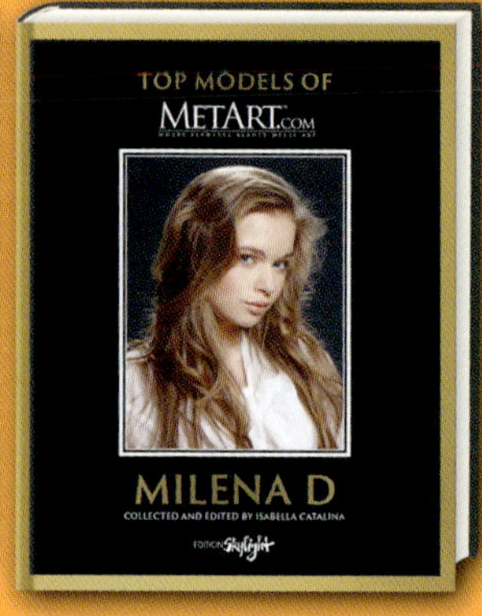

MILENA D

ISBN 978-3-03766-696-8

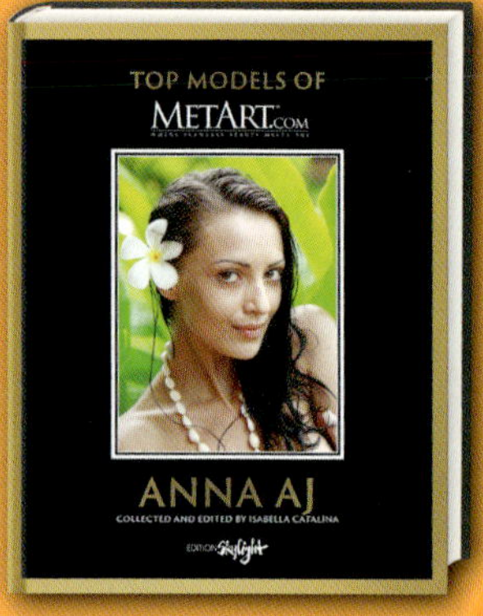

ANNA AJ

ISBN 978-3-03766-695-1

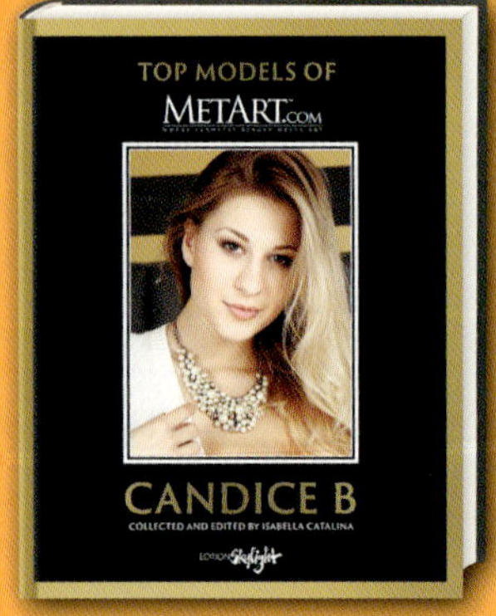

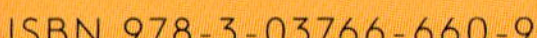

CANDICE B

ISBN 978-3-03766-660-9

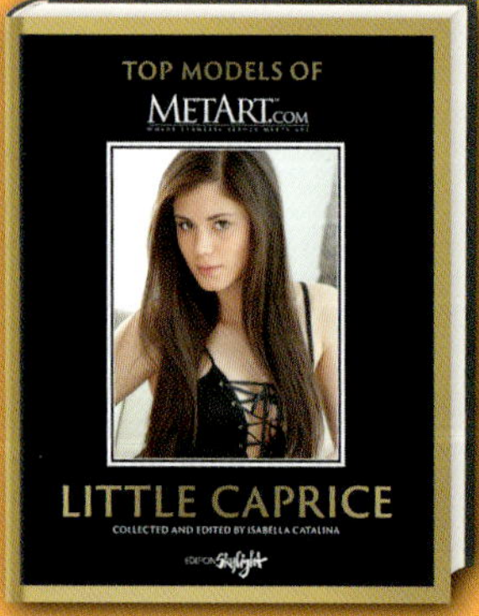

LITTLE CAPRICE

ISBN 978-3-03766-659-3

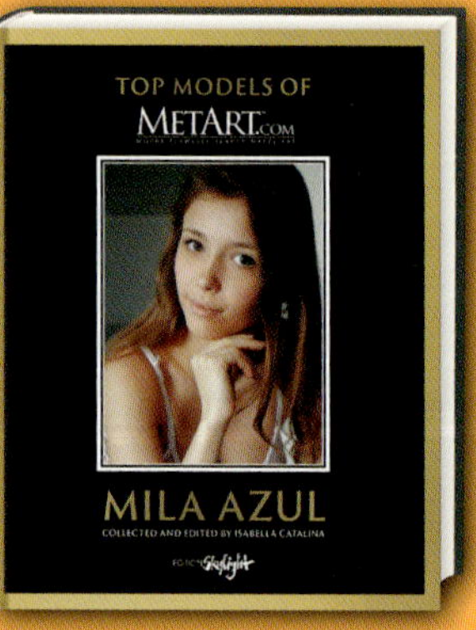

MILA AZUL

ISBN 978-3-03766-680-7

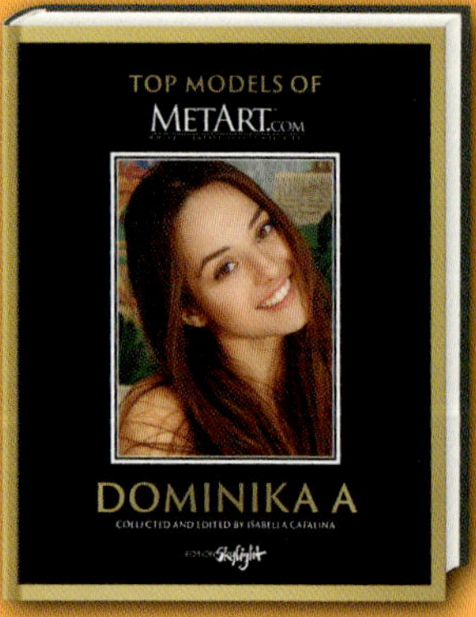

DOMINIKA A

ISBN 978-3-03766-679-1

WWW.EDITION-SKYLIGHT.COM